W9-AOW-612

Complete MathSmart

Revised and Updated!

Grade 3

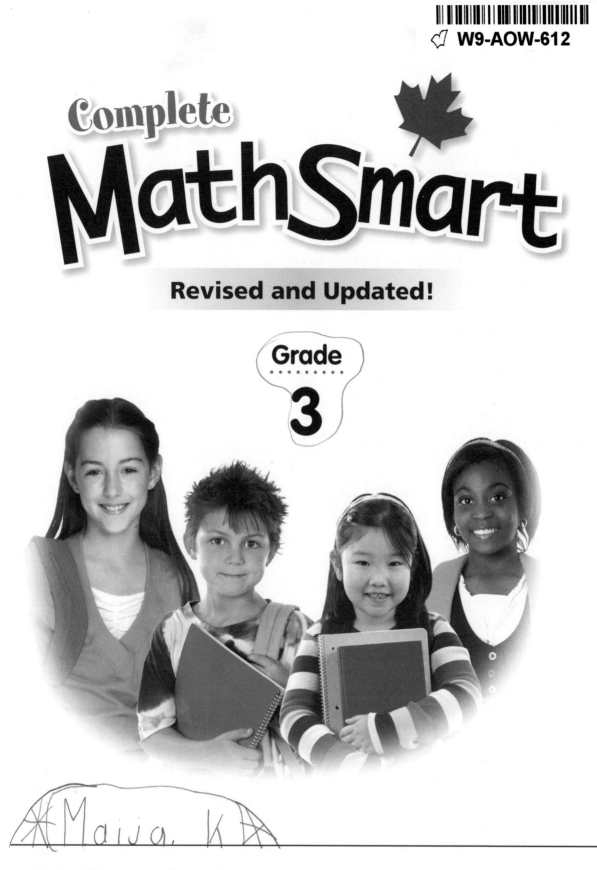

Maiya K.

Copyright © 2012 Popular Book Company (Canada) Limited

Printed in China

ISBN: 978-1-897164-13-6

ontents

Section I

	Overview	5
1.	Addition and Subtraction	6
2.	4-digit Numbers	10
3.	Multiplication	12
4.	Division	16
5.	More about Multiplication and Division	20
	Midway Review	22
6.	Money	26
7.	Measurement	30
8.	Fractions and Decimals	32
9.	Probability	36
10.	Graphs	38
	Final Review	42

Section II

	Overview	47
1.	Introducing Multiplication	48
2.	Multiplying by 2 or 5	52
3.	Multiplying by 3 or 4	56
4.	Multiplying by 6 or 7	60
5.	Multiplication Facts to 49	64
6.	Multiplying by 8, 9, 0 or 1	68
7.	More Multiplying	72
8.	Introducing Division	76
	Midway Review	80
9.	Multiplication and Division Fact Families	84
10.	Dividing by 1, 2 or 3	88
11.	Dividing by 4 or 5	92
12.	Dividing by 6 or 7	96
13.	Dividing by 8 or 9	100
14.	Division with Remainders	104
15.	More Dividing	108
16.	More Multiplying and Dividing	112
	Final Review	116

Section III

	Overview	121
	Review	122
1.	Numbers to 100	126

ISBN: 978-1-897164-13-6

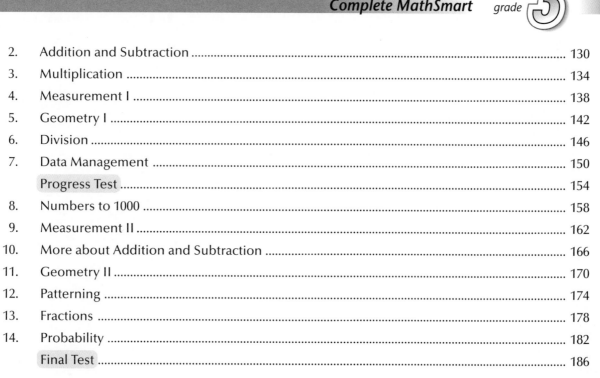
2.   Addition and Subtraction 130
3.   Multiplication 134
4.   Measurement I 138
5.   Geometry I 142
6.   Division 146
7.   Data Management 150
     Progress Test 154
8.   Numbers to 1000 158
9.   Measurement II 162
10. More about Addition and Subtraction 166
11. Geometry II 170
12. Patterning 174
13. Fractions 178
14. Probability 182
     Final Test 186

Section IV

     Overview 193
1.   Numeration 194
2.   Addition and Subtraction 196
3.   Multiplication 200
4.   Division 204
5.   Fractions 208
6.   Money 212
     Midway Review 216
7.   Capacity and Mass 220
8.   Length 224
9.   Patterns 228
10. Geometry 232
11. Pictographs 236
12. Bar Graphs 238
     Final Review 240

Parents' Guide 245
Answers 249

ISBN: 978-1-897164-13-6

Overview

In Grade 2, children developed arithmetic skills which included addition and subtraction up to 100 as well as writing and ordering 2-digit and 3-digit numbers.

In this section, children develop these skills further to include ordering, and adding and subtracting 4-digit numbers. Multiplication of 1-digit numbers and division of 2-digit numbers by 1-digit numbers are introduced and practised. The concepts of Fractions and Decimals are also explained.

Money applications include the use of decimals and sums up to $10. Measurement skills are expanded to include standard units for recording perimeter, area, capacity, volume and mass.

Organizing data and constructing pictographs and bar graphs are practised. Children are also encouraged to use mathematical language to discuss probability.

Addition and Subtraction

The table shows the number of students in 5 high schools. Read the table and answer the questions.

	Allentown School	Brownsville School	Cedarbrae School	Davisville School	Eagletown School
Number of students	1050	1025	1330	1040	1245

① Which school has the largest number of students?

_____

② Which school has the smallest number of students?

_____

③ 426 students in Allentown School are girls. How many boys are in Allentown School?

_____ = _____   _____ boys

④ 50 students are transferred from Brownsville School to Cedarbrae School. How many students are now at Brownsville School?

_____ = _____   _____ students

⑤ How many students are now at Cedarbrae School?

_____ = _____   _____ students

⑥ 250 students of Davisville School go to school by bus. How many students of the school do not go to school by bus?

_____ = _____   _____ students

⑦ 319 students of Eagletown School wear glasses. How many students of the school do not wear glasses?

_____ = _____   _____ students

ISBN: 978-1-897164-13-6

Uncle William recorded the number of sandwiches and pitas sold last month. Look at his record and answer the questions.

	Roast Beef	Chicken Salad	Turkey Breast
Sandwich	582	394	1325
Pita	1429	1066	849

⑧ How many roast beef sandwiches and pitas were sold?

_____ = _____

_____ roast beef sandwiches and pitas were sold.

⑨ How many chicken salad sandwiches and pitas were sold?

_____ = _____

_____ chicken salad sandwiches and pitas were sold.

⑩ How many turkey breast sandwiches and pitas were sold?

_____ = _____

_____ turkey breast sandwiches and pitas were sold.

⑪ How many sandwiches were sold?

_____ = _____

_____ sandwiches were sold.

⑫ How many pitas were sold?

_____ = _____

_____ pitas were sold.

⑬ How many fewer sandwiches than pitas were sold?

_____ = _____

_____ fewer sandwiches than pitas were sold.

Find the sums or differences. Match the letters with the answers to see what Charlie says.

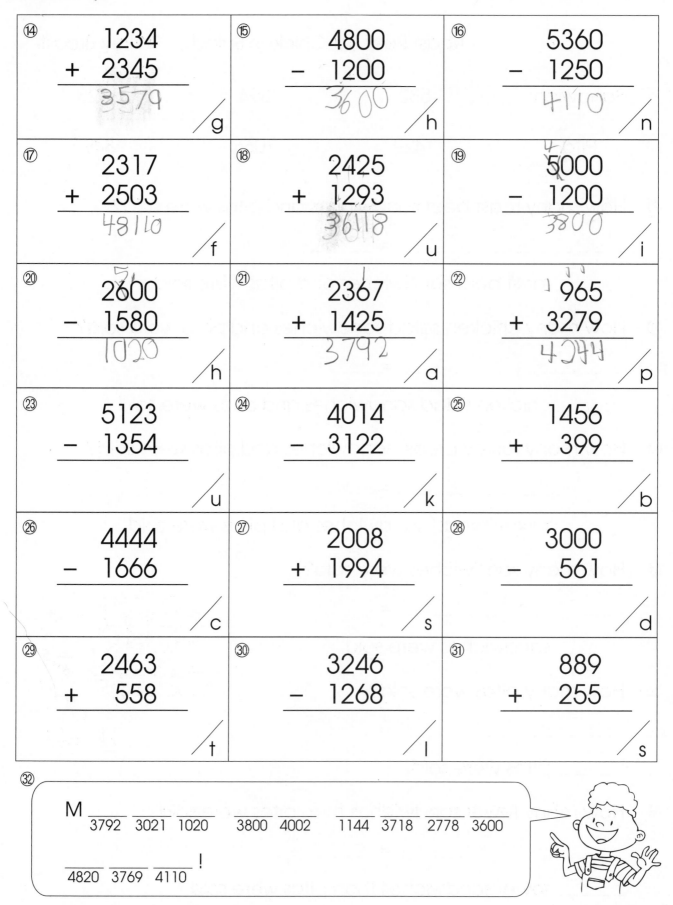

⑭
```
  1234
+ 2345
  3579
```
/g

⑮
```
  4800
- 1200
  3600
```
/h

⑯
```
  5360
- 1250
  4110
```
/n

⑰
```
  2317
+ 2503
  48110
```
/f

⑱
```
  2425
+ 1293
  36118
```
/u

⑲
```
  5000
- 1200
  3800
```
/i

⑳
```
  2600
- 1580
  1020
```
/h

㉑
```
  2367
+ 1425
  3792
```
/a

㉒
```
   965
+ 3279
  4244
```
/p

㉓
```
  5123
- 1354
```
/u

㉔
```
  4014
- 3122
```
/k

㉕
```
  1456
+  399
```
/b

㉖
```
  4444
- 1666
```
/c

㉗
```
  2008
+ 1994
```
/s

㉘
```
  3000
-  561
```
/d

㉙
```
  2463
+  558
```
/t

㉚
```
  3246
- 1268
```
/l

㉛
```
   889
+  255
```
/s

㉜

M ____ ____ ____   ____ ____   ____ ____ ____
  3792 3021 1020 3800 4002 1144 3718 2778 3600

____ ____ ____ !
4820 3769 4110

The Smart Girls performed in 4 cities last year. The table shows the attendance at each of their concerts. Look at the table and answer the questions.

City	Attendance
Toronto	3590
Montreal	2945
Calgary	1782
Vancouver	2595

㉝ How many people in total attended the concert in Toronto or Montreal?

_____ = _____   _____ people

㉞ How many people in total attended the concert in Calgary or Vancouver?

_____ = _____   _____ people

㉟ How many more people attended the concert in Vancouver than in Calgary?

_____ = _____   _____ more people

㊱ 1827 girls attended the concert in Montreal. How many boys attended that concert?

_____ = _____   _____ boys

㊲ The band expects to have 260 more people attending their concert in Toronto this year. How many people are expected?

_____ = _____   _____ people

㊳ The band expects to have 290 fewer people attending their concert in Calgary this year. How many people are expected?

_____ = _____   _____ people

ISBN: 978-1-897164-13-6

 **4-digit Numbers**

Write the numbers. Then put the numbers in order.

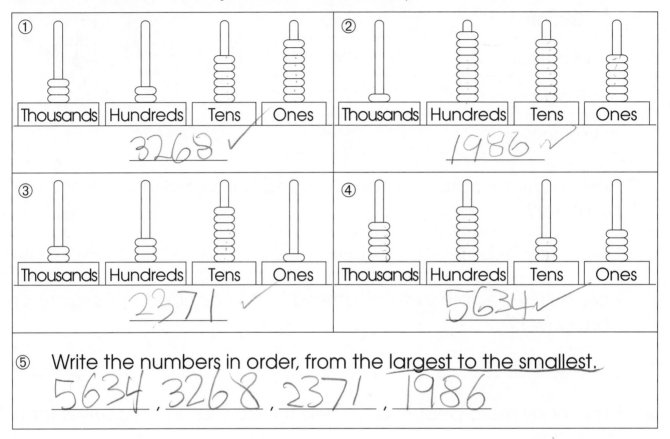

①
Thousands	Hundreds	Tens	Ones

3268 ✓

②
Thousands	Hundreds	Tens	Ones

1986 ✓

③
Thousands	Hundreds	Tens	Ones

2371 ✓

④
Thousands	Hundreds	Tens	Ones

5634 ✓

⑤ Write the numbers in order, from the largest to the smallest.

5634 , 3268 , 2371 , 1986

Write the numbers or words.

⑥ The largest 4-digit number with 5, 6, 1 and 4 _____

⑦ The smallest 4-digit number with 3, 0, 8 and 6 _____

⑧ The largest 4-digit odd number with 5, 9, 2 and 3 _____

⑨ The smallest 4-digit even number with 1, 7, 4 and 2 _____

⑩ The number 2341 in words _____

⑪ The number 4102 in words _____

⑫ The number 7009 in words _____

ISBN: 978-1-897164-13-6

Riverview School is collecting pennies for a local hospital. See how many pennies each jar can hold. Then answer the questions.

⑬ Grade 1 fill 1 big jar and 2 medium jars. How many pennies do they collect?

 1200 pennies

⑭ Grade 2 fill 2 big jars and 5 small jars. How many pennies do they collect?

 2050 pennies

⑮ Grade 3 fill 3 big jars and 4 medium jars. How many pennies do they collect?

 3400 pennies

⑯ Grade 4 fill 2 big jars, 2 small jars and collect 5 more pennies. How many pennies do they collect?

2205 pennies

⑰ Grade 5 collect 3000 pennies. How many big jars do they fill?

 3 big jars

⑱ Grade 6 collect 900 pennies. How many medium jars do they fill?

 9 medium jars

⑲ Which grade collects the most pennies?

Grade 3

⑳ 9380 pennies are collected. How many jars of different sizes can be filled, using the fewest jars?

ISBN: 978-1-897164-13-6

 Multiplication

Count and write the number of pictures on the cards to complete the tables. Then fill in the blanks.

①

a. Number of cards	1	2	3	4	5	6
Total number of ♡						

b. There are _____ threes.   c. _____ x 3 = _____

②

a. Number of cards	1	2	3	4	5	6	7
Total number of ☆							

b. There are _____ fours.   c. _____ x 4 = _____

③

a. Number of cards	1	2	3	4	5	6
Total number of △						

b. There are _____ eights.   c. _____ x 8 = _____

④

a. Number of cards	1	2	3	4	5
Total number of ♛					

b. There are _____ sevens.   c. _____ x 7 = _____

⑤

a. Number of cards	1	2	3	4	5	6	7	8
Total number of ✕								

b. There are _____ twos.   c. _____ x 2 = _____

ISBN: 978-1-897164-13-6

Count the number of animals in each picture. Then check ✔ the correct answers and fill in the blanks.

⑥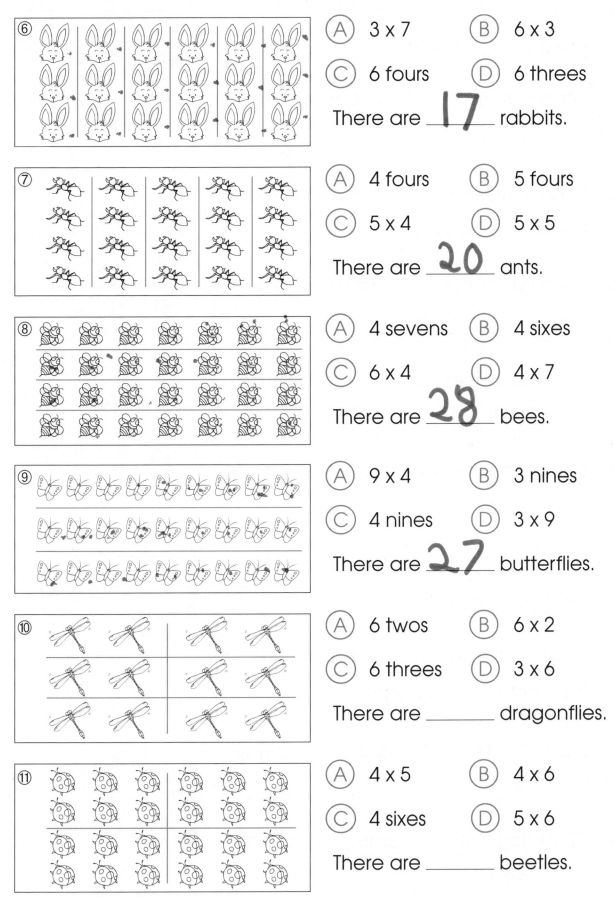

(A) 3 x 7　　(B) 6 x 3

(C) 6 fours　　(D) 6 threes

There are __17__ rabbits.

⑦

(A) 4 fours　　(B) 5 fours

(C) 5 x 4　　(D) 5 x 5

There are __20__ ants.

⑧

(A) 4 sevens　　(B) 4 sixes

(C) 6 x 4　　(D) 4 x 7

There are __28__ bees.

⑨

(A) 9 x 4　　(B) 3 nines

(C) 4 nines　　(D) 3 x 9

There are __27__ butterflies.

⑩

(A) 6 twos　　(B) 6 x 2

(C) 6 threes　　(D) 3 x 6

There are _____ dragonflies.

⑪

(A) 4 x 5　　(B) 4 x 6

(C) 4 sixes　　(D) 5 x 6

There are _____ beetles.

ISBN: 978-1-897164-13-6

Look at the pictures. Then write the numbers to complete each sentence.

⑫ a. Each cat has __8__ whiskers. 8 cats have _____ whiskers.

b. Each cat has _____ eyes. 8 cats have _____ eyes.

⑬ a. Each flower has _____ leaves. 9 flowers have _____ leaves.

b. Each flower has _____ petals. 9 flowers have _____ petals.

⑭ a. Each bracelet has _____ big beads. 6 bracelets have _____ big beads.

b. Each bracelet has _____ small beads. 6 bracelets have _____ small beads.

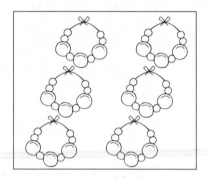

⑮ a. Each tray holds _____ cakes. 3 trays hold _____ cakes.

b. Each tray holds _____ doughnuts. 3 trays hold _____ doughnuts.

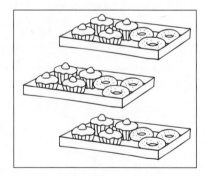

⑯ a. Each dog has _____ legs. 7 dogs have _____ legs.

b. Each dog has _____ ears. 7 dogs have _____ ears.

  ISBN: 978-1-897164-13-6

16
+16
32

See what Adam takes when he goes camping. Help him solve the problems.

⑰ A box holds 6 eggs. How many eggs are there in 3 boxes?

_____ X _____ = _____

There are _____ eggs in 3 boxes.

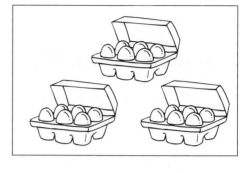

⑱ A pack has 8 sausages. How many sausages are there in 4 packs?

_____ X _____ = _____

There are _____ sausages in 4 packs.

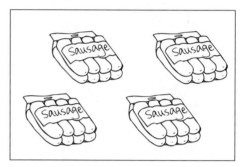

⑲ A bag has 5 buns. How many buns are there in 5 bags?

_____ X _____ = _____

There are _____ buns in 5 bags.

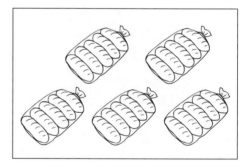

⑳ A pack has 8 batteries. How many batteries are there in 7 packs?

_____ X _____ = _____

There are _____ batteries in 7 packs.

㉑ A bunch has 9 bananas. How many bananas are there in 5 bunches?

_____ X _____ = _____

There Are _____ bananas in 5 bunches.

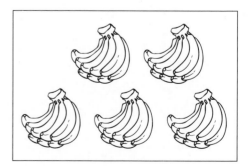

ISBN: 978-1-897164-13-6

Division

Look at the pictures. Write the numbers.

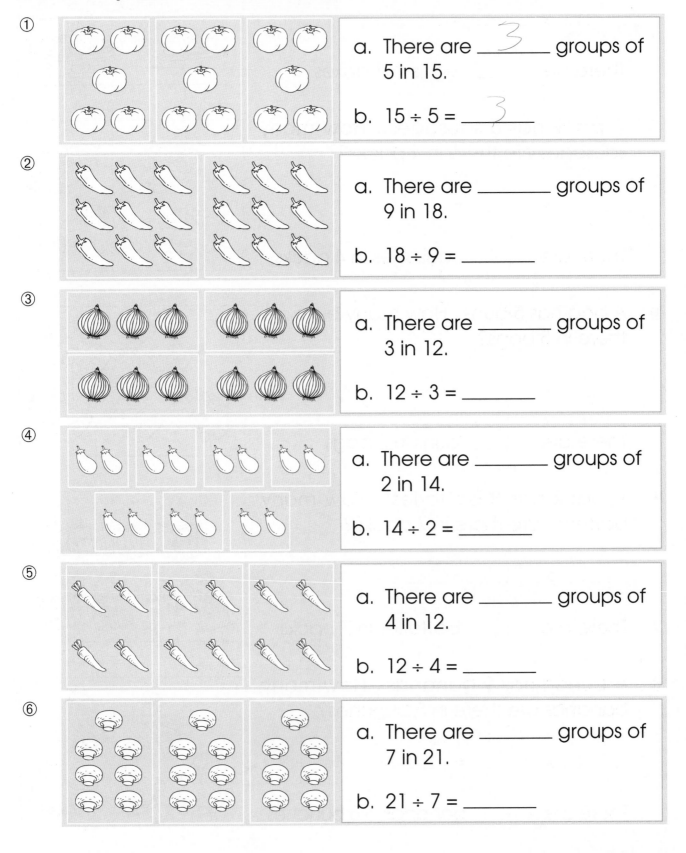

① a. There are ___3___ groups of 5 in 15.

   b. 15 ÷ 5 = ___3___

② a. There are _____ groups of 9 in 18.

   b. 18 ÷ 9 = _____

③ a. There are _____ groups of 3 in 12.

   b. 12 ÷ 3 = _____

④ a. There are _____ groups of 2 in 14.

   b. 14 ÷ 2 = _____

⑤ a. There are _____ groups of 4 in 12.

   b. 12 ÷ 4 = _____

⑥ a. There are _____ groups of 7 in 21.

   b. 21 ÷ 7 = _____

   ISBN: 978-1-897164-13-6

See how the children divide their stickers. Help them circle each group of stickers and write the numbers.

⑦ Wayne divides 18 stickers into 2 equal groups.

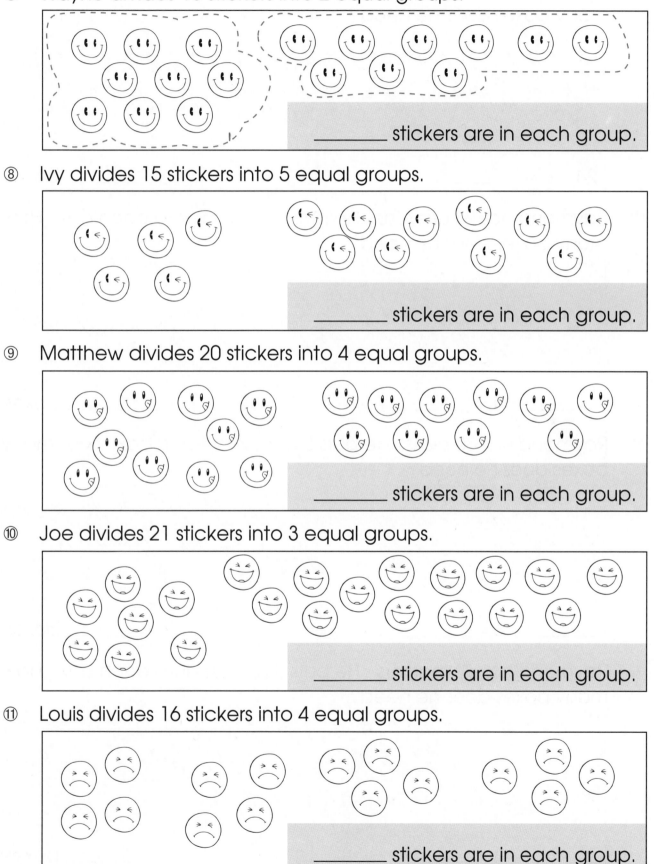

_____ stickers are in each group.

⑧ Ivy divides 15 stickers into 5 equal groups.

_____ stickers are in each group.

⑨ Matthew divides 20 stickers into 4 equal groups.

_____ stickers are in each group.

⑩ Joe divides 21 stickers into 3 equal groups.

_____ stickers are in each group.

⑪ Louis divides 16 stickers into 4 equal groups.

_____ stickers are in each group.

ISBN: 978-1-897164-13-6

Raymond puts his stationery into boxes. Help him circle each group of stationery and write the numbers.

⑫ Raymond has 24 pencils. He puts 6 pencils into each box. How many boxes does he need?

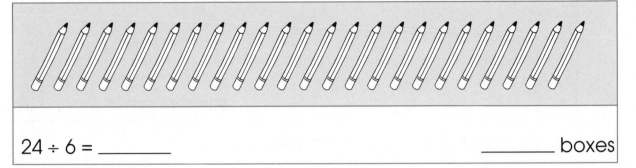

24 ÷ 6 = _____   _____ boxes

⑬ Raymond has 28 crayons. He puts 4 crayons into each box. How many boxes does he need?

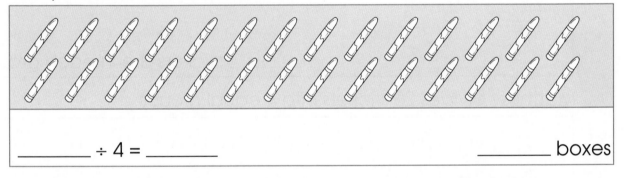

_____ ÷ 4 = _____   _____ boxes

⑭ Raymond has 30 pens. He puts 5 pens into each box. How many boxes does he need?

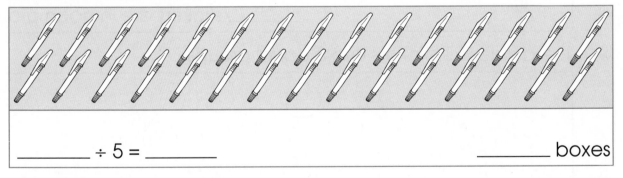

_____ ÷ 5 = _____   _____ boxes

⑮ Raymond has 40 markers. He puts 8 markers into each box. How many boxes does he need?

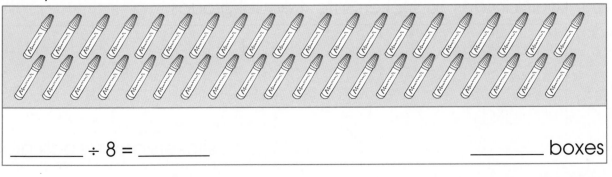

_____ ÷ 8 = _____   _____ boxes

   ISBN: 978-1-897164-13-6

Answer the questions.

⑯ Put 18 cookies into 6 jars. How many cookies are there in each jar?

$18 \div 6 =$ _____   _____ cookies are in each jar.

⑰ Put 24 muffins into 4 boxes. How many muffins are there in each box?

_____ $\div\ 4 =$ _____   _____ muffins are in each box.

⑱ Put 26 doughnuts into 3 bags. How many doughnuts are there in each bag? How many doughnuts are left over?

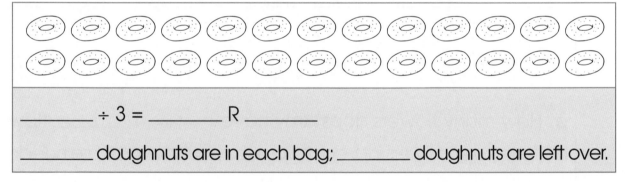

_____ $\div\ 3 =$ _____ R _____

_____ doughnuts are in each bag; _____ doughnuts are left over.

⑲ Put 23 pretzels into 5 baskets. How many pretzels are there in each basket? How many pretzels are left over?

_____ $\div\ 5 =$ _____ R _____

_____ pretzels are in each basket; _____ pretzels are left over.

ISBN: 978-1-897164-13-6

See what the children have. Help them solve the problems.

①

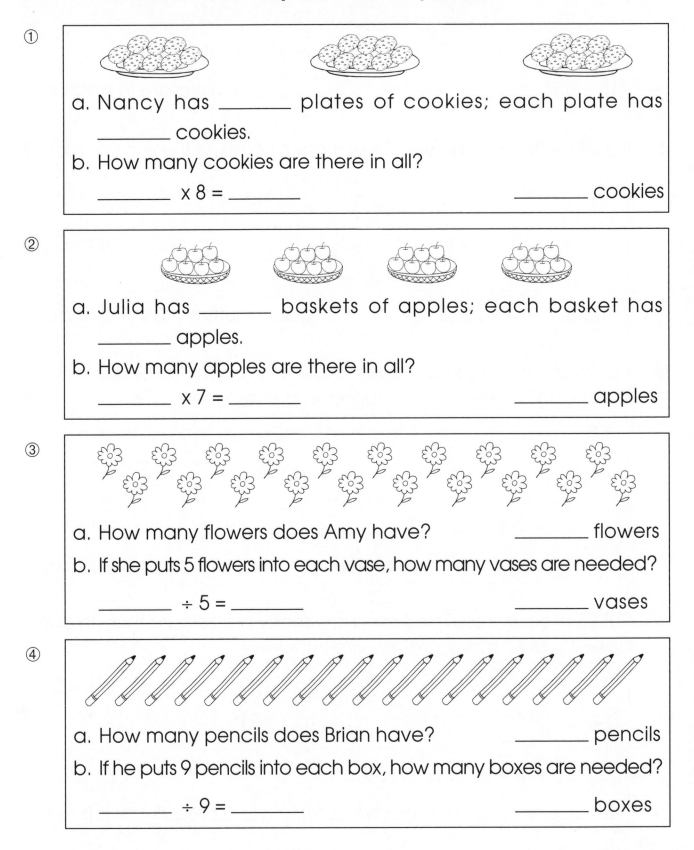

a. Nancy has _____ plates of cookies; each plate has _____ cookies.

b. How many cookies are there in all?

_____ x 8 = _____   _____ cookies

②

a. Julia has _____ baskets of apples; each basket has _____ apples.

b. How many apples are there in all?

_____ x 7 = _____   _____ apples

③

a. How many flowers does Amy have?   _____ flowers

b. If she puts 5 flowers into each vase, how many vases are needed?

_____ ÷ 5 = _____   _____ vases

④

a. How many pencils does Brian have?   _____ pencils

b. If he puts 9 pencils into each box, how many boxes are needed?

_____ ÷ 9 = _____   _____ boxes

ISBN: 978-1-897164-13-6

Answer the questions.

⑤ Jim cuts a pizza into 8 slices. If he gets 48 slices, how many pizzas has he cut?

_____ ÷ _____ = _____   _____ pizzas

⑥ Ivan has 3 bags of marbles. Each bag contains 9 marbles. How many marbles does Ivan have?

_____ x _____ = _____   _____ marbles

⑦ Each page of a photo album has 3 photos. How many photos are there on 8 pages?

_____ x _____ = _____   _____ photos

⑧ Each box holds 4 muffins. How many boxes are needed to hold 36 muffins?

_____ ÷ _____ = _____   _____ boxes

⑨ Each child has 7 pennies. How many pennies do 6 children have?

_____ x _____ = _____   _____ pennies

⑩ Joe has 25 baseball cards. He puts 5 cards into a pile. How many piles can he get?

_____ ÷ _____ = _____   _____ piles

⑪ A pack has 6 stickers. How many stickers are there in 3 packs?

_____ x _____ = _____   _____ stickers

ISBN: 978-1-897164-13-6

Midway Review

Fill in the missing numbers.

① 1169, 1170, _____ , _____ , 1173, _____ , 1175

② 2588, 2688, _____ , _____ , 2988, _____ , 3188

③ 9214, _____ , 7214, _____ , 5214, _____ , 3214

④ 4016, _____ , 4012, _____ , 4008, _____ , 4004

Use the following numbers to answer the questions.

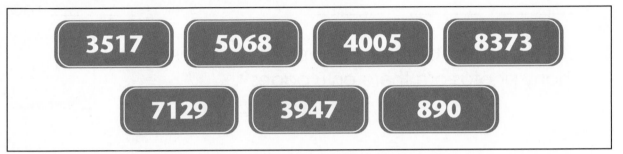

3517   5068   4005   8373

7129   3947   890

⑤ How many numbers are bigger than 5000?   _____

⑥ Which number is smaller than 4000 but bigger than 3600?   _____

⑦ Which number has 5 in its thousands place?   _____

⑧ Which number has 3 in its hundreds place?   _____

⑨ How many even numbers are there?   _____

⑩ What is the sum of the smallest and the biggest numbers?   _____

⑪ What is the difference between the smallest and the biggest numbers?   _____

⑫ Write the biggest number in words.

_____

⑬ Write the smallest number in words.

_____

ISBN: 978-1-897164-13-6

The table shows how many stamps each child has. Help the children fill in the boxes on the number line and answer the questions.

	Eva	Molly	Brad	Mary	George
Number of stamps	927	2018	1806	1446	1129

⑭ Put the names and numbers in the boxes to show how many stamps each child has.

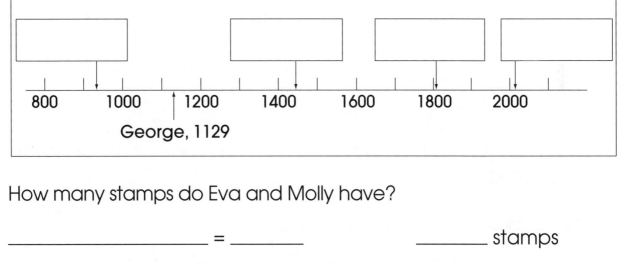

⑮ How many stamps do Eva and Molly have?

_____ = _____ _____ stamps

⑯ How many more stamps does Molly have than Eva?

_____ = _____ _____ more stamps

⑰ How many stamps do Brad and Mary have?

_____ = _____ _____ stamps

⑱ How many fewer stamps does Mary have than Brad?

_____ = _____ _____ fewer stamps

⑲ How many stamps do the boys have?

_____ = _____ _____ stamps

⑳ How many stamps do the girls have?

_____ = _____ _____ stamps

Answer the questions.

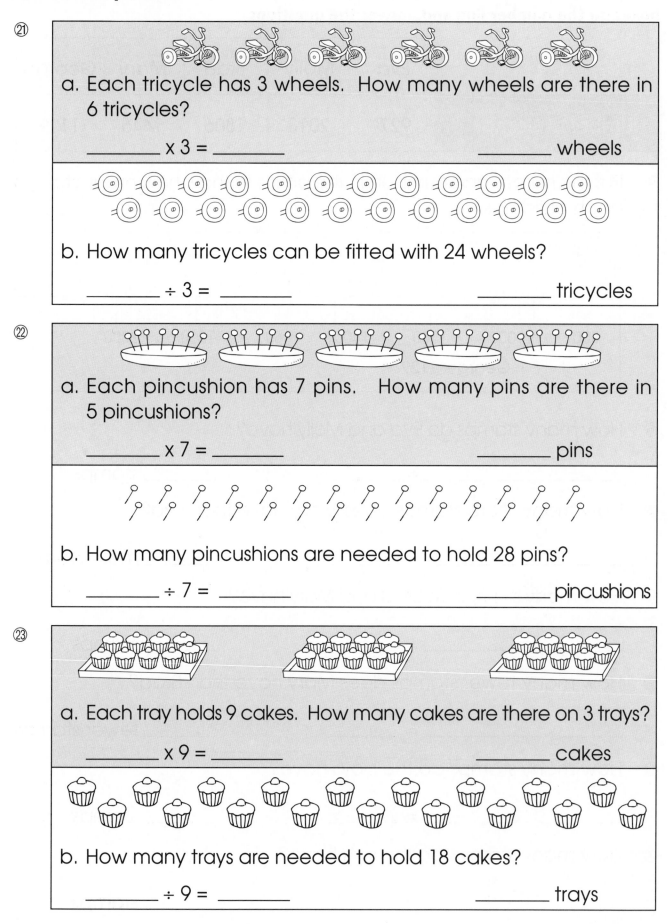

21.

a. Each tricycle has 3 wheels. How many wheels are there in 6 tricycles?

_____ x 3 = _____   _____ wheels

b. How many tricycles can be fitted with 24 wheels?

_____ ÷ 3 = _____   _____ tricycles

22.

a. Each pincushion has 7 pins.   How many pins are there in 5 pincushions?

_____ x 7 = _____   _____ pins

b. How many pincushions are needed to hold 28 pins?

_____ ÷ 7 = _____   _____ pincushions

23.

a. Each tray holds 9 cakes. How many cakes are there on 3 trays?

_____ x 9 = _____   _____ cakes

b. How many trays are needed to hold 18 cakes?

_____ ÷ 9 = _____   _____ trays

    ISBN: 978-1-897164-13-6

Look at the pictures. Write the numbers.

㉔
a. $3 \times 4 = $ _____ b. $2 \times 6 = $ _____

c. $12 \div 3 = $ _____ d. $12 \div 2 = $ _____

㉕
a. $2 \times 9 = $ _____ b. $3 \times 6 = $ _____

c. $18 \div 2 = $ _____ d. $18 \div 6 = $ _____

㉖
a. $3 \times 8 = $ _____ b. $6 \times 4 = $ _____

c. $24 \div 8 = $ _____ d. $24 \div 6 = $ _____

Answer the questions.

㉗ 8 flowers are divided into 2 equal groups. How many flowers are there in each group?

_____ $\div$ 2 = _____   _____ flowers

㉘ Each box holds 6 sandwiches. How many sandwiches are there in 9 boxes?

_____ x 6 = _____   _____ sandwiches

㉙ Mrs Feler divides 63 markers equally among 7 children. How many markers can each child get?

_____ $\div$ 7 = _____   _____ markers

㉚ Each row has 9 chairs. How many chairs are there in 4 rows?

_____ x 9 = _____   _____ chairs

Check ✔ the correct number of coins to pay for each toy in 2 different ways.

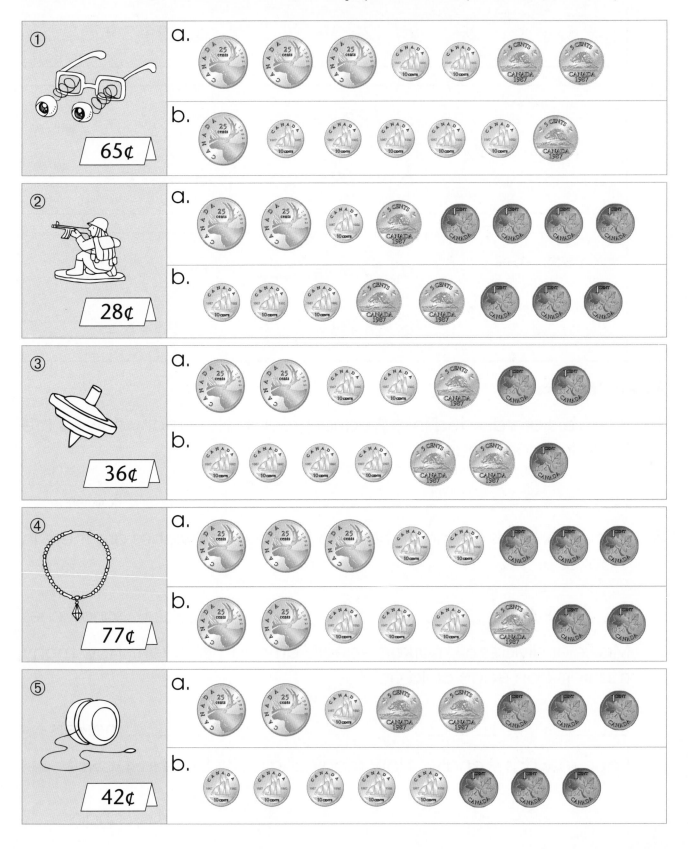

ISBN: 978-1-897164-13-6

Write how much money each child has. Then see what they buy and write how much they have left.

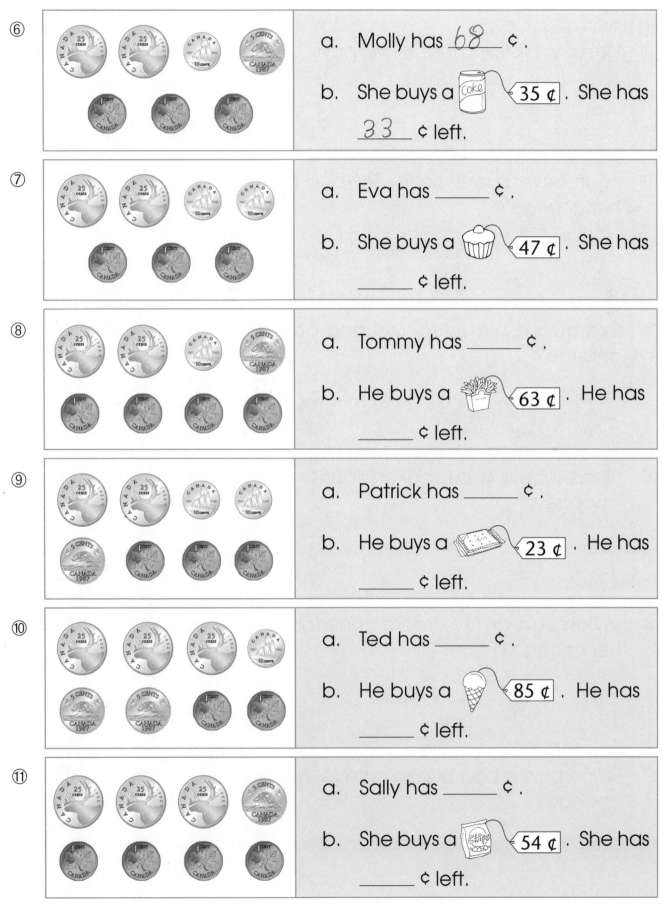

⑥

a. Molly has _68_ ¢.

b. She buys a [Coke] ⟨ 35 ¢ ⟩. She has _33_ ¢ left.

⑦

a. Eva has _____ ¢.

b. She buys a ⟨ 47 ¢ ⟩. She has _____ ¢ left.

⑧

a. Tommy has _____ ¢.

b. He buys a ⟨ 63 ¢ ⟩. He has _____ ¢ left.

⑨

a. Patrick has _____ ¢.

b. He buys a ⟨ 23 ¢ ⟩. He has _____ ¢ left.

⑩

a. Ted has _____ ¢.

b. He buys a ⟨ 85 ¢ ⟩. He has _____ ¢ left.

⑪

a. Sally has _____ ¢.

b. She buys a [chips] ⟨ 54 ¢ ⟩. She has _____ ¢ left.

ISBN: 978-1-897164-13-6

See how much the customers pay for their food. Help the cashier check ✔ the fewest coins to show the change.

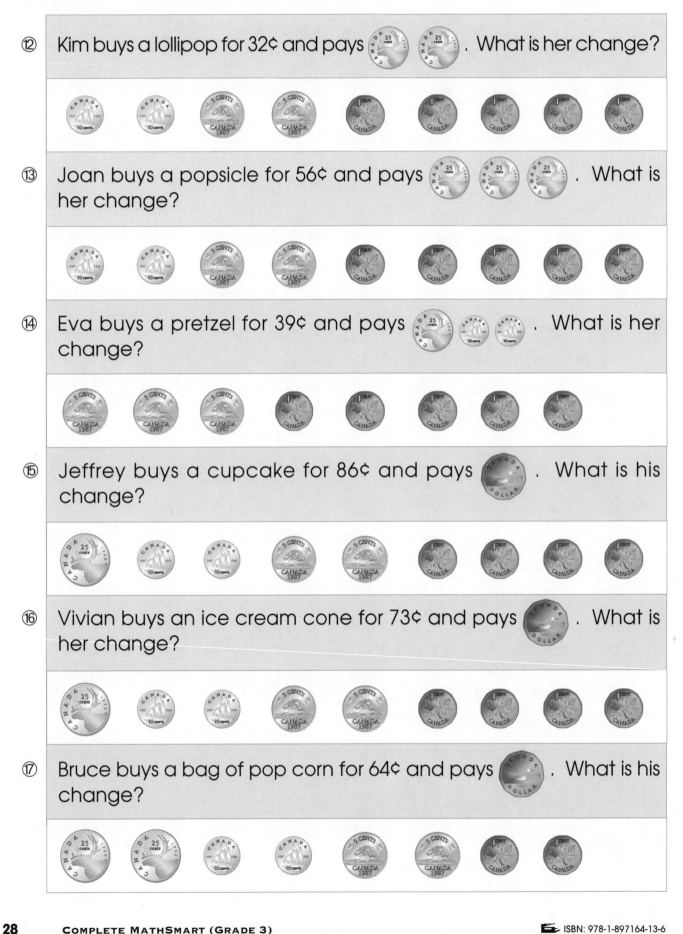

⑫ Kim buys a lollipop for 32¢ and pays ⬤⬤ . What is her change?

⑬ Joan buys a popsicle for 56¢ and pays ⬤⬤⬤ . What is her change?

⑭ Eva buys a pretzel for 39¢ and pays ⬤⬤⬤ . What is her change?

⑮ Jeffrey buys a cupcake for 86¢ and pays ⬤ . What is his change?

⑯ Vivian buys an ice cream cone for 73¢ and pays ⬤ . What is her change?

⑰ Bruce buys a bag of pop corn for 64¢ and pays ⬤ . What is his change?

Mrs Ford works in a bakery. Help her solve the problems.

⑱ a. Mike buys 2 bread rolls for 16¢ each. How much does he need to pay?

_____ = _____

_____ ¢

b. What is his change from 50¢ ?

_____ = _____

_____ ¢

⑲ a. Mr Jenn buys 2 cinnamon buns for 37¢ each. How much does he need to pay?

_____ = _____   _____ ¢

b. What is his change from 80¢ ?

_____ = _____   _____ ¢

⑳ a. Mrs Winter buys 3 chocolate chip cookies for 18¢ each. How much does she need to pay?

_____ = _____   _____ ¢

b. What is her change from $1?

_____ = _____   _____ ¢

㉑ a. Pam buys 3 brownies for 29¢ each. How much does she need to pay?

_____ = _____   _____ ¢

b. What is her change from $1?

_____ = _____   _____ ¢

ISBN: 978-1-897164-13-6

Measurement

Circle the correct answers.

①	Which is a better unit for measuring the length of a dining table?		
②	Which is a better unit for measuring the weight of an apple?		
③	Which is a better unit for measuring the length of a football field?	centimetre	metre
④	Which is a better unit for measuring the time you sleep every night?	second	hour
⑤	Which is a better unit for measuring the time you take to brush your teeth?	minute	hour
⑥	How many minutes are there in 1 hour?	30	60
⑦	How many hours are there in 1 day?	24	25

Find the perimeter of each shape.

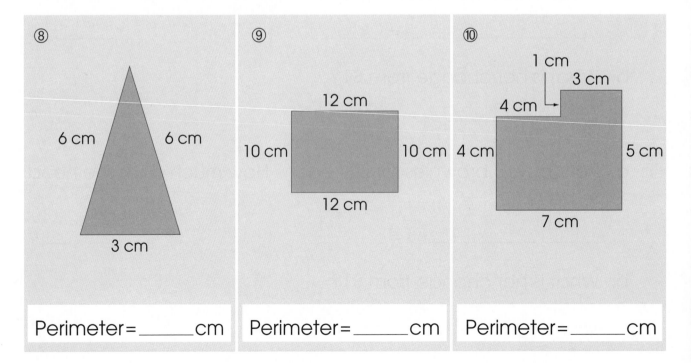

⑧

6 cm　6 cm

3 cm

Perimeter = _____ cm

⑨

12 cm

10 cm　10 cm

12 cm

Perimeter = _____ cm

⑩

1 cm

3 cm

4 cm

4 cm　　5 cm

7 cm

Perimeter = _____ cm

ISBN: 978-1-897164-13-6

Mrs Ling wants to bake a cake. Look at the ingredients, times and temperatures. Answer the questions.

⑪ Which ingredient is the heaviest? _____

⑫ Which ingredient is the lightest? _____

⑬ Which is heavier, the sugar or the cocoa? _____

⑭ Draw the hands on the clock faces to show the time Mrs Ling starts to bake her cake and the time the cake is done.

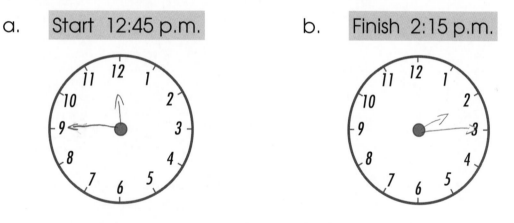

a. Start 12:45 p.m.

b. Finish 2:15 p.m.

⑮ How long did it take to bake the cake? _____

⑯ Write the temperatures in the kitchen and in the living room.

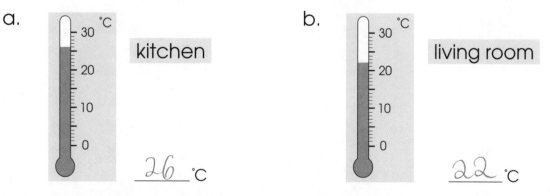

a. kitchen   _26_ °C

b. living room   _22_ °C

⑰ Which place has a higher temperature, the kitchen or the living room? _____

8 Fractions and Decimals

Colour $\frac{2}{3}$ of each shape.

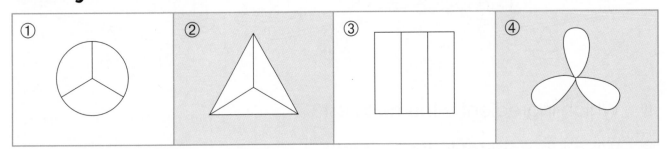

Colour $\frac{1}{4}$ of each shape or group of shapes.

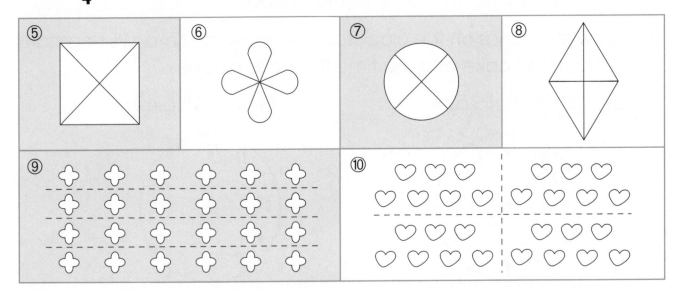

Write a fraction for the shaded part of each shape or group of shapes.

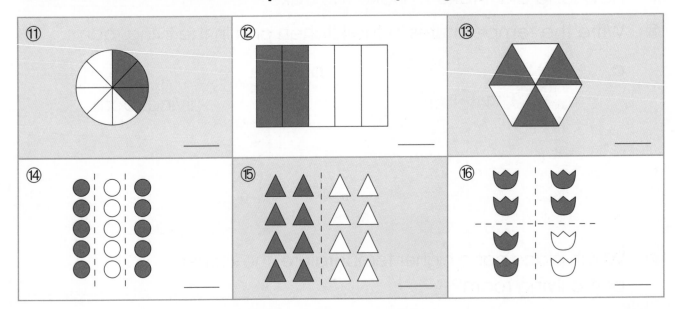

ISBN: 978-1-897164-13-6

Colour the shapes to show each fraction. Write 'greater' or 'smaller' to complete each sentence.

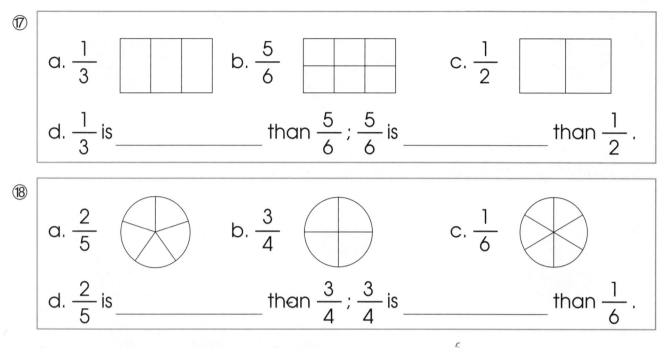

⑰
a. $\frac{1}{3}$ b. $\frac{5}{6}$ c. $\frac{1}{2}$

d. $\frac{1}{3}$ is _____ than $\frac{5}{6}$; $\frac{5}{6}$ is _____ than $\frac{1}{2}$.

⑱
a. $\frac{2}{5}$ b. $\frac{3}{4}$ c. $\frac{1}{6}$

d. $\frac{2}{5}$ is _____ than $\frac{3}{4}$; $\frac{3}{4}$ is _____ than $\frac{1}{6}$.

Look at the children. Write the fractions.

⑲ How many children are there? _____ children

⑳ What fraction of the children are smiling? _____

㉑ What fraction of the children wear glasses? _____

㉒ What fraction of the children are boys? _____

㉓ What fraction of the children have curly hair? _____

㉔ What fraction of the children have long hair? _____

㉕ What fraction of the children with straight hair wear glasses? _____

ISBN: 978-1-897164-13-6

Write a decimal number of the shaded part of each shape. Then answer the questions.

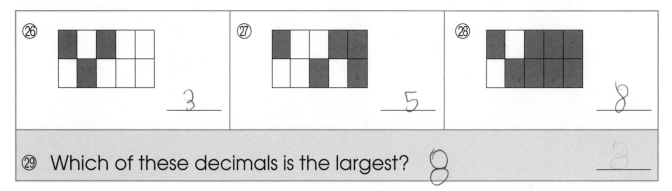

㉖ _3_

㉗ _5_

㉘ _8_

㉙ Which of these decimals is the largest? 8 _8_

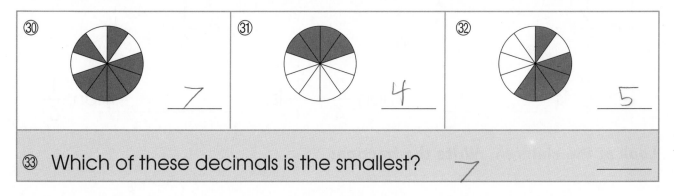

㉚ _7_

㉛ _4_

㉜ _5_

㉝ Which of these decimals is the smallest? 7 ___

Colour the shapes to show each decimal number.

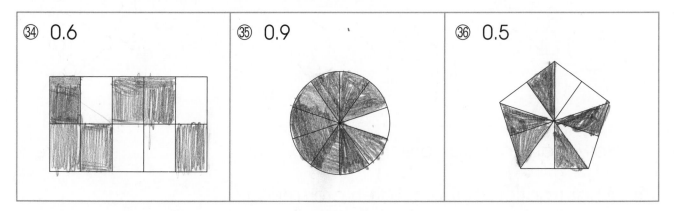

㉞ 0.6

㉟ 0.9

㊱ 0.5

Write a decimal number in words of the shaded part of each shape.

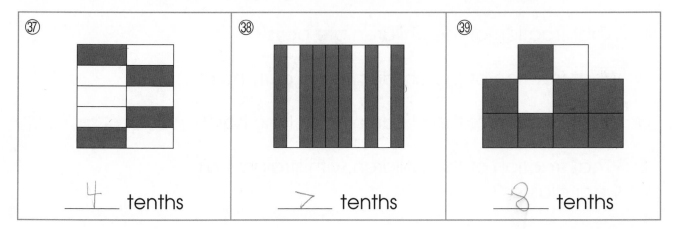

㊲ _4_ tenths

㊳ _7_ tenths

㊴ _8_ tenths

Help the children write the amounts they have in decimals. Then fill in the blanks.

㊵ Kathy has 235¢ in her piggy bank.
She has $ ________ .

㊶ Paul has 261¢ in his piggy bank.
He has $ ________ .

㊷ Kathy has ________ more/less money than Paul.

㊸ 2.35 is ________ greater/smaller than 2.61.

㊹ Pat has 309¢ in her piggy bank. She has $ ________ .

㊺ Raymond has 325¢ in his piggy bank. He has $ ________ .

㊻ Pat has ________ more/less money than Raymond.

㊼ 3.09 is ________ greater/smaller than 3.25.

㊽ Susan has 75¢ in her piggy bank. She has $ ________ .

㊾ Katie has 250¢ in her piggy bank. She has $ ________ .

㊿ Jake has 175¢ in his piggy bank. He has $ ________ .

(51) Susan has ________ more/less money than Katie.

(52) Katie has ________ more/less money than Jake.

(53) 0.75 is ________ greater/smaller than 2.50.

(54) 2.50 is ________ greater/smaller than 1.75.

ISBN: 978-1-897164-13-6

Probability

Pam shuffles all her cards and lets Jimmy pick one. Answer the questions.

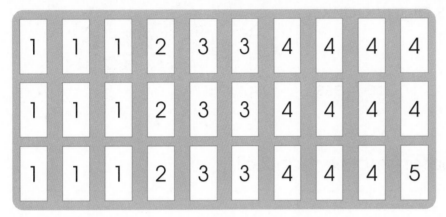

① Are all the numbers equally likely to be picked? _____

② Which number is Jimmy most likely to pick? _____

③ Which number is Jimmy most unlikely to pick? _____

④ Is there a greater chance to pick a $\boxed{1}$ or a $\boxed{2}$? _____

⑤ Is there a smaller chance to pick a $\boxed{3}$ or a $\boxed{4}$? _____

⑥ Is there any chance to pick a $\boxed{7}$? _____

⑦ If the number card Jimmy picks is the same as the one he guesses, he will win the game. What number should Jimmy guess to have the greatest chance to win the game? _____

⑧ What number does Jimmy guess if he has the smallest chance to win? _____

⑨ If Pam takes away all the $\boxed{4}$, what number should Jimmy guess to have the greatest chance to win the game? _____

ISBN: 978-1-897164-13-6

Look at Jason's spinners and check ✔ the correct answers.

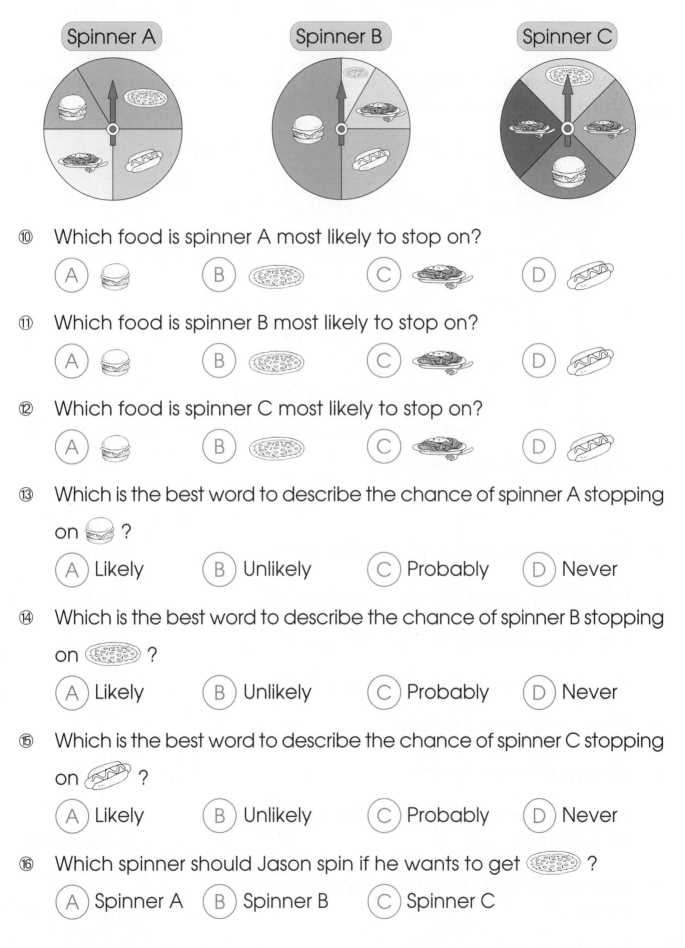

⑩ Which food is spinner A most likely to stop on?

Ⓐ   Ⓑ   Ⓒ   Ⓓ

⑪ Which food is spinner B most likely to stop on?

Ⓐ   Ⓑ   Ⓒ   Ⓓ

⑫ Which food is spinner C most likely to stop on?

Ⓐ   Ⓑ   Ⓒ   Ⓓ

⑬ Which is the best word to describe the chance of spinner A stopping on   ?

Ⓐ Likely   Ⓑ Unlikely   Ⓒ Probably   Ⓓ Never

⑭ Which is the best word to describe the chance of spinner B stopping on   ?

Ⓐ Likely   Ⓑ Unlikely   Ⓒ Probably   Ⓓ Never

⑮ Which is the best word to describe the chance of spinner C stopping on   ?

Ⓐ Likely   Ⓑ Unlikely   Ⓒ Probably   Ⓓ Never

⑯ Which spinner should Jason spin if he wants to get   ?

Ⓐ Spinner A   Ⓑ Spinner B   Ⓒ Spinner C

ISBN: 978-1-897164-13-6

Graphs

Five children each tossed a penny 10 times and recorded the number of heads they got. Use the graph to answer the questions.

Number of Heads Each Child Got

Freda	🪙🪙🪙🪙🪙
Gerrie	🪙🪙🪙🪙🪙🪙🪙
Helen	🪙🪙🪙🪙🪙
Iris	🪙🪙🪙🪙
Lianne	🪙🪙🪙🪙🪙

① What is the title of the graph?

_____

② How many times did Iris get a head? _____ times

③ How many times did Helen get a head? _____ times

④ How many times did Gerrie get a tail? _____ times

⑤ How many times did Lianne get a tail? _____ times

⑥ Who got the most heads? _____

⑦ Who got the most tails? _____

⑧ How many times more did Gerrie get a head than Freda? _____ times more

⑨ How many times fewer did Gerrie get a tail than Iris? _____ times fewer

ISBN: 978-1-897164-13-6

Use the graph to answer the questions.

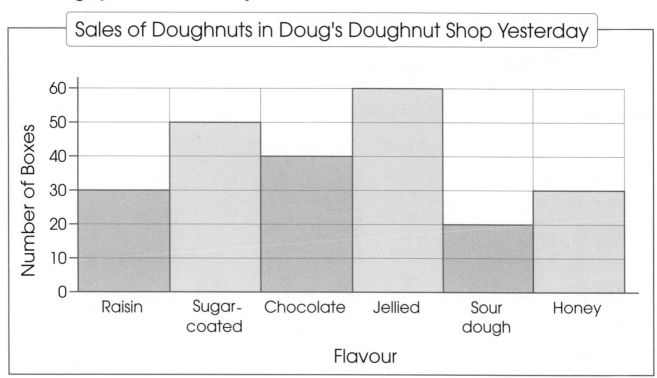

Sales of Doughnuts in Doug's Doughnut Shop Yesterday

⑩ What is the title of the graph?

_____

⑪ What type of graph is it?   _____

⑫ How many boxes of raisin doughnuts
were sold?   _____ boxes

⑬ How many boxes of sugar-coated
doughnuts were sold?   _____ boxes

⑭ Which was the most popular
doughnut?   _____ doughnut

⑮ Which was the least popular
doughnut?   _____ doughnut

⑯ Which kind of doughnut had the
same sales as raisin doughnut?   _____ doughnut

⑰ If each box holds 6 doughnuts,
how many chocolate doughnuts   _____ chocolate
were sold in all?   doughnuts

Mrs Feler records the favourite summer activities in her class. Use her graph to complete the table and answer the questions.

Favourite Summer Activities in Mrs Feler's Class

⑱

Favourite Activity	Swimming	Soccer	Cycling	Hiking
Number of Children				

⑲ Which is the most popular summer activity? _____

⑳ Which is the least popular summer activity? _____

㉑ How many children are there in Mrs Feler's class? _____ children

Use the table above to complete the graph.

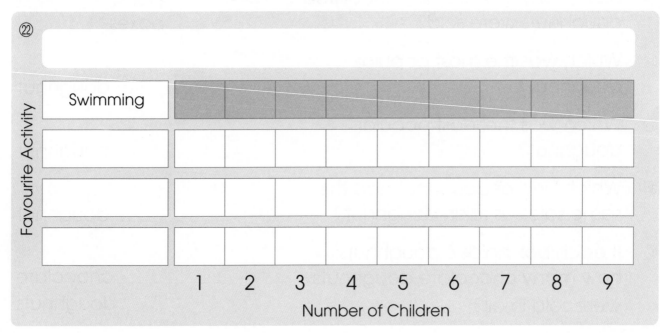

㉒

Favourite Activity

Swimming

Number of Children

1 2 3 4 5 6 7 8 9

   ISBN: 978-1-897164-13-6

The students of Riverview School were asked whether they had been to Florida. Use the chart below to complete the graph.

	Grade 1	Grade 2	Grade 3	Grade 4
Number of students	ⅢⅢ Ⅲ	ⅢⅢ ⅢⅢ Ⅱ	ⅢⅢ ⅢⅢ ⅢⅢ Ⅰ	ⅢⅢ ⅢⅢ ⅢⅢ

㉓

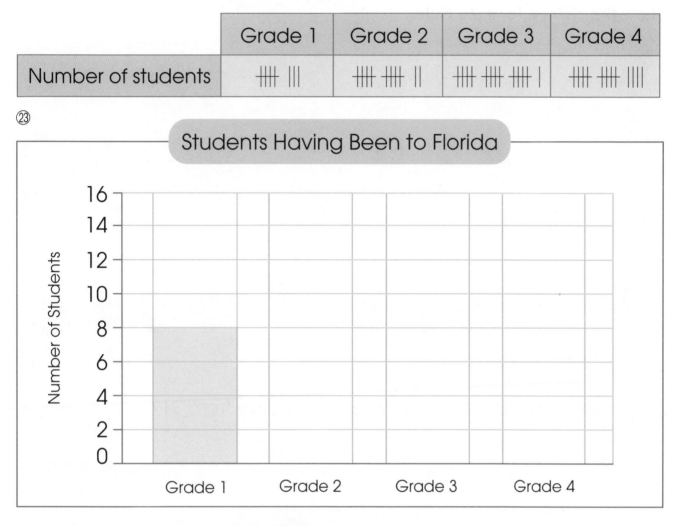

㉔ What is the title of the graph?

_____

㉕ Which grade has the most students who have been to Florida? .... Grade _____

㉖ Which grade has 8 students who have been to Florida? .... Grade _____

㉗ How many Grade 4 students have been to Florida? .... _____ students

㉘ If 7 girls in Grade 2 have been to Florida, how many boys in Grade 2 have been to Florida? ...... _____ boys

㉙ How many students have been to Florida? .... _____ students

ISBN: 978-1-897164-13-6

Final Review

Write the price of each snack. Then calculate and check ✔ the fewest coins to show the change for each child.

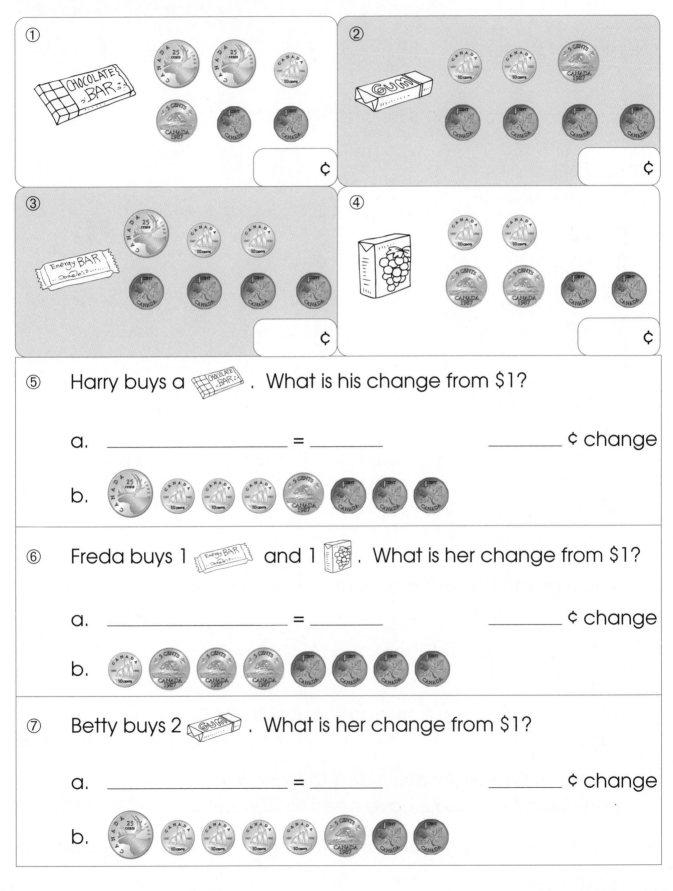

① CHOCOLATE BAR

_____ ¢

② GUM

_____ ¢

③ Energy BAR

_____ ¢

④

_____ ¢

⑤ Harry buys a [CHOCOLATE BAR]. What is his change from $1?

a. _____ = _____ _____ ¢ change

b.

⑥ Freda buys 1 [Energy BAR] and 1 [ ]. What is her change from $1?

a. _____ = _____ _____ ¢ change

b.

⑦ Betty buys 2 [GUM]. What is her change from $1?

a. _____ = _____ _____ ¢ change

b.

ISBN: 978-1-897164-13-6

Draw the clock hands to show the times and calculate the perimeter of each digital clock.

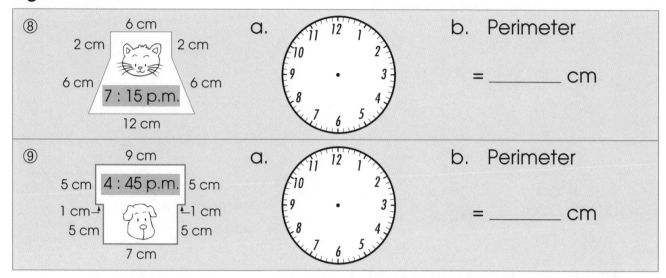

⑧ 6 cm / 2 cm / 2 cm / 6 cm / 6 cm / 7 : 15 p.m. / 12 cm

a.

b. Perimeter

= _____ cm

⑨ 9 cm / 5 cm / 4 : 45 p.m. / 5 cm / 1 cm / 1 cm / 5 cm / 5 cm / 7 cm

a.

b. Perimeter

= _____ cm

Measure and write the lengths of the bracelets. Then answer the questions.

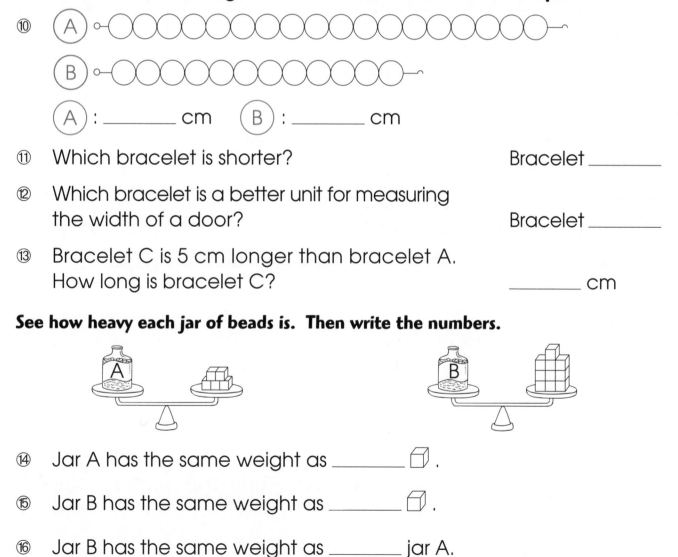

⑩ (A)

(B)

(A) : _____ cm   (B) : _____ cm

⑪ Which bracelet is shorter?   Bracelet _____

⑫ Which bracelet is a better unit for measuring the width of a door?   Bracelet _____

⑬ Bracelet C is 5 cm longer than bracelet A. How long is bracelet C?   _____ cm

See how heavy each jar of beads is. Then write the numbers.

⑭ Jar A has the same weight as _____ ▢ .

⑮ Jar B has the same weight as _____ ▢ .

⑯ Jar B has the same weight as _____ jar A.

Look at the graph. Then answer the questions.

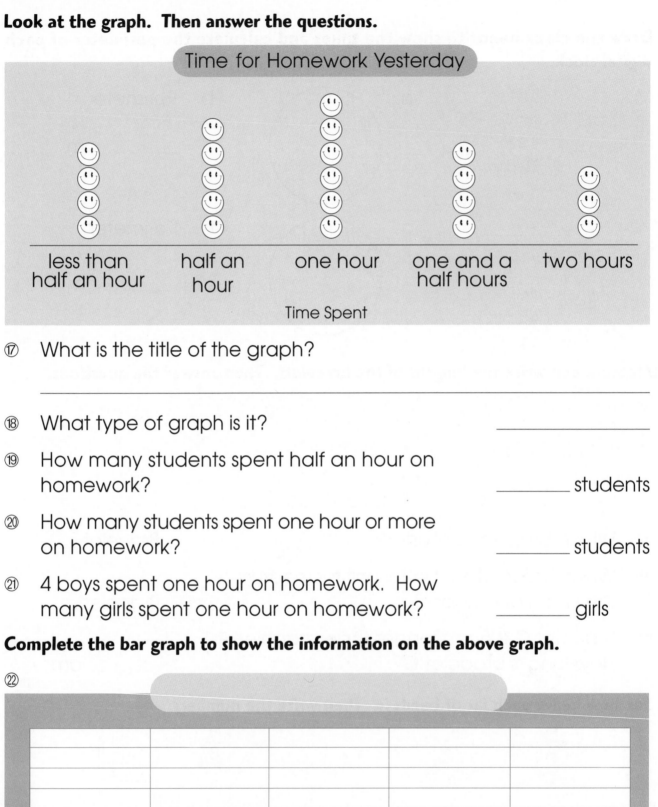

Time for Homework Yesterday

less than half an hour | half an hour | one hour | one and a half hours | two hours

Time Spent

⑰ What is the title of the graph?

_____

⑱ What type of graph is it?   _____

⑲ How many students spent half an hour on homework?   _____ students

⑳ How many students spent one hour or more on homework?   _____ students

㉑ 4 boys spent one hour on homework. How many girls spent one hour on homework?   _____ girls

Complete the bar graph to show the information on the above graph.

㉒

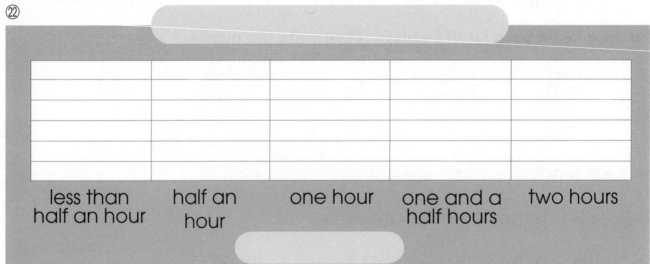

less than half an hour | half an hour | one hour | one and a half hours | two hours

ISBN: 978-1-897164-13-6

Write a fraction and a decimal for the shaded part of each shape.

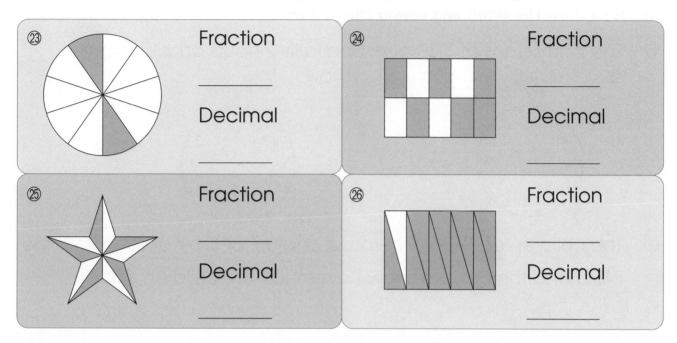

㉓ Fraction

_____

Decimal

_____

㉔ Fraction

_____

Decimal

_____

㉕ Fraction

_____

Decimal

_____

㉖ Fraction

_____

Decimal

_____

Peter picks one marble from the bag. Help him answer the questions.

㉗ Are all the marbles equally likely to be picked? _____

㉘ What colour is Peter most likely to pick? _____

㉙ What colour is Peter most unlikely to pick? _____

㉚ Is there any chance to pick a (Yellow)? _____

㉛ Is there any chance to pick a (Blue)? _____

㉜ Is there a greater chance to pick a (Black) or a (Red)? _____

㉝ How many marbles are there in the bag? _____ marbles

㉞ What fraction of the marbles are red? _____

㉟ What fraction of the marbles are yellow? _____

ISBN: 978-1-897164-13-6

Danielle invites some friends to her birthday party. Help Danielle draw the clock hands to show the times and colour the pictures.

㊱ The party starts at 3:30 p.m. and lasts 2 hours and 15 minutes.

a.

Start

b.

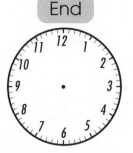

End

㊲ The children eat $\frac{5}{8}$ of the pizza and 0.7 of the cake. Colour the pizza and the cake to show how much the children eat.

Pizza

a.

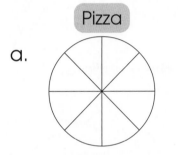

Cake

b.

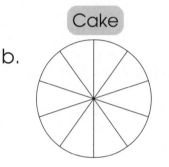

Use the graph to answer the questions.

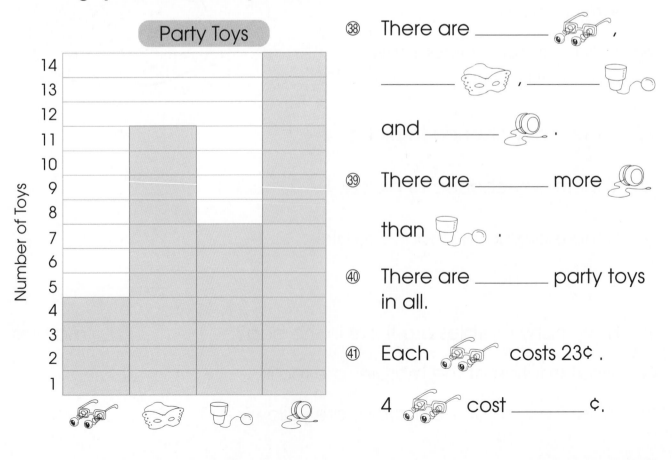

Party Toys

Number of Toys

㊳ There are _____ ,

_____ , _____

and _____ .

㊴ There are _____ more

than .

㊵ There are _____ party toys in all.

㊶ Each costs 23¢.

4 cost _____ ¢.

ISBN: 978-1-897164-13-6

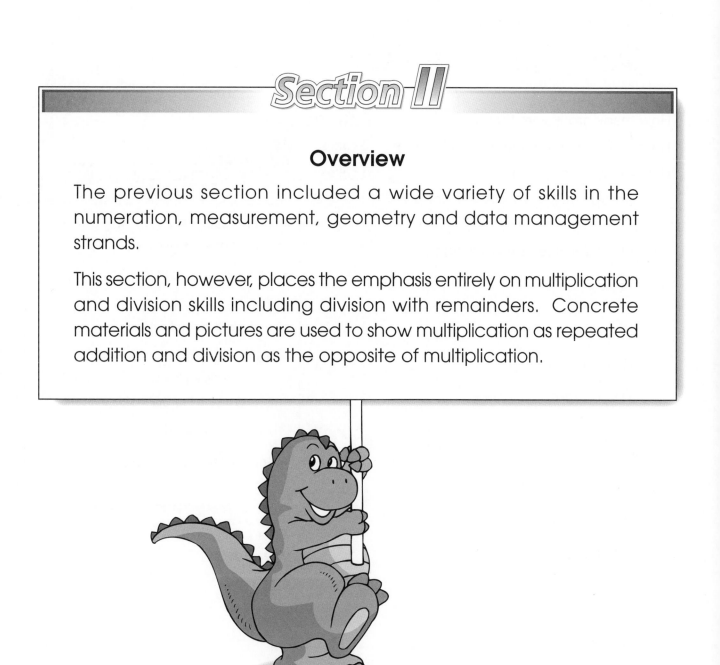

Section II

Overview

The previous section included a wide variety of skills in the numeration, measurement, geometry and data management strands.

This section, however, places the emphasis entirely on multiplication and division skills including division with remainders. Concrete materials and pictures are used to show multiplication as repeated addition and division as the opposite of multiplication.

Introducing Multiplication

EXAMPLE

How many cakes are there on 4 plates?

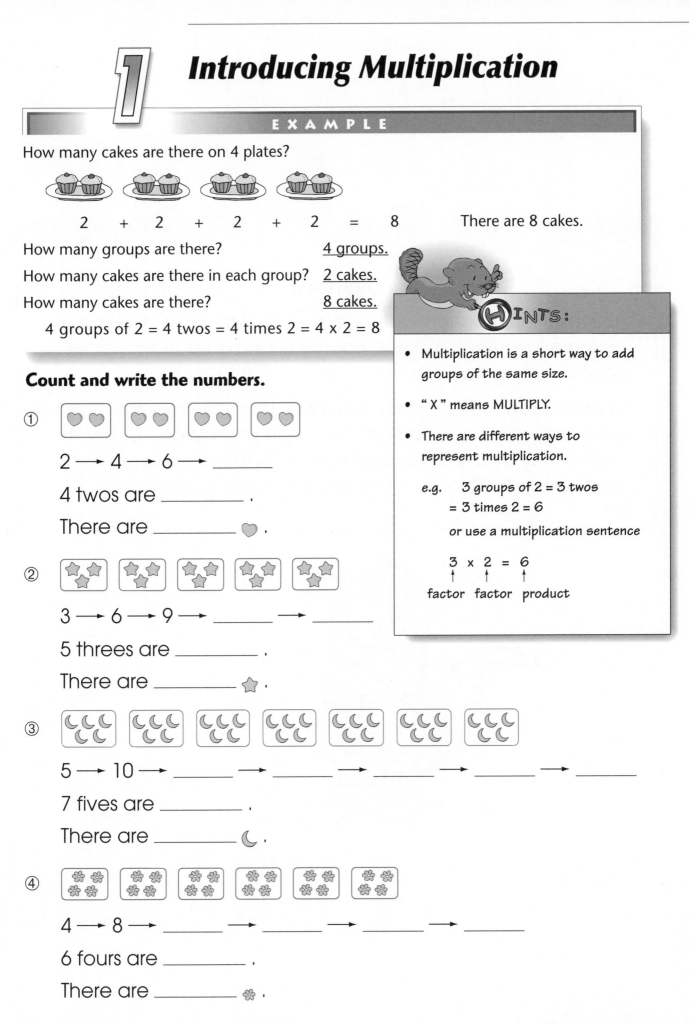

2 + 2 + 2 + 2 = 8   There are 8 cakes.

How many groups are there?   4 groups.

How many cakes are there in each group?   2 cakes.

How many cakes are there?   8 cakes.

4 groups of 2 = 4 twos = 4 times 2 = 4 x 2 = 8

HINTS:

- Multiplication is a short way to add groups of the same size.

- " X " means MULTIPLY.

- There are different ways to represent multiplication.

  e.g.   3 groups of 2 = 3 twos
          = 3 times 2 = 6

  or use a multiplication sentence

  3 x 2 = 6
  factor factor product

Count and write the numbers.

①

2 → 4 → 6 → _____

4 twos are _____ .

There are _____ ♥ .

②

3 → 6 → 9 → _____ → _____

5 threes are _____ .

There are _____ ☆ .

③

5 → 10 → _____ → _____ → _____ → _____ → _____

7 fives are _____ .

There are _____ ☾ .

④

4 → 8 → _____ → _____ → _____ → _____

6 fours are _____ .

There are _____ ✿ .

   ISBN: 978-1-897164-13-6

Add and complete.

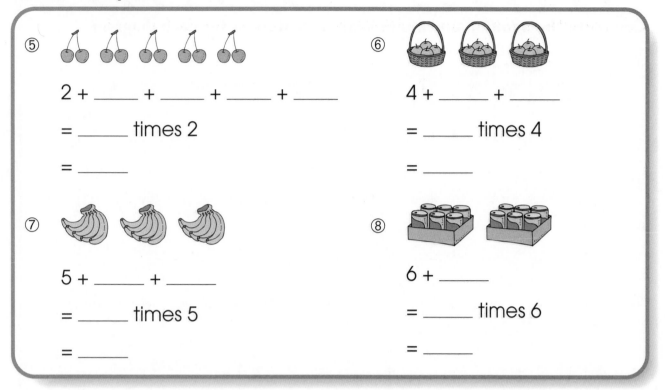

⑤ 2 + _____ + _____ + _____ + _____

= _____ times 2

= _____

⑥ 4 + _____ + _____

= _____ times 4

= _____

⑦ 5 + _____ + _____

= _____ times 5

= _____

⑧ 6 + _____

= _____ times 6

= _____

Circle the correct number of shapes in each diagram. Complete the statements.

⑨ Circle in groups of 4.

_____ fours are _____ .

_____ times 4 = _____

⑩ Circle in groups of 6.

_____ sixes are _____ .

_____ times 6 = _____

⑪ Circle in groups of 7.

_____ sevens are _____ .

_____ times 7 = _____

⑫ Circle in groups of 3.

_____ threes are _____ .

_____ times 3 = _____

ISBN: 978-1-897164-13-6

Complete the addition and multiplication sentences for each diagram.

⑬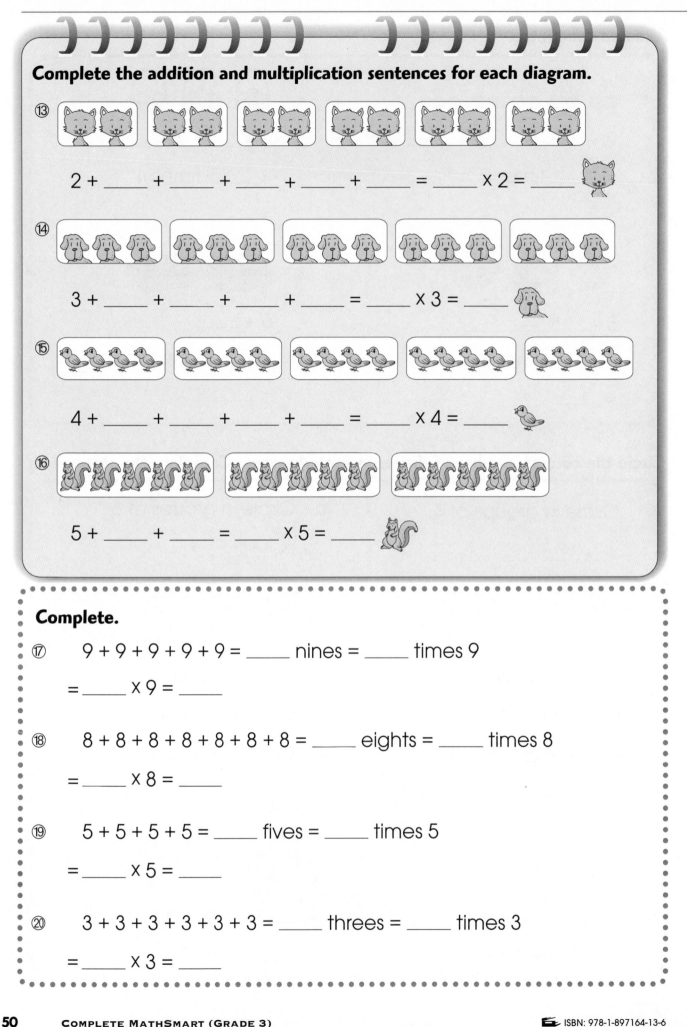

2 + ____ + ____ + ____ + ____ + ____ = ____ x 2 = ____

⑭

3 + ____ + ____ + ____ + ____ = ____ x 3 = ____

⑮

4 + ____ + ____ + ____ + ____ = ____ x 4 = ____

⑯

5 + ____ + ____ = ____ x 5 = ____

Complete.

⑰ 9 + 9 + 9 + 9 + 9 = ____ nines = ____ times 9

= ____ x 9 = ____

⑱ 8 + 8 + 8 + 8 + 8 + 8 + 8 = ____ eights = ____ times 8

= ____ x 8 = ____

⑲ 5 + 5 + 5 + 5 = ____ fives = ____ times 5

= ____ x 5 = ____

⑳ 3 + 3 + 3 + 3 + 3 + 3 = ____ threes = ____ times 3

= ____ x 3 = ____

ISBN: 978-1-897164-13-6

Match. Write the letters in the ○.

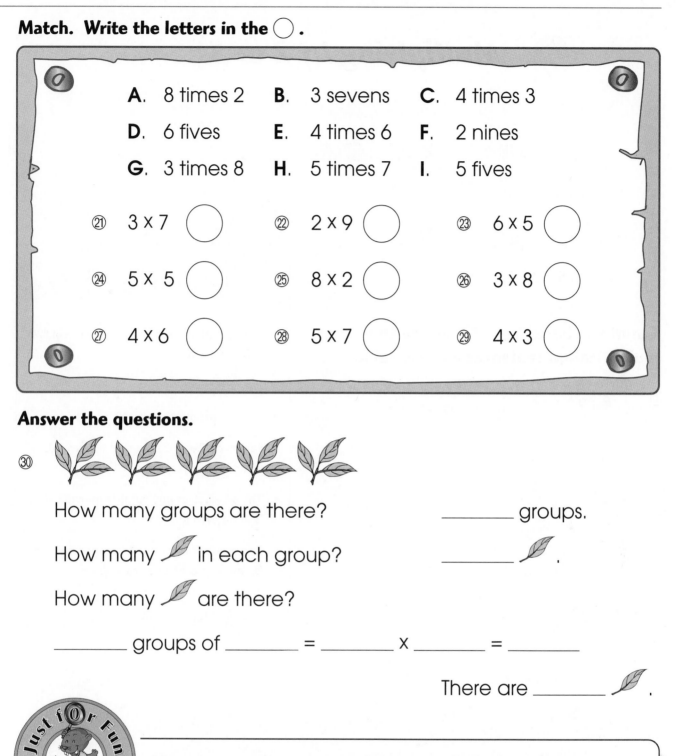

A. 8 times 2	**B.** 3 sevens	**C.** 4 times 3
D. 6 fives	**E.** 4 times 6	**F.** 2 nines
G. 3 times 8	**H.** 5 times 7	**I.** 5 fives

㉑ 3 x 7 ○   ㉒ 2 x 9 ○   ㉓ 6 x 5 ○

㉔ 5 x 5 ○   ㉕ 8 x 2 ○   ㉖ 3 x 8 ○

㉗ 4 x 6 ○   ㉘ 5 x 7 ○   ㉙ 4 x 3 ○

Answer the questions.

㉚

How many groups are there?   _____ groups.

How many 🌿 in each group?   _____ 🌿 .

How many 🌿 are there?

_____ groups of _____ = _____ x _____ = _____

There are _____ 🌿 .

Move one stick in each problem to make the number sentences true.

① I ╋ II ╋ III = IIII

② IIIIII ━ II ━ I = I

ISBN: 978-1-897164-13-6

Multiplying by 2 or 5

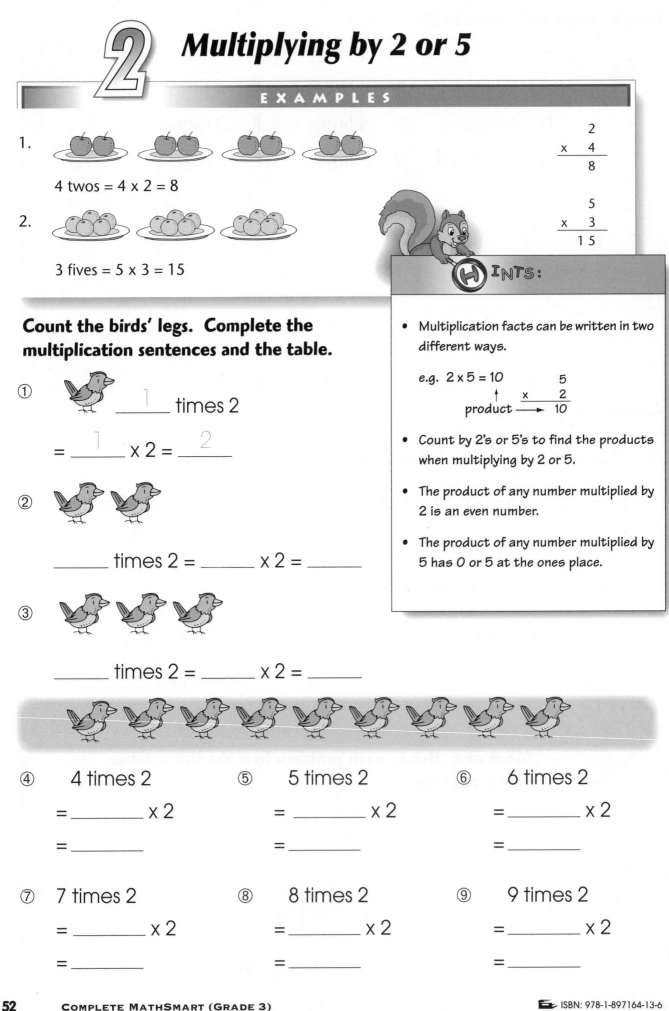

1.

4 twos = 4 x 2 = 8

$$\begin{array}{r} 2 \\ \times\ 4 \\ \hline 8 \end{array}$$

2.

3 fives = 5 x 3 = 15

$$\begin{array}{r} 5 \\ \times\ 3 \\ \hline 1\ 5 \end{array}$$

HINTS:

- Multiplication facts can be written in two different ways.

  e.g. 2 x 5 = 10
  $$\begin{array}{r} 5 \\ \times\ 2 \\ \hline 10 \end{array}$$
  product ⟶ 10

- Count by 2's or 5's to find the products when multiplying by 2 or 5.

- The product of any number multiplied by 2 is an even number.

- The product of any number multiplied by 5 has 0 or 5 at the ones place.

Count the birds' legs. Complete the multiplication sentences and the table.

① _____1_____ times 2

= _____1_____ x 2 = _____2_____

②

_____ times 2 = _____ x 2 = _____

③

_____ times 2 = _____ x 2 = _____

④ 4 times 2

= _____ x 2

= _____

⑤ 5 times 2

= _____ x 2

= _____

⑥ 6 times 2

= _____ x 2

= _____

⑦ 7 times 2

= _____ x 2

= _____

⑧ 8 times 2

= _____ x 2

= _____

⑨ 9 times 2

= _____ x 2

= _____

ISBN: 978-1-897164-13-6

⑩

x	1	2	3	4	5	6	7	8	9
2									

Count the number of flowers. Complete the multiplication sentences and the table below.

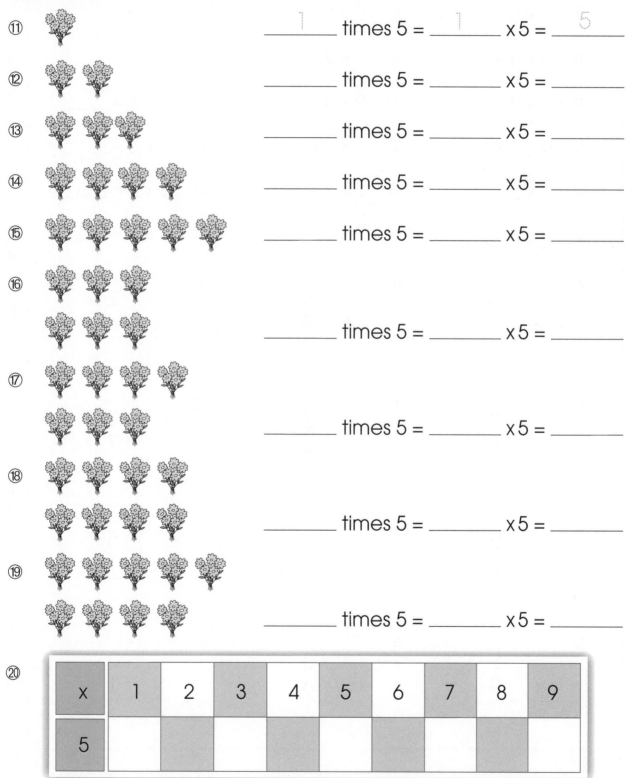

⑪ _____1_____ times 5 = _____1_____ x 5 = _____5_____

⑫ _____ times 5 = _____ x 5 = _____

⑬ _____ times 5 = _____ x 5 = _____

⑭ _____ times 5 = _____ x 5 = _____

⑮ _____ times 5 = _____ x 5 = _____

⑯ _____ times 5 = _____ x 5 = _____

⑰ _____ times 5 = _____ x 5 = _____

⑱ _____ times 5 = _____ x 5 = _____

⑲ _____ times 5 = _____ x 5 = _____

⑳

x	1	2	3	4	5	6	7	8	9
5									

ISBN: 978-1-897164-13-6

Do the multiplication.

㉑ $8 \times 2 =$ _____   ㉒ $4 \times 5 =$ _____   ㉓ $7 \times 5 =$ _____

㉔ $5 \times 2 =$ _____   ㉕ $3 \times 5 =$ _____   ㉖ $6 \times 2 =$ _____

㉗ $5 \times 5 =$ _____   ㉘ $2 \times 2 =$ _____   ㉙ $4 \times 2 =$ _____

㉚ $8 \times 5 =$ _____   ㉛ $3 \times 2 =$ _____   ㉜ $2 \times 5 =$ _____

㉝ $1 \times 2 =$ _____   ㉞ $9 \times 5 =$ _____   ㉟ $6 \times 5 =$ _____

㊱ $9 \times 2 =$ _____   ㊲ $1 \times 5 =$ _____   ㊳ $7 \times 2 =$ _____

㊴ $2 \times 5 =$ _____   ㊵ $5 \times 2 =$ _____   ㊶ $3 \times 2 =$ _____

㊷ $9 \times 2 =$ _____   ㊸ $8 \times 2 =$ _____   ㊹ $5 \times 5 =$ _____

㊺
$$\begin{array}{r} 5 \\ \times \quad 3 \\ \hline \end{array}$$

㊻
$$\begin{array}{r} 5 \\ \times \quad 8 \\ \hline \end{array}$$

㊼
$$\begin{array}{r} 2 \\ \times \quad 4 \\ \hline \end{array}$$

㊽
$$\begin{array}{r} 2 \\ \times \quad 6 \\ \hline \end{array}$$

㊾
$$\begin{array}{r} 2 \\ \times \quad 2 \\ \hline \end{array}$$

㊿
$$\begin{array}{r} 2 \\ \times \quad 7 \\ \hline \end{array}$$

(51)
$$\begin{array}{r} 5 \\ \times \quad 7 \\ \hline \end{array}$$

(52)
$$\begin{array}{r} 5 \\ \times \quad 4 \\ \hline \end{array}$$

(53)
$$\begin{array}{r} 5 \\ \times \quad 1 \\ \hline \end{array}$$

(54)
$$\begin{array}{r} 2 \\ \times \quad 9 \\ \hline \end{array}$$

(55)
$$\begin{array}{r} 5 \\ \times \quad 6 \\ \hline \end{array}$$

(56)
$$\begin{array}{r} 2 \\ \times \quad 1 \\ \hline \end{array}$$

ISBN: 978-1-897164-13-6

Solve the problems. Show your work.

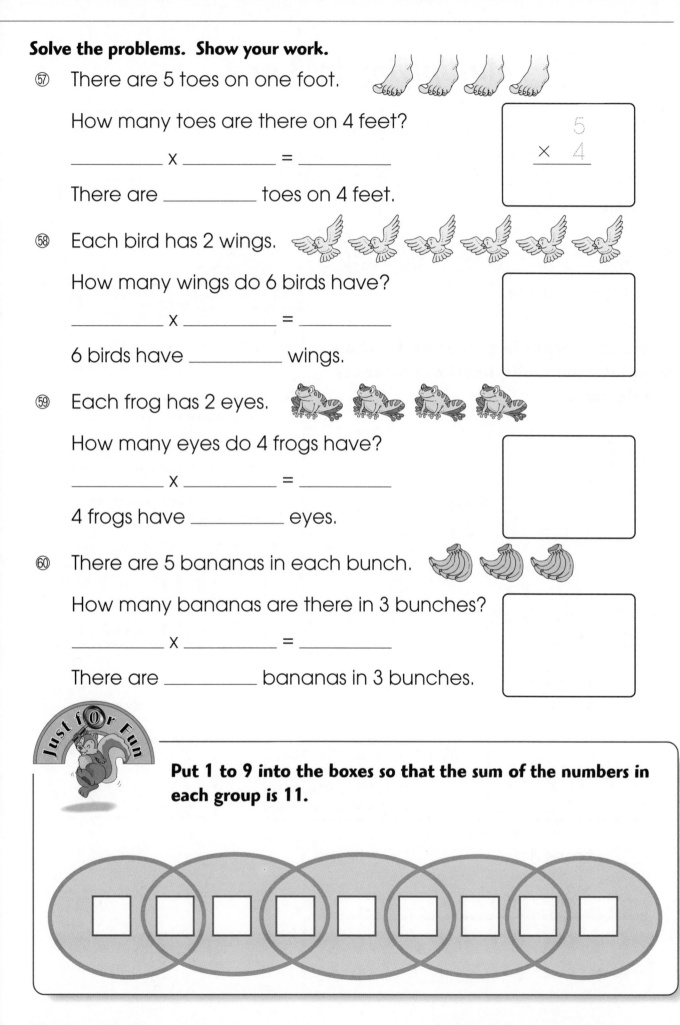

㊗ There are 5 toes on one foot.

How many toes are there on 4 feet?

_____ x _____ = _____

There are _____ toes on 4 feet.

$$\begin{array}{r} 5 \\ \times\ 4 \\ \hline \end{array}$$

㊙ Each bird has 2 wings.

How many wings do 6 birds have?

_____ x _____ = _____

6 birds have _____ wings.

㊡ Each frog has 2 eyes.

How many eyes do 4 frogs have?

_____ x _____ = _____

4 frogs have _____ eyes.

㊤ There are 5 bananas in each bunch.

How many bananas are there in 3 bunches?

_____ x _____ = _____

There are _____ bananas in 3 bunches.

Just for Fun

Put 1 to 9 into the boxes so that the sum of the numbers in each group is 11.

Multiplying by 3 or 4

1.

5 threes = 5 x 3 = 15

$$\begin{array}{r} 3 \\ \times\ 5 \\ \hline 1\ 5 \end{array}$$

2.

6 fours = 6 x 4 = 24

$$\begin{array}{r} 4 \\ \times\ 6 \\ \hline 2\ 4 \end{array}$$

Circle the shapes in groups of 3. Then complete the multiplication sentences and the table.

HINTS:

- Count by 3's or 4's to find the products when multiplying by 3 or 4.
- The product of any number multiplied by 4 is an even number.
- The product of any even number multipled by 3 is an even number.
- The product of any odd number multiplied by 3 is an odd number.

① ____1____ times 3
= ___1___ X 3 = ___3___

② _____ times 3
= _____ X 3 = _____

③ _____ times 3
= _____ X 3 = _____

④ _____ times 3
= _____ X 3 = _____

⑤ _____ times 3
= _____ X 3 = _____

⑥ _____ times 3
= _____ X 3 = _____

⑦ _____ times 3
= _____ X 3 = _____

⑧ _____ times 3
= _____ X 3 = _____

ISBN: 978-1-897164-13-6

⑨

x	1	2	3	4	5	6	7	8	9
3									

Count the number of wings on the dragonflies. Then complete the multiplication sentences.

⑩ 1 dragonfly has 4 wings.   1 x 4 = _____

⑪ 2 dragonflies have _____ wings.   2 x 4 = _____

⑫ 3 dragonflies have _____ wings.   _____ x 4 = _____

⑬ 4 dragonflies have _____ wings.   _____ x 4 = _____

⑭ 5 dragonflies have _____ wings.   _____ x 4 = _____

⑮ 6 dragonflies have _____ wings.   _____ x 4 = _____

⑯ 7 dragonflies have _____ wings.   _____ x 4 = _____

⑰ 8 dragonflies have _____ wings.   _____ x 4 = _____

⑱ 9 dragonflies have _____ wings.   _____ x 4 = _____

Little Frog jumps 4 spaces every time. Complete its path and list the numbers it lands on.

⑲

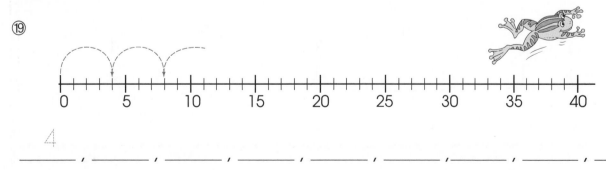

4

_____ , _____ , _____ , _____ , _____ , _____ , _____ , _____ , _____

ISBN: 978-1-897164-13-6

Do the multiplication.

20. $5 \times 3 =$ _____   21. $7 \times 4 =$ _____   22. $4 \times 4 =$ _____

23. $3 \times 3 =$ _____   24. $2 \times 3 =$ _____   25. $3 \times 4 =$ _____

26. $6 \times 4 =$ _____   27. $8 \times 4 =$ _____   28. $7 \times 3 =$ _____

29. $1 \times 4 =$ _____   30. $4 \times 3 =$ _____   31. $6 \times 3 =$ _____

32. $8 \times 3 =$ _____   33. $9 \times 4 =$ _____   34. $5 \times 4 =$ _____

35. $9 \times 3 =$ _____   36. $1 \times 3 =$ _____   37. $2 \times 4 =$ _____

38. $5 \times 4 =$ _____   39. $6 \times 4 =$ _____   40. $9 \times 3 =$ _____

41. $7 \times 3 =$ _____   42. $3 \times 3 =$ _____   43. $8 \times 4 =$ _____

44.
$$\begin{array}{r} 3 \\ \times\ 8 \\ \hline \end{array}$$

45.
$$\begin{array}{r} 4 \\ \times\ 9 \\ \hline \end{array}$$

46.
$$\begin{array}{r} 3 \\ \times\ 6 \\ \hline \end{array}$$

47.
$$\begin{array}{r} 4 \\ \times\ 7 \\ \hline \end{array}$$

48.
$$\begin{array}{r} 4 \\ \times\ 4 \\ \hline \end{array}$$

49.
$$\begin{array}{r} 3 \\ \times\ 5 \\ \hline \end{array}$$

50.
$$\begin{array}{r} 4 \\ \times\ 3 \\ \hline \end{array}$$

51.
$$\begin{array}{r} 3 \\ \times\ 1 \\ \hline \end{array}$$

52.
$$\begin{array}{r} 3 \\ \times\ 2 \\ \hline \end{array}$$

53.
$$\begin{array}{r} 4 \\ \times\ 1 \\ \hline \end{array}$$

54.
$$\begin{array}{r} 3 \\ \times\ 4 \\ \hline \end{array}$$

55.
$$\begin{array}{r} 4 \\ \times\ 2 \\ \hline \end{array}$$

     ISBN: 978-1-897164-13-6

Solve the problems. Show your work.

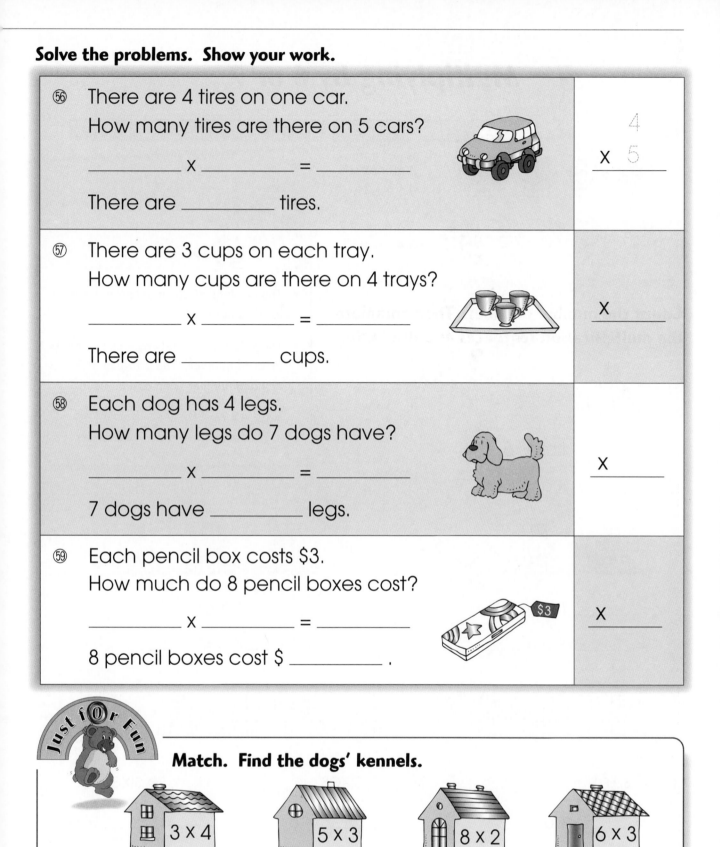

56 There are 4 tires on one car.
How many tires are there on 5 cars?

_____ x _____ = _____

There are _____ tires.

4
x 5
_____

57 There are 3 cups on each tray.
How many cups are there on 4 trays?

_____ x _____ = _____

There are _____ cups.

x
_____

58 Each dog has 4 legs.
How many legs do 7 dogs have?

_____ x _____ = _____

7 dogs have _____ legs.

x
_____

59 Each pencil box costs $3.
How much do 8 pencil boxes cost?

_____ x _____ = _____

8 pencil boxes cost $ _____ .

x
_____

Just for Fun

Match. Find the dogs' kennels.

3 x 4   5 x 3   8 x 2   6 x 3

16   12   18   15

ISBN: 978-1-897164-13-6

4 Multiplying by 6 or 7

1. 4 groups of 6
= 4 x 6 = 24

2. 5 groups of 7
= 5 x 7 = 35

HINTS:

- The product of any number and 6 is an even number.

- The product of 7 and any even number is an even number. The product of 7 and any odd number is an odd number.

  e.g. $4 \times 7 = 28$ ← even number

  $3 \times 7 = 21$ ← odd number

Count the number of cubes. Then complete the multiplication sentences and the table.

① ___1___ times 6

= ___1___ x 6 = ___6___

② _____ times 6

= _____ x 6 = _____

③ _____ times 6

= _____ x 6 = _____

④ 4 sixes

= _____ x 6

= _____

⑤ 5 sixes

= _____ x 6

= _____

⑥ 6 sixes

= _____ x 6

= _____

⑦ 7 sixes

= _____ x 6

= _____

⑧ 8 sixes

= _____ x 6

= _____

⑨ 9 sixes

= _____ x 6

= _____

ISBN: 978-1-897164-13-6

⑩

X	1	2	3	4	5	6	7	8	9
6									

Count the number of stars on the cards. Then complete the multiplication sentences.

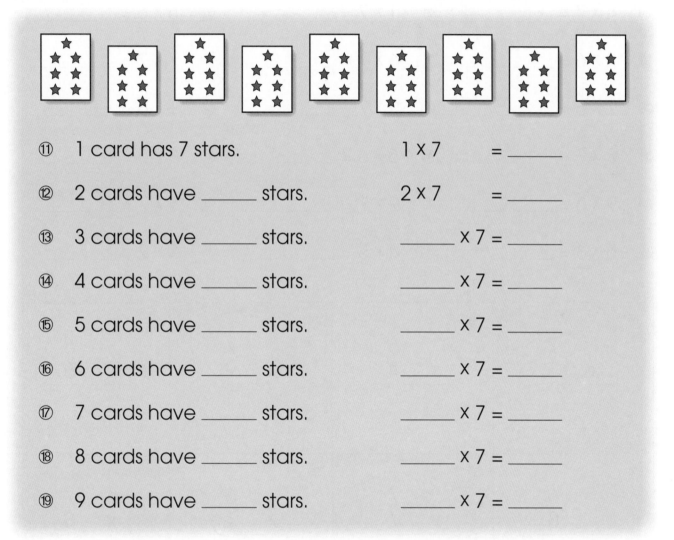

⑪ 1 card has 7 stars.   1 × 7   = _____

⑫ 2 cards have _____ stars.   2 × 7   = _____

⑬ 3 cards have _____ stars.   _____ × 7 = _____

⑭ 4 cards have _____ stars.   _____ × 7 = _____

⑮ 5 cards have _____ stars.   _____ × 7 = _____

⑯ 6 cards have _____ stars.   _____ × 7 = _____

⑰ 7 cards have _____ stars.   _____ × 7 = _____

⑱ 8 cards have _____ stars.   _____ × 7 = _____

⑲ 9 cards have _____ stars.   _____ × 7 = _____

Count by 7's. Help Little Butterfly find its path through the flowers. Colour its path.

⑳

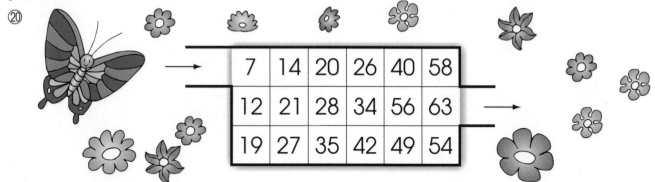

7	14	20	26	40	58
12	21	28	34	56	63
19	27	35	42	49	54

Do the Multiplication.

㉑ 4 x 6 = ______	㉒ 5 x 7 = ______	㉓ 3 x 7 = ______
㉔ 3 x 6 = ______	㉕ 6 x 6 = ______	㉖ 8 x 7 = ______
㉗ 2 x 7 = ______	㉘ 8 x 6 = ______	㉙ 9 x 6 = ______
㉚ 4 x 7 = ______	㉛ 1 x 7 = ______	㉜ 5 x 6 = ______
㉝ 2 x 6 = ______	㉞ 6 x 7 = ______	㉟ 7 x 7 = ______
㊱ 7 x 6 = ______	㊲ 9 x 7 = ______	㊳ 1 x 6 = ______
㊴ 3 x 7 = ______	㊵ 5 x 6 = ______	㊶ 3 x 6 = ______
㊷ 9 x 6 = ______	㊸ 2 x 7 = ______	㊹ 5 x 7 = ______
㊺ 5 x 3 = ______	㊻ 4 x 5 = ______	㊼ 3 x 2 = ______

㊽ 7 x 1	㊾ 6 x 4	㊿ 7 x 9	(51) 6 x 6
(52) 6 x 8	(53) 7 x 7	(54) 6 x 1	(55) 7 x 8
(56) 7 x 6	(57) 6 x 2	(58) 7 x 4	(59) 6 x 7

ISBN: 978-1-897164-13-6

Solve the problems. Show your work.

60 A little bee has 6 legs.
    How many legs do 8 bees have?

    _____ = _____

    8 bees have _____ legs.

61 There are 7 buttons on a shirt.
    How many buttons are there on 5 shirts?

    _____ = _____

    There are _____ buttons on 5 shirts.

62 There are 6 shelves in a cupboard.
    How many shelves are there in 4 cupboards?

    _____ = _____

    There are _____ shelves in 4 cupboards.

63 There are 7 cakes on a plate.
    How many cakes are there on 6 plates?

    _____ = _____

    There are _____ cakes.

Just for Fun

Write + or – in the ○ to make the number sentences true.

① 3 ○ 2 ○ 1 = 0
② 3 ○ 2 ○ 1 = 2
③ 3 ○ 2 ○ 1 = 4
④ 3 ○ 2 ○ 1 = 6

Multiplication Facts to 49

EXAMPLES

1. 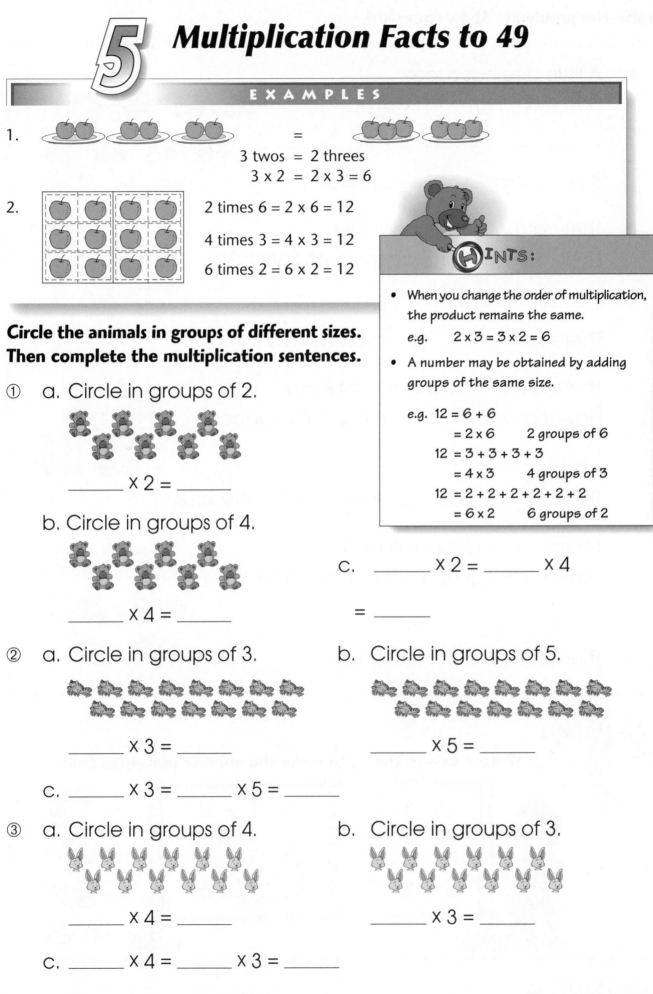 =

   3 twos = 2 threes
   3 x 2 = 2 x 3 = 6

2. 2 times 6 = 2 x 6 = 12

   4 times 3 = 4 x 3 = 12

   6 times 2 = 6 x 2 = 12

HINTS:

- When you change the order of multiplication, the product remains the same.

  e.g.   2 x 3 = 3 x 2 = 6

- A number may be obtained by adding groups of the same size.

  e.g. 12 = 6 + 6
   = 2 x 6   2 groups of 6
   12 = 3 + 3 + 3 + 3
   = 4 x 3   4 groups of 3
   12 = 2 + 2 + 2 + 2 + 2 + 2
   = 6 x 2   6 groups of 2

Circle the animals in groups of different sizes. Then complete the multiplication sentences.

① a. Circle in groups of 2.

   _____ X 2 = _____

   b. Circle in groups of 4.

   _____ X 4 = _____

   c. _____ X 2 = _____ X 4

   = _____

② a. Circle in groups of 3.

   _____ X 3 = _____

   c. _____ X 3 = _____ X 5 = _____

   b. Circle in groups of 5.

   _____ X 5 = _____

③ a. Circle in groups of 4.

   _____ X 4 = _____

   c. _____ X 4 = _____ X 3 = _____

   b. Circle in groups of 3.

   _____ X 3 = _____

ISBN: 978-1-897164-13-6

Complete the following multiplication sentences.

④ 2 x 5 = _____

5 x 2 = _____

2 x 5 = _____ x 2

⑤ 6 x 3 = _____

3 x 6 = _____

6 x 3 = 3 x _____

⑥ 4 x 7 = _____

7 x 4 = _____

_____ x 7 = 7 x 4

⑦ 2 x 7 = _____

7 x 2 = _____

2 x _____ = 7 x 2

⑧ 5 x 6 = _____

6 x 5 = _____

5 x _____ = 6 x _____

⑨ 4 x 5 = _____

5 x 4 = _____

_____ x 5 = _____ x 4

⑩ 3 x _____ = 7 x 3

= _____

⑪ _____ x 6 = 6 x 4

= _____

⑫ 2 x 6 = _____ x 2

= _____

⑬ 5 x 7 = 7 x _____

= _____

⑭ 4 x _____ = 6 x 4

= _____

⑮ 2 x _____ = 9 x 2

= _____

Write True (T) or False (F) in the (   ).

⑯ 5 + 2 = 2 x 5   (   )

⑰ 2 + 2 = 2 x 2   (   )

⑱ 3 x 7 = 7 x 3   (   )

⑲ 2 + 6 = 6 + 2   (   )

⑳ 6 + 7 = 7 + 6   (   )

㉑ 5 + 5 = 2 + 5   (   )

㉒ 6 + 6 = 6 x 2   (   )

㉓ 3 x 4 = 4 x 3   (   )

Circle the insects in groups of different sizes and complete the multiplication sentences.

㉔ a. Circle in groups of 2.

_____ groups of 2

= _____ x 2

= _____

b. Circle in groups of 3.

_____ groups of 3

= _____ x 3

= _____

c. Circle in groups of 6.

_____ groups of 6

= _____ x 6

= _____

d. _____ x 2 = _____ x 3 = _____ x 6 = _____

㉕ a. Circle in groups of 3.

_____ groups of 3

= _____ x 3

= _____

b. Circle in groups of 4.

_____ groups of 4

= _____ x 4

= _____

c. Circle in groups of 6.

_____ groups of 6

= _____ x 6

= _____

d. _____ x 3 = _____ x 4 = _____ x 6 = _____

ISBN: 978-1-897164-13-6

Answer the questions. Fill in the missing numbers.

㉖  A bag of sweets is shared equally among 7 children. Each child has 6 sweets.

If it is shared equally among 6 children, each child can have _____ sweets.

㉗  A bag of cookies is shared equally among 6 children. Each child has 5 cookies.

If it is shared equally among 5 children, each child can have _____ cookies.

㉘ A box of lollipops is shared equally among 5 girls. Each girl has 4 lollipops.

If it is shared equally among 4 girls, each girl has _____ lollipops.

㉙ 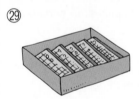 Sally puts her chocolate bars equally into 3 boxes. Each box has 5 chocolate bars.

If she puts the chocolate bars equally into 5 boxes, each box will have _____ chocolate bars.

㉚  Tom has enough money to buy 6 chocolate bars at $3 each.

He can buy _____ chocolate bars if the price of each chocolate bar is reduced to $2.

Match the cakes with the boxes.

6 Multiplying by 8, 9, 0 or 1

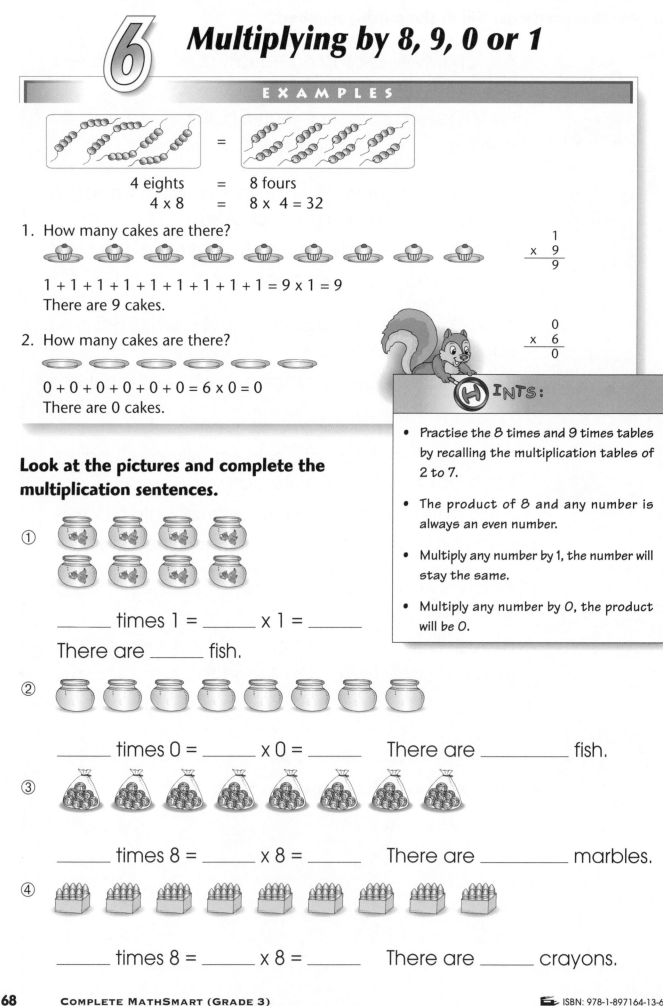

4 eights   =   8 fours
4 x 8   =   8 x 4 = 32

1. How many cakes are there?

$$\begin{array}{r} 1 \\ \times\ 9 \\ \hline 9 \end{array}$$

1 + 1 + 1 + 1 + 1 + 1 + 1 + 1 + 1 = 9 x 1 = 9
There are 9 cakes.

2. How many cakes are there?

$$\begin{array}{r} 0 \\ \times\ 6 \\ \hline 0 \end{array}$$

0 + 0 + 0 + 0 + 0 + 0 = 6 x 0 = 0
There are 0 cakes.

HINTS:

- Practise the 8 times and 9 times tables by recalling the multiplication tables of 2 to 7.

- The product of 8 and any number is always an even number.

- Multiply any number by 1, the number will stay the same.

- Multiply any number by 0, the product will be 0.

Look at the pictures and complete the multiplication sentences.

① _____ times 1 = _____ x 1 = _____
There are _____ fish.

② _____ times 0 = _____ x 0 = _____   There are _____ fish.

③ _____ times 8 = _____ x 8 = _____   There are _____ marbles.

④ _____ times 8 = _____ x 8 = _____   There are _____ crayons.

   ISBN: 978-1-897164-13-6

Complete the multiplication sentences and multiplication table.

⑤   1 times eight = 1 x 8 = 8 x _____ = _____

⑥   2 times eight = 2 x 8 = 8 x _____ = _____

⑦   3 times eight = 3 x 8 = 8 x _____ = _____

⑧   4 times eight = 4 x 8 = 8 x _____ = _____

⑨   5 times eight = 5 x 8 = 8 x _____ = _____

⑩   6 times eight = 6 x 8 = 8 x _____ = _____

⑪   7 times eight = 7 x 8 = 8 x _____ = _____

⑫

x	1	2	3	4	5	6	7	8	9
8									

⑬   1 x 9 = 9 x _____

= _____

⑭   2 x 9 = 9 x _____

= _____

⑮   3 x 9 = 9 x _____

= _____

⑯   4 x 9 = 9 x _____

= _____

⑰   5 x 9 = 9 x _____

= _____

⑱   6 x 9 = 9 x _____

= _____

⑲   7 x 9 = 9 x _____

= _____

⑳   8 x 9 = 9 x _____

= _____

㉑   9 + 9 + 9 + 9 + 9 + 9 + 9 + 9 + 9

= 9 x 9 = _____

ISBN: 978-1-897164-13-6

Do the multiplication.

㉒
$$\begin{array}{r} 1 \\ \times\ 4 \\ \hline \end{array}$$

㉓
$$\begin{array}{r} 0 \\ \times\ 5 \\ \hline \end{array}$$

㉔
$$\begin{array}{r} 0 \\ \times\ 8 \\ \hline \end{array}$$

㉕
$$\begin{array}{r} 1 \\ \times\ 3 \\ \hline \end{array}$$

㉖
$$\begin{array}{r} 8 \\ \times\ 3 \\ \hline \end{array}$$

㉗
$$\begin{array}{r} 9 \\ \times\ 4 \\ \hline \end{array}$$

㉘
$$\begin{array}{r} 8 \\ \times\ 8 \\ \hline \end{array}$$

㉙
$$\begin{array}{r} 9 \\ \times\ 2 \\ \hline \end{array}$$

㉚
$$\begin{array}{r} 9 \\ \times\ 9 \\ \hline \end{array}$$

㉛
$$\begin{array}{r} 8 \\ \times\ 2 \\ \hline \end{array}$$

㉜
$$\begin{array}{r} 9 \\ \times\ 6 \\ \hline \end{array}$$

㉝
$$\begin{array}{r} 8 \\ \times\ 9 \\ \hline \end{array}$$

㉞
$$\begin{array}{r} 0 \\ \times\ 9 \\ \hline \end{array}$$

㉟
$$\begin{array}{r} 1 \\ \times\ 8 \\ \hline \end{array}$$

㊱
$$\begin{array}{r} 0 \\ \times\ 6 \\ \hline \end{array}$$

㊲
$$\begin{array}{r} 1 \\ \times\ 7 \\ \hline \end{array}$$

㊳
$$\begin{array}{r} 1 \\ \times\ 5 \\ \hline \end{array}$$

㊴
$$\begin{array}{r} 9 \\ \times\ 3 \\ \hline \end{array}$$

㊵
$$\begin{array}{r} 8 \\ \times\ 4 \\ \hline \end{array}$$

㊶
$$\begin{array}{r} 0 \\ \times\ 2 \\ \hline \end{array}$$

㊷
$$\begin{array}{r} 9 \\ \times\ 5 \\ \hline \end{array}$$

㊸
$$\begin{array}{r} 0 \\ \times\ 7 \\ \hline \end{array}$$

㊹
$$\begin{array}{r} 1 \\ \times\ 6 \\ \hline \end{array}$$

㊺
$$\begin{array}{r} 8 \\ \times\ 7 \\ \hline \end{array}$$

ISBN: 978-1-897164-13-6

Solve the problems. Show your work.

㊻ There are 9 apples in a basket.

How many apples are there in 6 baskets?

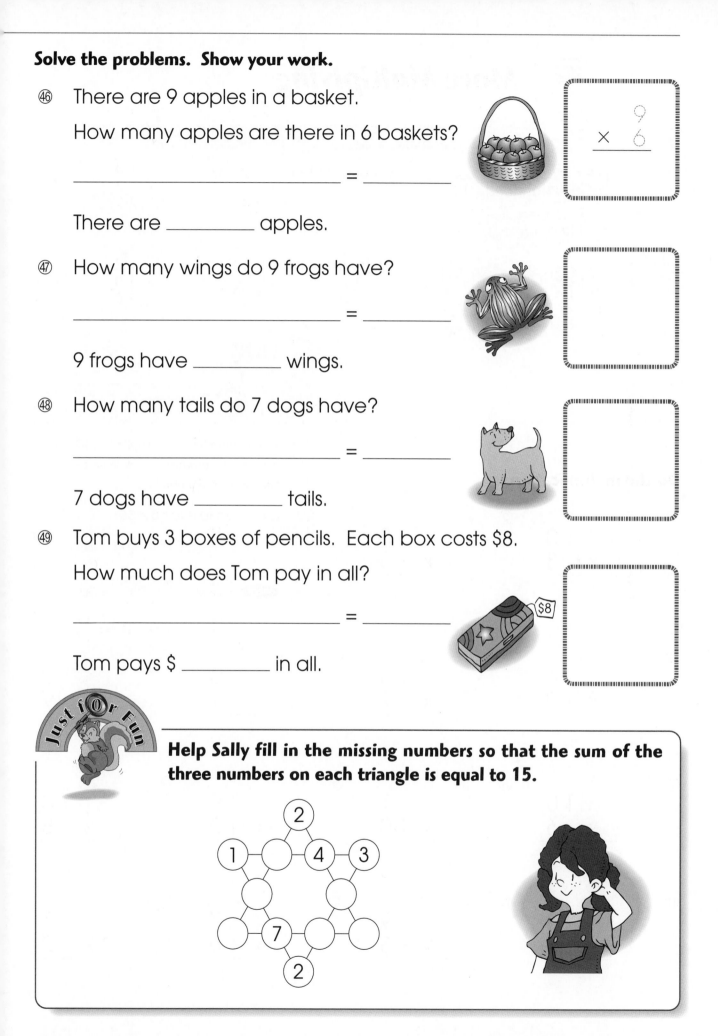

_____ = _____

There are _____ apples.

㊼ How many wings do 9 frogs have?

_____ = _____

9 frogs have _____ wings.

㊽ How many tails do 7 dogs have?

_____ = _____

7 dogs have _____ tails.

㊾ Tom buys 3 boxes of pencils. Each box costs \$8.

How much does Tom pay in all?

_____ = _____

Tom pays \$ _____ in all.

Just f☻r Fun

Help Sally fill in the missing numbers so that the sum of the three numbers on each triangle is equal to 15.

7 More Multiplying

EXAMPLES

1.

2 groups of ten $= 2 \times 10$
$= 20$

$$\begin{array}{r} 1\,0 \\ \times\ \ 2 \\ \hline 2\,0 \end{array}$$

2.

10 groups of two $= 10 \times 2$
$= 20$

$$\begin{array}{r} 2 \\ \times\ 1\,0 \\ \hline 2\,0 \end{array}$$

HINTS:

- When a number is multiplied by 10, you can get the product by adding a zero to the right of the number.

  e.g. $5 \times 10 = 10 \times 5 = 50$

     5 tens   10 fives   write a zero to the right of 5

  check 5 tens = | tens | ones |
  |---|---|
  | 5 | 0 | = 50

Do the multiplication.

①
$$\begin{array}{r} 1\,0 \\ \times\ \ 3 \\ \hline \end{array}$$

②
$$\begin{array}{r} 5 \\ \times\ 1\,0 \\ \hline \end{array}$$

③
$$\begin{array}{r} 4 \\ \times\ 1\,0 \\ \hline \end{array}$$

④
$$\begin{array}{r} 1\,0 \\ \times\ \ 7 \\ \hline \end{array}$$

⑤
$$\begin{array}{r} 3 \\ \times\ \ 1 \\ \hline \end{array}$$

⑥
$$\begin{array}{r} 0 \\ \times\ \ 9 \\ \hline \end{array}$$

⑦
$$\begin{array}{r} 1\,0 \\ \times\ \ 6 \\ \hline \end{array}$$

⑧
$$\begin{array}{r} 1 \\ \times\ 1\,0 \\ \hline \end{array}$$

⑨
$$\begin{array}{r} 9 \\ \times\ 1\,0 \\ \hline \end{array}$$

⑩
$$\begin{array}{r} 1\,0 \\ \times\ \ 8 \\ \hline \end{array}$$

⑪
$$\begin{array}{r} 8 \\ \times\ \ 7 \\ \hline \end{array}$$

⑫
$$\begin{array}{r} 9 \\ \times\ \ 3 \\ \hline \end{array}$$

⑬
$$\begin{array}{r} 7 \\ \times\ \ 6 \\ \hline \end{array}$$

⑭
$$\begin{array}{r} 5 \\ \times\ \ 2 \\ \hline \end{array}$$

ISBN: 978-1-897164-13-6

Complete the following multiplication table.

⑮

✕	1	2	3	4	5	6	7	8	9	10
1	1									
2		4								
3			9							
4				16						
5					25					
6						36				
7							49			
8								64		
9									81	
10										100

Find the flags for each child.   Write the letters on the flags.

A	6 x 2	B	5 x 6	C	4 x 3
D	4 x 4	E	3 x 10	F	8 x 2

⑯   ⑰   ⑱

ISBN: 978-1-897164-13-6

Write 2 multiplication sentences for each picture.

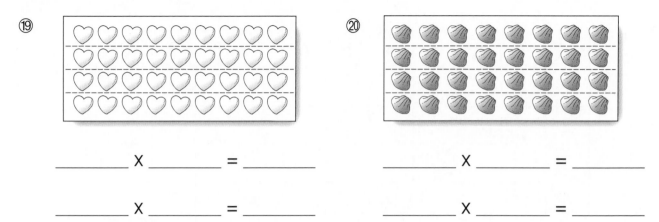

⑲

_____ X _____ = _____

_____ X _____ = _____

⑳

_____ X _____ = _____

_____ X _____ = _____

Complete the following multiplication sentences.

㉑ 7 X 6 = _____

㉒ 3 X 9 = _____

㉓ 8 X 5 = _____

㉔ 0 X 4 = _____

㉕ 9 X 1 = _____

㉖ 7 X 10 = _____

㉗ 5 X 9 = _____

㉘ 6 X 3 = _____

㉙ 9 X 8 = _____

㉚ 2 X 7 = _____

㉛ 2 X 0 X 5 = _____

㉜ 1 X 3 X 6 = _____

㉝ 3 X 3 X 10 = _____

㉞ 4 X 1 X 7 = _____

㉟ _____ X 7 = 7 X 3

= _____

㊱ 8 X _____ = 2 X 4

= _____

㊲ _____ X 4 = 2 X _____

= 12

㊳ 5 X _____ = 0 X 7

= _____

㊴ 4 X _____ = 5 X _____

= 40

㊵ _____ X 2 = 5 X 4

= _____

ISBN: 978-1-897164-13-6

Solve the problems. Show your work.

㊶ How many legs do 10 snails have?

_____ = _____   _____ legs.

㊷ A ladybird has 6 legs. How many legs do 5 ladybirds have?

_____ = _____   _____ legs.

㊸ A butterfly has 4 wings. How many wings do 8 butterflies have?

_____ = _____   _____ wings.

㊹ There are 6 chocolate bars in a box. How many chocolate bars are there in 7 boxes?

_____ = _____   _____ bars.

㊺ There are 9 pears in a bag. How many pears are there in 4 bags?

_____ = _____   _____ pears.

㊻ Notebooks are sold for $3 each. Sally buys 7 notebooks. How much does she pay in all?

_____ = _____ $ _____ .

Fill in the numbers to make each number sentence true.

① Use the same number in all boxes.

$\boxed{} + \boxed{} = \boxed{} \times \boxed{}$

② The sum of three different numbers is equal to their product.

$\boxed{} + \boxed{} + \boxed{} = \boxed{} \times \boxed{} \times \boxed{}$

 **Introducing Division**

There are 8 cakes. Put them on the plates in groups of 2. How many plates are needed?

Circle the cakes in groups of 2.
How many cakes are there? <u>8 cakes.</u>
How many cakes in each group? <u>2 cakes.</u>
How many groups are there? <u>4 groups.</u>

There are 4 groups of two in 8.
4 plates are needed for 8 cakes with 2 cakes on each plate.

 **INTS:**

- Division is to share things equally into groups of the same size.

- " ÷ " means DIVIDE.

- Use a division sentence to represent division.

  e.g. 4 groups of two in eight is expressed as:

  $$8 \div 2 = 4$$
  dividend divisor quotient

Group the goodies and complete each statement.

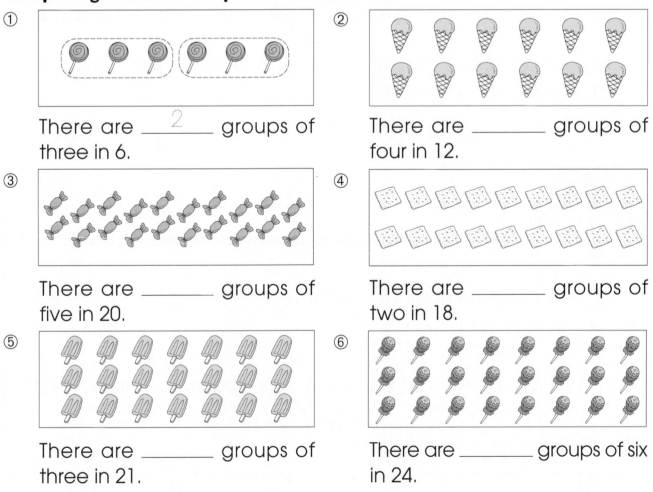

① There are ___2___ groups of three in 6.

② There are _____ groups of four in 12.

③ There are _____ groups of five in 20.

④ There are _____ groups of two in 18.

⑤ There are _____ groups of three in 21.

⑥ There are _____ groups of six in 24.

Help the children divide the stationery equally among themselves. Complete each statement.

⑦ Divide 18  equally among 3 children. Each child has _____ .

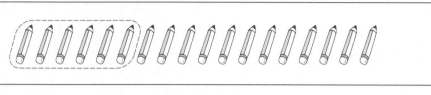

⑧ Divide 20  equally among 4 children. Each child has _____ .

⑨ Divide 30  equally among 5 children. Each child has _____ .

⑩ Divide 24  equally among 6 children. Each child has _____ .

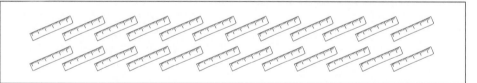

⑪ Divide 32  equally among 4 children. Each child has _____ .

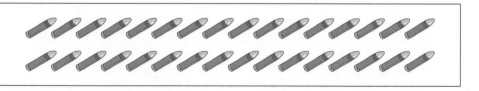

⑫ Divide 32  equally among 6 children. Each child has _____ with _____ left over.

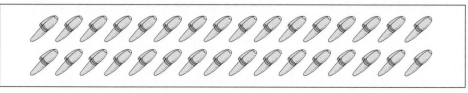

ISBN: 978-1-897164-13-6

Aunt Mary has 24 boxes of juice. Fill in the blanks to show how she divides the juice equally among the children.

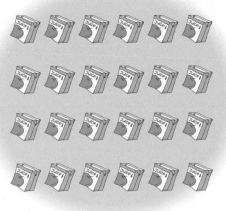

⑬ If each child gets 3 boxes, the juice can be shared among _____ children.

⑭ If each child gets 4 boxes, the juice can be shared among _____ children.

⑮ If each child gets 5 boxes, the juice can be shared among _____ children with _____ boxes left over.

Complete the division sentence for each picture.

⑯

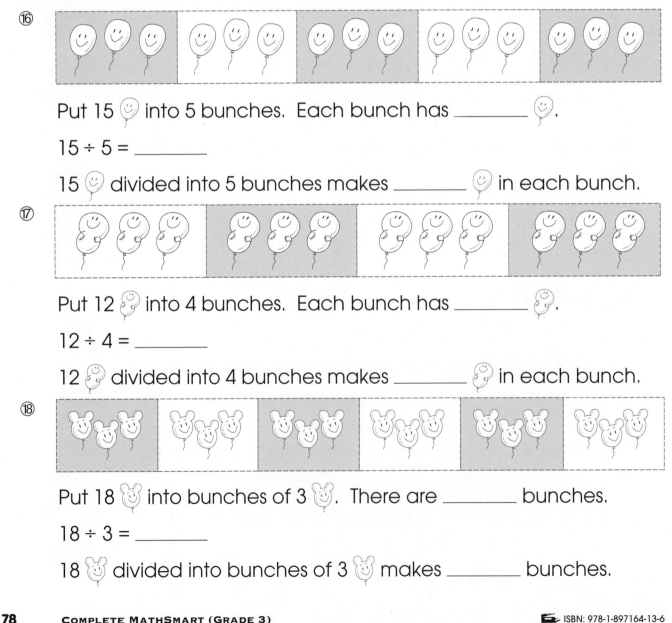

Put 15 ☺ into 5 bunches. Each bunch has _____ ☺.

15 ÷ 5 = _____

15 ☺ divided into 5 bunches makes _____ ☺ in each bunch.

⑰

Put 12 ☺ into 4 bunches. Each bunch has _____ ☺.

12 ÷ 4 = _____

12 ☺ divided into 4 bunches makes _____ ☺ in each bunch.

⑱

Put 18 ☺ into bunches of 3 ☺. There are _____ bunches.

18 ÷ 3 = _____

18 ☺ divided into bunches of 3 ☺ makes _____ bunches.

ISBN: 978-1-897164-13-6

Count and complete the division sentence for each picture.

⑲ ____6____ 🐜 divided into 2 equal groups.

____6____ ÷ ____2____ = _____

There are _____ 🐜 in each group.

⑳ _____ 🐞 divided into groups of 4.

_____ ÷ _____ = _____

There are _____ groups of 🐞.

㉑ _____ 🦋 divided into 3 equal groups.

_____ ÷ _____ = _____

There are _____ 🦋 in each group.

㉒ _____ 🐝 divided into groups of 5.

_____ ÷ _____ = _____

There are _____ groups of 🐝.

㉓ _____ 🦗 divided into groups of 3.

_____ ÷ _____ = _____

There are _____ groups of 🦗.

㉔ _____ 🕷 divided into 5 equal groups.

_____ ÷ _____ = _____

There are _____ 🕷 in each group.

Just for Fun

Fill in the missing numbers to continue the multiplication.

The number in each box is the product of the multiplication sentence on the left of ⟶.

① 2 x 3 ⟶ [ ] x 4 ⟶ [ ] x 0 ⟶ [ ]

② 3 x 3 ⟶ [ ] x 5 ⟶ [ ] x 1 ⟶ [ ]

ISBN: 978-1-897164-13-6

Midway

Fill in the missing numbers.

① 0 ____ ____ 6 8 10 ____ ____

② 6 9 12 ____ ____ ____ 24 ____

③ 15 20 ____ ____ 35 ____ ____

④ 6 12 ____ ____ 30 36 ____ ____

⑤ 14 ____ ____ 35 42 ____ ____

⑥ ____ 8 12 ____ ____ 24 ____ 32

⑦ ____ 27 36 45 ____ ____ ____

⑧ 16 ____ ____ 40 48 56 ____ ____

Circle the correct answers.

⑨ When a number is multiplied by this number, the ones place of the product is always a 5 or a 0.

| 0 | 1 | 2 | 3 | 4 | 5 | 6 | 7 | 8 | 9 |

⑩ When a number is multiplied by this number, the product is the same as that number.

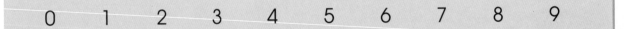

| 0 | 1 | 2 | 3 | 4 | 5 | 6 | 7 | 8 | 9 |

⑪ When a number is multiplied by this number, the product is always 0.

| 0 | 1 | 2 | 3 | 4 | 5 | 6 | 7 | 8 | 9 |

⑫ When a number is multiplied by any of these numbers, the product is always an even number.

| 0 | 1 | 2 | 3 | 4 | 5 | 6 | 7 | 8 | 9 |

 ISBN: 978-1-897164-13-6

Do the multiplication.

⑬ 8×7	⑭ 0×6	⑮ 10×5	⑯ 6×5
⑰ 9×1	⑱ 2×7	⑲ 3×8	⑳ 4×3
㉑ 3×10	㉒ 1×8	㉓ 7×5	㉔ 2×9
㉕ 6×4	㉖ 5×9	㉗ 3×6	㉘ 7×4

㉙ 2 x 5 = ________ ㉚ 3 x 7 = ________ ㉛ 9 x 3 = ________

㉜ 8 x 0 = ________ ㉝ 5 x 4 = ________ ㉞ 2 x 6 = ________

㉟ 7 x 9 = ________ ㊱ 1 x 7 = ________ ㊲ 4 x 8 = ________

㊳ 9 x 2 = ________ ㊴ 3 x 2 = ________ ㊵ 8 x 5 = ________

㊶ 8 x 6 = ________ ㊷ 9 x 4 = ________ ㊸ 6 x 9 = ________

ISBN: 978-1-897164-13-6

Complete the multiplication sentences.

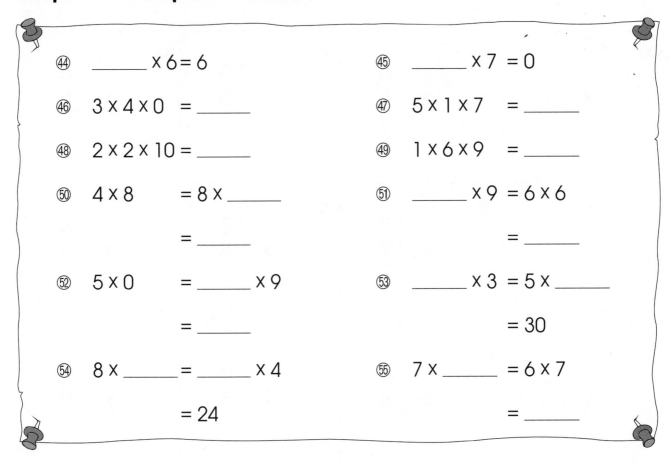

44. _____ × 6 = 6

45. _____ × 7 = 0

46. 3 × 4 × 0 = _____

47. 5 × 1 × 7 = _____

48. 2 × 2 × 10 = _____

49. 1 × 6 × 9 = _____

50. 4 × 8 = 8 × _____

   = _____

51. _____ × 9 = 6 × 6

   = _____

52. 5 × 0 = _____ × 9

   = _____

53. _____ × 3 = 5 × _____

   = 30

54. 8 × _____ = _____ × 4

   = 24

55. 7 × _____ = 6 × 7

   = _____

In each group, put a X in the ◯ beside the number sentence that is different.

56. A. 4 eights ◯
    B. 4 + 8 ◯
    C. 8 + 8 + 8 + 8 ◯
    D. 8 × 4 ◯

57. A. 5 zeros ◯
    B. 0 × 5 ◯
    C. 0 + 0 + 0 + 0 + 0 ◯
    D. 1 × 5 ◯

58. A. 6 + 6 + 6 + 6 + 6 ◯
    B. 6 × 5 ◯
    C. 5 times 6 ◯
    D. 5 + 5 + 5 + 5 + 5 ◯

59. A. 7 + 8 ◯
    B. 7 × 8 ◯
    C. 8 sevens ◯
    D. 7 times 8 ◯

   ISBN: 978-1-897164-13-6

Count and complete the division sentence for each picture.

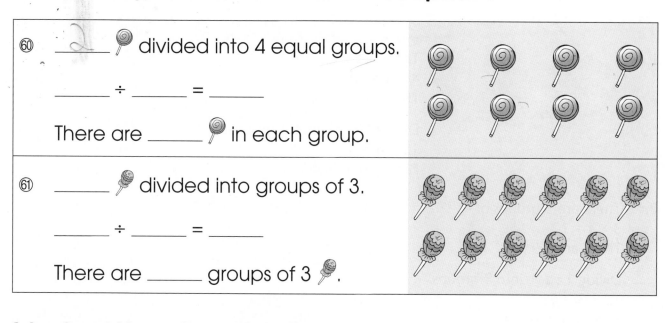

⑥⓪ ___2___ 🍭 divided into 4 equal groups. _____ ÷ _____ = _____ There are _____ 🍭 in each group.	
⑥① _____ 🍭 divided into groups of 3. _____ ÷ _____ = _____ There are _____ groups of 3 🍭.	

Solve the problems. Show your work.

⑥② Divide 6 bags of candy among 3 children. How many bags of candy does each child have?

_____ = _____   _____ bags of candy.

⑥③ A dragonfly has 4 wings. How many wings do 6 dragonflies have?

_____ = _____   _____ wings.

⑥④ A cupboard has 5 shelves with 8 cups on each shelf. How many cups are there in the cupboard ?

_____ = _____   _____ cups.

⑥⑤ A box of ice lollies costs $7. Sally buys 3 boxes for her birthday party. How much does Sally pay for the ice lollies ?

_____ = _____ $ _____ .

⑥⑥ 4 children share a box of chocolates. Each child gets 3 chocolates. How many chocolates does each child get if the same box of chocolates is shared among 3 children?

Each child gets _____ chocolates.

Multiplication and Division Fact Families

1. There are 4 groups of 3 🥕.
   $4 \times 3 = 12$
   There are 12 🥕.

   Divide 12 🥕 into 4 groups.
   $12 \div 4 = 3$
   Each group has 3 🥕.

2. There are 3 groups of 4 🥕.
   $3 \times 4 = 12$
   There are 12 🥕.

   Divide 12 🥕 into 3 groups.
   $12 \div 3 = 4$
   Each group has 4 🥕.

HINTS:

- Get familiar with the multiplication facts to be ready for division.

- There are 2 multiplication facts and 2 division facts for a fact family using the same 3 numbers.

  e.g. $3 \times 5 = 15$ $15 \div 5 = 3$
        $5 \times 3 = 15$ $15 \div 3 = 5$

Look at the pictures. Complete the multiplication and division sentences.

① _____ $\times 4 = 12$ $12 \div$ _____ $= 4$

② _____ $\times 3 = 15$ $15 \div$ _____ $= 3$

③ _____ $\times 6 = 18$ $18 \div$ _____ $= 6$

④ _____ $\times 5 = 20$ $20 \div$ _____ $= 5$

⑤ _____ $\times 7 = 35$ $35 \div$ _____ $= 7$

⑥ _____ $\times 8 = 16$ $16 \div$ _____ $= 8$

⑦ _____ $\times 3 = 12$ $12 \div$ _____ $= 3$

   ISBN: 978-1-897164-13-6

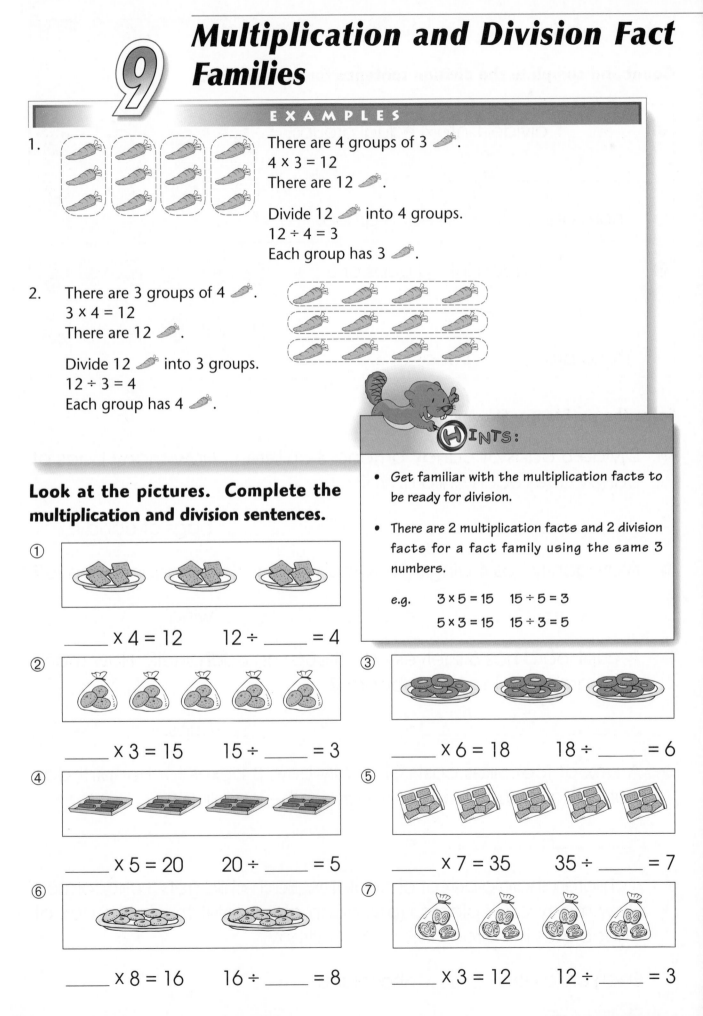

Write a fact family for each picture.

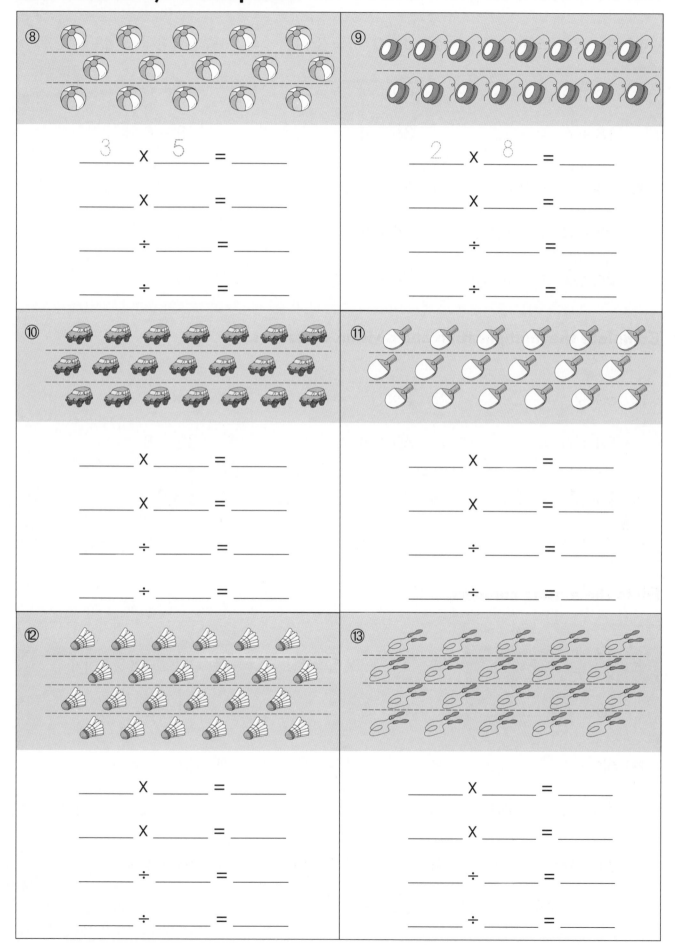

⑧

_____ 3 _____ X _____ 5 _____ = _____

_____ X _____ = _____

_____ ÷ _____ = _____

_____ ÷ _____ = _____

⑨

_____ 2 _____ X _____ 8 _____ = _____

_____ X _____ = _____

_____ ÷ _____ = _____

_____ ÷ _____ = _____

⑩

_____ X _____ = _____

_____ X _____ = _____

_____ ÷ _____ = _____

_____ ÷ _____ = _____

⑪

_____ X _____ = _____

_____ X _____ = _____

_____ ÷ _____ = _____

_____ ÷ _____ = _____

⑫

_____ X _____ = _____

_____ X _____ = _____

_____ ÷ _____ = _____

_____ ÷ _____ = _____

⑬

_____ X _____ = _____

_____ X _____ = _____

_____ ÷ _____ = _____

_____ ÷ _____ = _____

ISBN: 978-1-897164-13-6

Find the quotients using multiplication facts.

⑭ $3 \times 6 = 18$

$18 \div 3 =$ _____

$18 \div 6 =$ _____

⑮ $4 \times 9 = 36$

$36 \div 9 =$ _____

$36 \div 4 =$ _____

⑯ $6 \times 8 = 48$

$48 \div 6 =$ _____

$48 \div 8 =$ _____

⑰ $7 \times 4 = 28$

$28 \div 4 =$ _____

$28 \div 7 =$ _____

⑱ $8 \times 3 = 24$

$24 \div 8 =$ _____

$24 \div 3 =$ _____

⑲ $5 \times 7 = 35$

$35 \div 5 =$ _____

$35 \div 7 =$ _____

Complete the multiplication and division sentences.

⑳ $6 \times 9 =$ _____

$54 \div 6 =$ _____

㉑ $8 \times 5 =$ _____

$40 \div 8 =$ _____

㉒ $4 \times 8 =$ _____

$32 \div 8 =$ _____

㉓ $9 \times 3 =$ _____

$27 \div 3 =$ _____

㉔ $7 \times 6 =$ _____

$42 \div 7 =$ _____

㉕ $5 \times 9 =$ _____

$45 \div 5 =$ _____

Fill in the missing numbers.

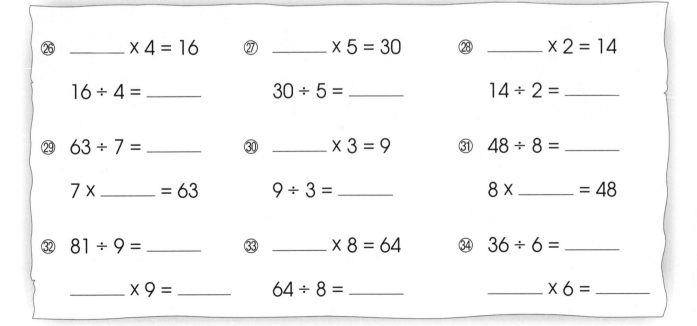

㉖ _____ $\times 4 = 16$

$16 \div 4 =$ _____

㉗ _____ $\times 5 = 30$

$30 \div 5 =$ _____

㉘ _____ $\times 2 = 14$

$14 \div 2 =$ _____

㉙ $63 \div 7 =$ _____

$7 \times$ _____ $= 63$

㉚ _____ $\times 3 = 9$

$9 \div 3 =$ _____

㉛ $48 \div 8 =$ _____

$8 \times$ _____ $= 48$

㉜ $81 \div 9 =$ _____

_____ $\times 9 =$ _____

㉝ _____ $\times 8 = 64$

$64 \div 8 =$ _____

㉞ $36 \div 6 =$ _____

_____ $\times 6 =$ _____

ISBN: 978-1-897164-13-6

Write the fact family for each group of numbers.

③⑤ 7   8   56

_____ X _____ = _____

_____ X _____ = _____

_____ ÷ _____ = _____

_____ ÷ _____ = _____

③⑥ 8   9   72

_____ X _____ = _____

_____ X _____ = _____

_____ ÷ _____ = _____

_____ ÷ _____ = _____

Write a multiplication sentence and a division sentence for each statement.

③⑦ There are 12 cakes in all. Put 2 cakes on a plate. There are 6 plates of cakes.

_____ X _____ = _____   _____ ÷ _____ = _____

③⑧ There are 40 stickers in all. Put 5 stickers on a page. There are 8 pages of stickers.

_____ X _____ = _____   _____ ÷ _____ = _____

③⑨ There are 30 children in all. Group 6 children into a team. There are 5 teams of children.

_____ X _____ = _____   _____ ÷ _____ = _____

④⓪ $45 is shared equally among 5 children. Each child gets $9.

_____ X _____ = _____   _____ ÷ _____ = _____

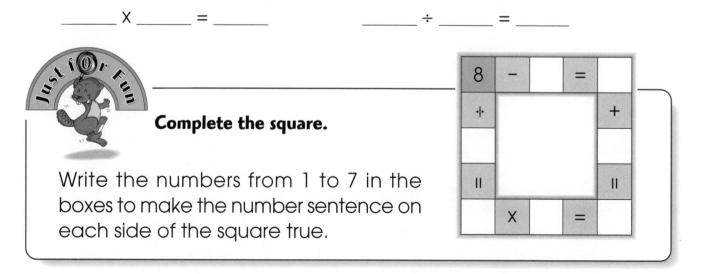

Just for Fun

Complete the square.

Write the numbers from 1 to 7 in the boxes to make the number sentence on each side of the square true.

8	–		=	
÷				+
=				=
	X		=	

ISBN: 978-1-897164-13-6

10 Dividing by 1, 2 or 3

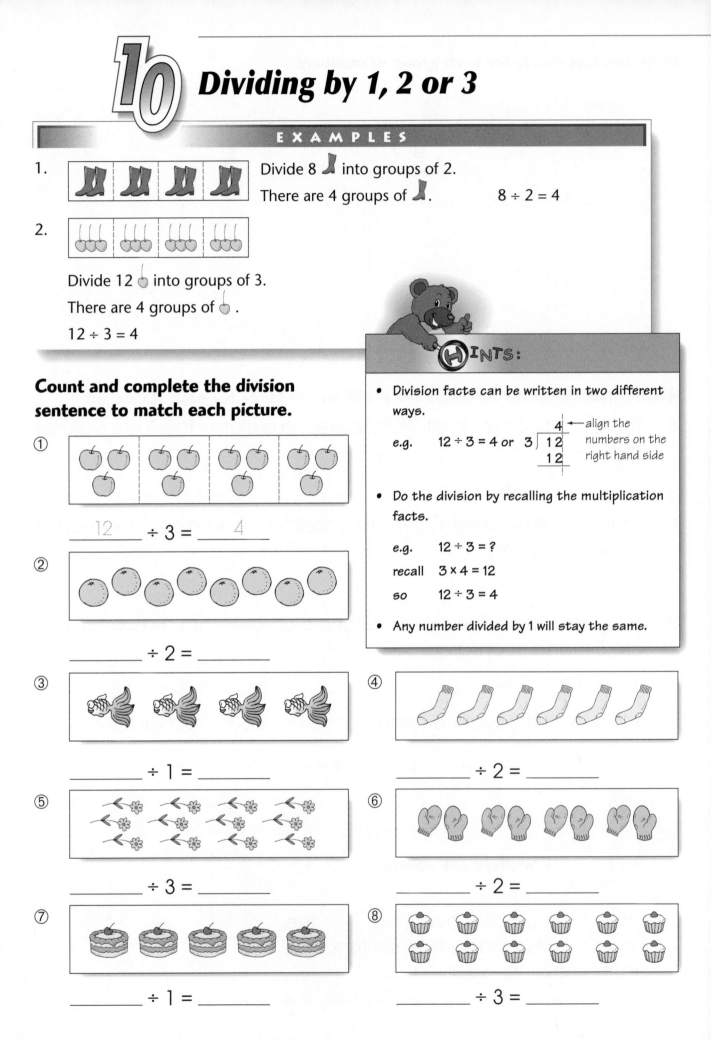

1. Divide 8 🥾 into groups of 2.
   There are 4 groups of 🥾. $8 \div 2 = 4$

2. Divide 12 🍒 into groups of 3.
   There are 4 groups of 🍒.
   $12 \div 3 = 4$

Count and complete the division sentence to match each picture.

HINTS:

- Division facts can be written in two different ways.

  e.g. $12 \div 3 = 4$ or $3\overline{)12}$ ← align the numbers on the right hand side

- Do the division by recalling the multiplication facts.

  e.g. $12 \div 3 = ?$
  recall $3 \times 4 = 12$
  so $12 \div 3 = 4$

- Any number divided by 1 will stay the same.

① _____ 12 _____ $\div 3 =$ _____ 4 _____

② _____ $\div 2 =$ _____

③ _____ $\div 1 =$ _____

④ _____ $\div 2 =$ _____

⑤ _____ $\div 3 =$ _____

⑥ _____ $\div 2 =$ _____

⑦ _____ $\div 1 =$ _____

⑧ _____ $\div 3 =$ _____

ISBN: 978-1-897164-13-6

Find the quotients using multiplication facts. Fill in the missing numbers.

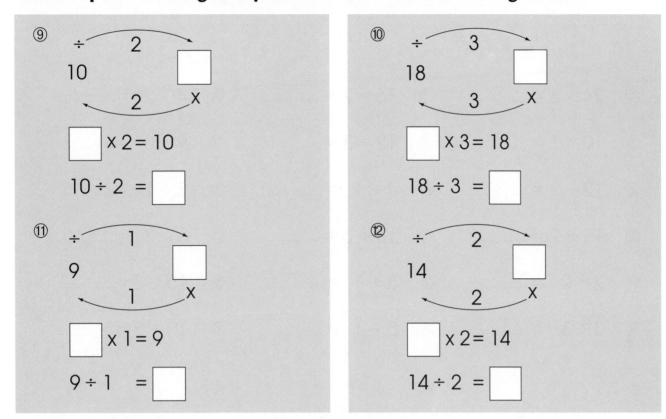

⑨ ÷ 2

10 □

2 ×

□ × 2 = 10

10 ÷ 2 = □

⑩ ÷ 3

18 □

3 ×

□ × 3 = 18

18 ÷ 3 = □

⑪ ÷ 1

9 □

1 ×

□ × 1 = 9

9 ÷ 1 = □

⑫ ÷ 2

14 □

2 ×

□ × 2 = 14

14 ÷ 2 = □

Find the quotients. Fill in the missing numbers.

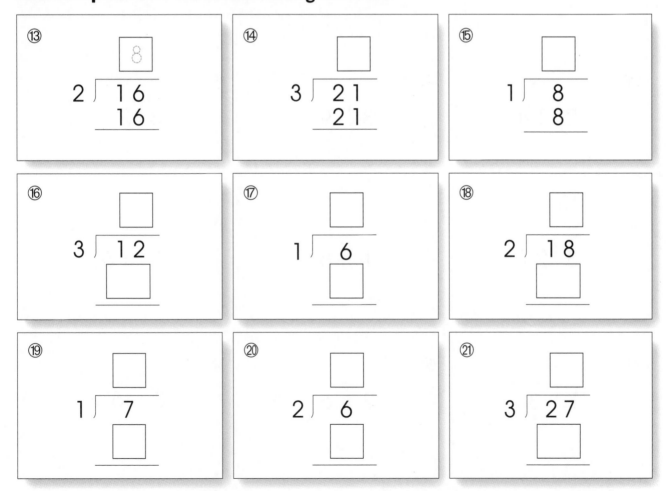

⑬
$$2\overline{)16}$$
   16
(quotient box: 8)

⑭
$$3\overline{)21}$$
   21

⑮
$$1\overline{)8}$$
   8

⑯
$$3\overline{)12}$$

⑰
$$1\overline{)6}$$

⑱
$$2\overline{)18}$$

⑲
$$1\overline{)7}$$

⑳
$$2\overline{)6}$$

㉑
$$3\overline{)27}$$

ISBN: 978-1-897164-13-6

Do the division.

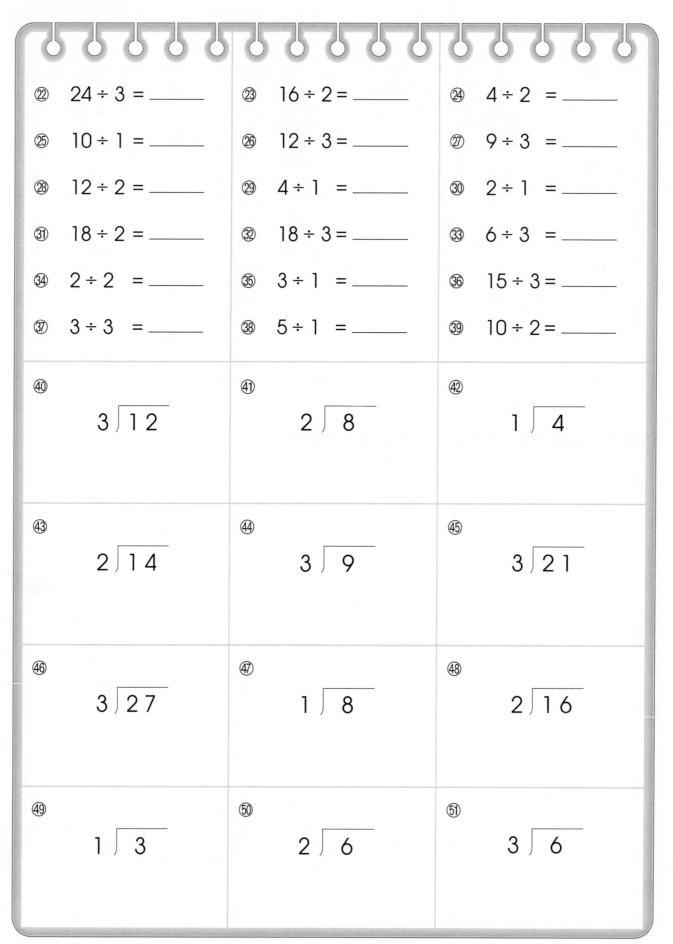

㉒ 24 ÷ 3 = ______

㉓ 16 ÷ 2 = ______

㉔ 4 ÷ 2 = ______

㉕ 10 ÷ 1 = ______

㉖ 12 ÷ 3 = ______

㉗ 9 ÷ 3 = ______

㉘ 12 ÷ 2 = ______

㉙ 4 ÷ 1 = ______

㉚ 2 ÷ 1 = ______

㉛ 18 ÷ 2 = ______

㉜ 18 ÷ 3 = ______

㉝ 6 ÷ 3 = ______

㉞ 2 ÷ 2 = ______

㉟ 3 ÷ 1 = ______

㊱ 15 ÷ 3 = ______

㊲ 3 ÷ 3 = ______

㊳ 5 ÷ 1 = ______

㊴ 10 ÷ 2 = ______

㊵ $3\overline{)12}$

㊶ $2\overline{)8}$

㊷ $1\overline{)4}$

㊸ $2\overline{)14}$

㊹ $3\overline{)9}$

㊺ $3\overline{)21}$

㊻ $3\overline{)27}$

㊼ $1\overline{)8}$

㊽ $2\overline{)16}$

㊾ $1\overline{)3}$

㊿ $2\overline{)6}$

(51) $3\overline{)6}$

ISBN: 978-1-897164-13-6

Solve the problems. Show your work.

(52) Mom divides a box of 24 chocolates among Tom and his 2 sisters. How many chocolates does each child have?

3) 24

________ ÷ ________ = ________

Each child has ________ chocolates.

(53) Tom has 16 balloons. He ties 2 balloons together in a bunch. How many bunches of balloons are there ?

________ ÷ ________ = ________

There are ________ bunches of balloons.

(54) Sally cuts 6 flowers from the garden. She puts 1 flower in each vase. How many vases does Sally need?

________ ÷ ________ = ________

She needs ________ vases.

(55) Tom and Sally share 12 lollipops between them. How many lollipops does each child have?

________ ÷ ________ = ________

Each child has ________ lollipops.

How many soldiers?

A number of soldiers are lining up in front of the Parliament Building. One soldier is holding a flag and the others are each holding a gun. Counting from the left, the 7th soldier is holding a flag. Counting from the right, the 10th soldier is holding a flag. How many soldiers are there in all?

________ soldiers.

ISBN: 978-1-897164-13-6

Dividing by 4 or 5

1. 8 ⦿ divided into groups of 4.
   There are 2 groups of ⦿. $8 \div 4 = 2$

2. 15 ⦿ divided into groups of 5.

   There are 3 groups of ⦿.

   $15 \div 5 = 3$

Count and complete the division sentence to match each picture.

HINTS:

- Align the quotient on the right hand side.

  $5\overline{)15}$ with 3 — ✗ $5\overline{)15}$ with 3 — ✓

- Dividing a number with 0 at the ones place by 5, the quotient is always an even number. Dividing a number with 5 at the ones place by 5, the quotient is always an odd number.

  e.g. $10 \div 5 = 2$ ← quotient is an even number

  0 at the ones place

  $35 \div 5 = 7$ ← quotient is an odd number

  5 at the ones place

① ___12___ ÷ 4 = ___3___

② _____ ÷ 5 = _____

③ _____ ÷ 5 = _____

④ _____ ÷ 4 = _____

⑤ _____ ÷ 4 = _____

⑥ _____ ÷ 5 = _____

⑦ _____ ÷ 4 = _____

Complete the multiplication table and use the multiplication facts to find the quotients.

⑧

	1	2	3	4	5	6	7	8	9
4			12						
5					25		35		

⑨ 10 ÷ 5 = _____

⑩ 16 ÷ 4 = _____

⑪ 12 ÷ 4 = _____

⑫ 32 ÷ 4 = _____

⑬ 24 ÷ 4 = _____

⑭ 20 ÷ 5 = _____

⑮ 40 ÷ 5 = _____

⑯ 35 ÷ 5 = _____

⑰ 36 ÷ 4 = _____

⑱ 20 ÷ 4 = _____

⑲ 45 ÷ 5 = _____

⑳ 28 ÷ 4 = _____

㉑ 30 ÷ 5 = _____

㉒ 4 ÷ 4 = _____

㉓ 15 ÷ 5 = _____

㉔ 5 ÷ 5 = _____

㉕ 25 ÷ 5 = _____

㉖ 8 ÷ 4 = _____

㉗ 4)‾1‾6‾

㉘ 5)‾3‾0‾

㉙ 4)‾2‾0‾

㉚ 5)‾4‾5‾

㉛ 4)‾3‾2‾

㉜ 5)‾2‾5‾

㉝ 4)‾3‾6‾

㉞ 5)‾4‾0‾

㉟ 4)‾2‾4‾

ISBN: 978-1-897164-13-6

Match the division sentences with the quotients.

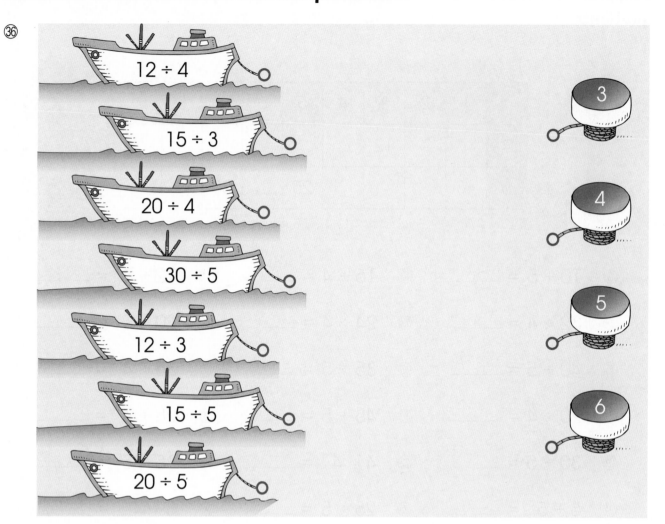

Fill in the boxes.

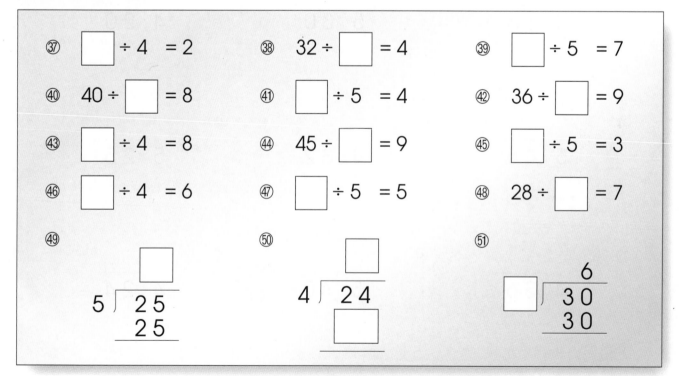

③⑦ $\boxed{} \div 4 = 2$ ③⑧ $32 \div \boxed{} = 4$ ③⑨ $\boxed{} \div 5 = 7$

④⓪ $40 \div \boxed{} = 8$ ④① $\boxed{} \div 5 = 4$ ④② $36 \div \boxed{} = 9$

④③ $\boxed{} \div 4 = 8$ ④④ $45 \div \boxed{} = 9$ ④⑤ $\boxed{} \div 5 = 3$

④⑥ $\boxed{} \div 4 = 6$ ④⑦ $\boxed{} \div 5 = 5$ ④⑧ $28 \div \boxed{} = 7$

④⑨

$5 \overline{)25}$
25

⑤⓪

$4 \overline{)24}$

⑤①

6
$\boxed{}\overline{)30}$
30

ISBN: 978-1-897164-13-6

Solve the problems. Show your work.

52   Dad plants 30 roses in 5 rows in the garden. How many roses are there in each row?

_____ ÷ _____ = _____

There are _____ roses in each row.

53   Tom buys 36 goldfish. He puts them in 4 bowls. How many goldfish are there in each bowl?

_____ ÷ _____ = _____

There are _____ goldfish in each bowl.

54   A chicken pie costs $4. How many chicken pies can be bought for $28?

_____ ÷ _____ = _____

_____ chicken pies can be bought.

55   20 boys and girls went to the movies in 5 cars. How many children were there in each car?

_____ ÷ _____ = _____

_____ children were in each car.

Just for Fun

Put + or − in the ◯ to make each number sentence true.

①   4 ◯ 3 ◯ 1 ◯ 2 = 0   ②   4 ◯ 3 ◯ 2 ◯ 1 = 2

③   4 ◯ 3 ◯ 2 ◯ 1 = 4   ④   4 ◯ 3 ◯ 2 ◯ 1 = 6

⑤   4 ◯ 3 ◯ 2 ◯ 1 = 8   ⑥   4 ◯ 3 ◯ 2 ◯ 1 = 10

12 Dividing by 6 or 7

EXAMPLES

1.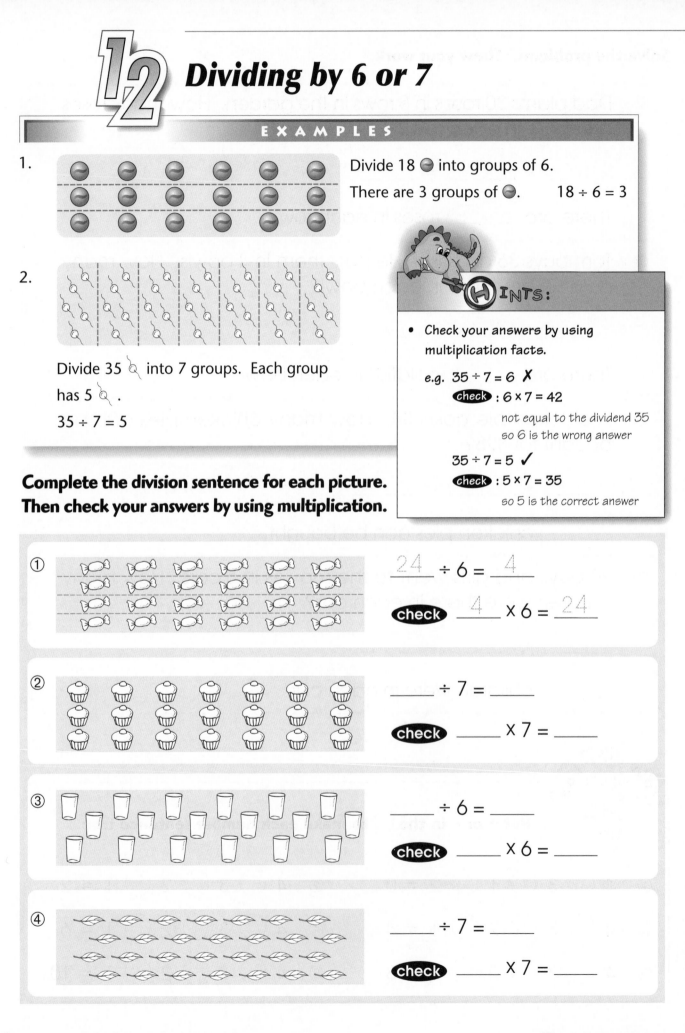

   Divide 18 ⬤ into groups of 6.
   There are 3 groups of ⬤. $18 ÷ 6 = 3$

2. Divide 35 🝆 into 7 groups. Each group
   has 5 🝆 .
   $35 ÷ 7 = 5$

HINTS:

- Check your answers by using multiplication facts.

   e.g. $35 ÷ 7 = 6$ ✗
   (check) : $6 × 7 = 42$
        not equal to the dividend 35
        so 6 is the wrong answer

   $35 ÷ 7 = 5$ ✓
   (check) : $5 × 7 = 35$
        so 5 is the correct answer

**Complete the division sentence for each picture.
Then check your answers by using multiplication.**

① ____24____ $÷ 6 =$ ___4___

   (check) ___4___ $× 6 =$ ___24___

② ____ $÷ 7 =$ ____

   (check) ____ $× 7 =$ ____

③ ____ $÷ 6 =$ ____

   (check) ____ $× 6 =$ ____

④ ____ $÷ 7 =$ ____

   (check) ____ $× 7 =$ ____

   ISBN: 978-1-897164-13-6

Do the division and check your answers using multiplication facts.

⑤ 63 ÷ 7 = _____

check

7 x _____ = 63

⑥ 36 ÷ 6 = _____

check

6 x _____ = 36

⑦ 49 ÷ 7 = _____

check

7 x _____ = 49

⑧ 54 ÷ 6 = _____

check

_____

⑨ 42 ÷ 7 = _____

check

_____

⑩ 24 ÷ 6 = _____

check

_____

⑪ 28 ÷ 7 = _____

check

_____

⑫ 30 ÷ 6 = _____

check

_____

⑬ 21 ÷ 7 = _____

check

_____

⑭ 18 ÷ 6 = _____

check

_____

⑮ 14 ÷ 7 = _____

check

_____

⑯ 48 ÷ 6 = _____

check

_____

Find the quotients.

⑰ 12 ÷ 6 = _____

⑱ 35 ÷ 7 = _____

⑲ 42 ÷ 6 = _____

⑳ 7 ÷ 7 = _____

㉑ 6 ÷ 6 = _____

㉒ 56 ÷ 7 = _____

㉓ 6)‾3‾6‾

㉔ 7)‾2‾1‾

㉕ 7)‾4‾9‾

㉖ 7)‾2‾8‾

㉗ 6)‾5‾4‾

㉘ 6)‾1‾8‾

Check the division sentences. Put a ✓ if the division sentence is true. Put a ✗ if the answer is wrong and write down the correct quotient.

	Division sentence	✓ or ✗	Correct quotient
㉙	$48 \div 6 = 8$		
㉚	$40 \div 5 = 6$		
㉛	$56 \div 7 = 8$		
㉜	$42 \div 7 = 9$		
㉝	$45 \div 5 = 9$		
㉞	$32 \div 4 = 7$		

Fill in the boxes.

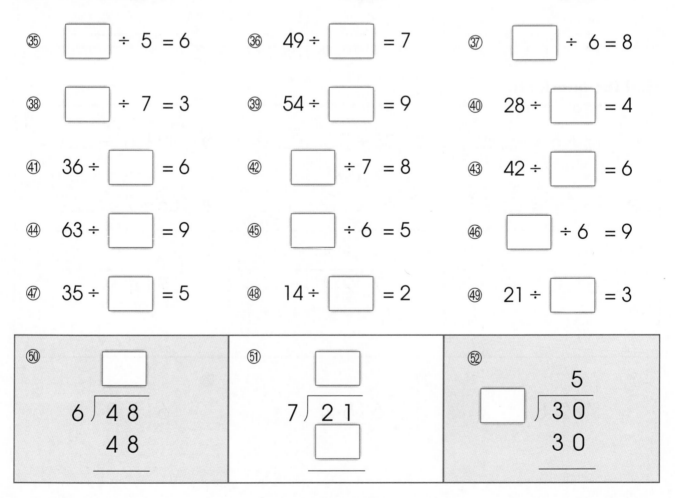

㉟ $\boxed{} \div 5 = 6$ ㊱ $49 \div \boxed{} = 7$ ㊲ $\boxed{} \div 6 = 8$

㊳ $\boxed{} \div 7 = 3$ ㊴ $54 \div \boxed{} = 9$ ㊵ $28 \div \boxed{} = 4$

㊶ $36 \div \boxed{} = 6$ ㊷ $\boxed{} \div 7 = 8$ ㊸ $42 \div \boxed{} = 6$

㊹ $63 \div \boxed{} = 9$ ㊺ $\boxed{} \div 6 = 5$ ㊻ $\boxed{} \div 6 = 9$

㊼ $35 \div \boxed{} = 5$ ㊽ $14 \div \boxed{} = 2$ ㊾ $21 \div \boxed{} = 3$

㊿ $6\overline{)48}$ 48

�;51 $7\overline{)21}$

㊫52 $\boxed{}\overline{)30}$ 5 30

ISBN: 978-1-897164-13-6

Solve the problems. Show your work and check your answers.

53 There are 54 soldiers lining up in 6 rows.

How many soldiers are there in each row?

_____ ÷ _____ = _____

There are _____ soldiers in each row.

54 Divide 56 marbles among 7 children.

How many marbles does each child have?

_____ ÷ _____ = _____

Each child has _____ marbles.

55 Sally cuts 24 tulips from the garden and puts them equally in 6 vases.

How many tulips does Sally put in each vase?

_____ ÷ _____ = _____

Sally puts _____ tulips in each vase.

56 Mom pays $35 for the sausage rolls at $7 each box. How many boxes of sausage rolls does Mom buy?

_____ ÷ _____ = _____

Mom buys _____ boxes of sausage rolls.

Just for Fun

Colour the two clocks that show the time Tom goes to bed and wakes up.

Ah! I've just slept for 2 hours.

A   B   C   D   E

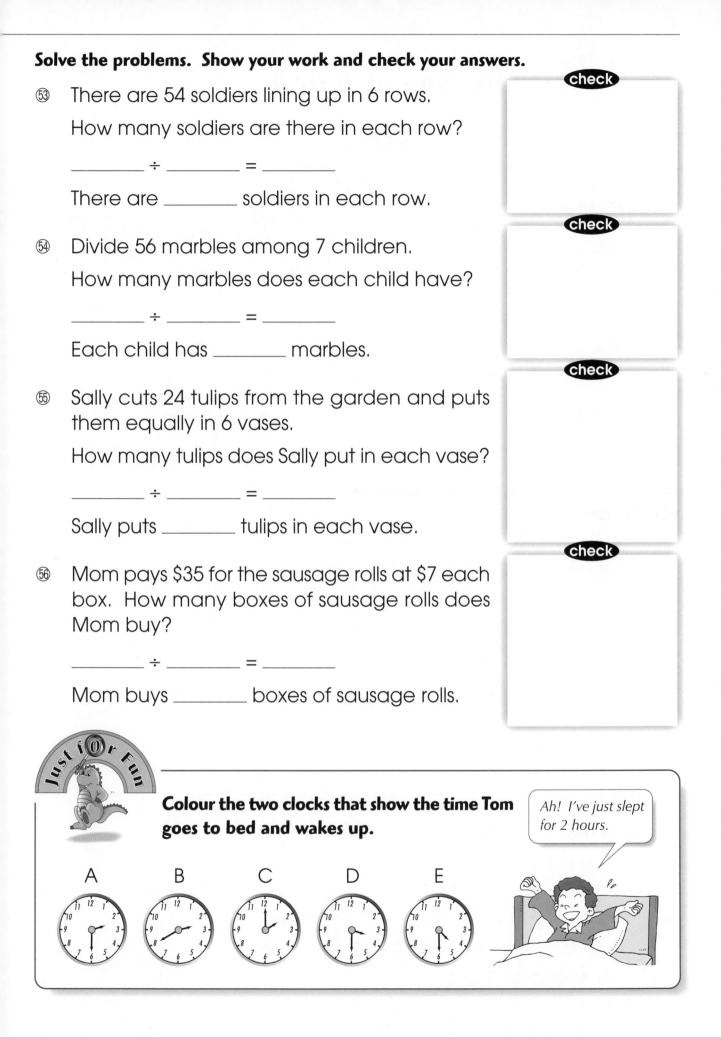

13 Dividing by 8 or 9

EXAMPLES

1.

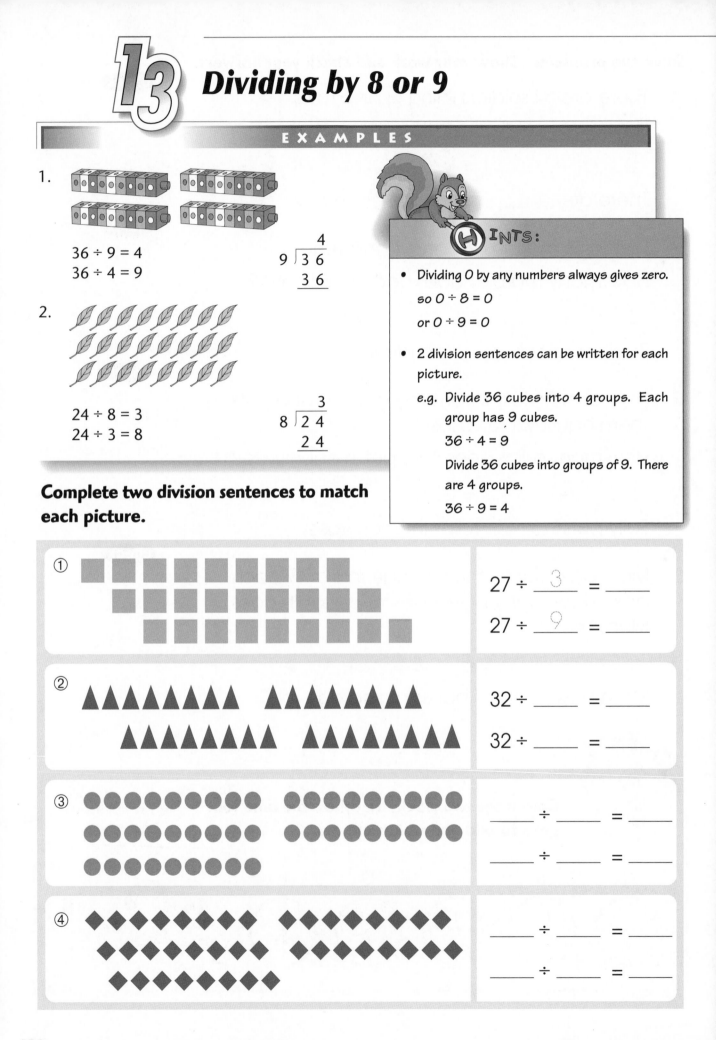

$36 \div 9 = 4$
$36 \div 4 = 9$

$$9 \overline{)\begin{array}{c} 4 \\ 3\,6 \\ \underline{3\,6} \end{array}}$$

2.

$24 \div 8 = 3$
$24 \div 3 = 8$

$$8 \overline{)\begin{array}{c} 3 \\ 2\,4 \\ \underline{2\,4} \end{array}}$$

HINTS:

- Dividing 0 by any numbers always gives zero.
  so $0 \div 8 = 0$
  or $0 \div 9 = 0$

- 2 division sentences can be written for each picture.
  e.g. Divide 36 cubes into 4 groups. Each group has 9 cubes.
  $36 \div 4 = 9$
  Divide 36 cubes into groups of 9. There are 4 groups.
  $36 \div 9 = 4$

Complete two division sentences to match each picture.

①
$27 \div \underline{\;\;3\;\;} = \underline{\;\;\;\;\;}$
$27 \div \underline{\;\;9\;\;} = \underline{\;\;\;\;\;}$

②
$32 \div \underline{\;\;\;\;\;} = \underline{\;\;\;\;\;}$
$32 \div \underline{\;\;\;\;\;} = \underline{\;\;\;\;\;}$

③
$\underline{\;\;\;\;\;} \div \underline{\;\;\;\;\;} = \underline{\;\;\;\;\;}$
$\underline{\;\;\;\;\;} \div \underline{\;\;\;\;\;} = \underline{\;\;\;\;\;}$

④
$\underline{\;\;\;\;\;} \div \underline{\;\;\;\;\;} = \underline{\;\;\;\;\;}$
$\underline{\;\;\;\;\;} \div \underline{\;\;\;\;\;} = \underline{\;\;\;\;\;}$

ISBN: 978-1-897164-13-6

Complete the division sentences.

⑤ $72 \div 9 =$ _____
$72 \div$ _____ $= 9$

⑥ $64 \div 8 =$ _____
$64 \div$ _____ $= 8$

⑦ $32 \div 8 =$ _____
$32 \div$ _____ $= 8$

⑧ $45 \div 9 =$ _____
$45 \div$ _____ $= 9$

⑨ $36 \div 9 =$ _____
$36 \div$ _____ $= 9$

⑩ $56 \div 8 =$ _____
$56 \div$ _____ $= 8$

⑪ $24 \div 8 =$ _____
$24 \div$ _____ $= 8$

⑫ $16 \div 8 =$ _____
$16 \div$ _____ $= 8$

⑬ $27 \div 9 =$ _____
$27 \div$ _____ $= 9$

⑭ $40 \div 8 =$ _____
$40 \div$ _____ $= 8$

⑮ $18 \div 9 =$ _____
$18 \div$ _____ $= 9$

⑯ $54 \div 9 =$ _____
$54 \div$ _____ $= 9$

⑰ $9 \div 9 =$ _____
$9 \div$ _____ $= 9$

⑱ $48 \div 8 =$ _____
$48 \div$ _____ $= 8$

⑲ $72 \div 8 =$ _____
$72 \div$ _____ $= 8$

⑳ $63 \div 9 =$ _____
$63 \div$ _____ $= 9$

㉑ $81 \div 9 =$ _____
$81 \div$ _____ $= 9$

㉒ $8 \div 8 =$ _____
$8 \div$ _____ $= 8$

㉓ $8\overline{)16}$ with handwritten 2 above and 16 below

㉔ $8\overline{)72}$

㉕ $9\overline{)36}$

㉖ $9\overline{)54}$

㉗ $9\overline{)45}$

㉘ $8\overline{)64}$

㉙ $8\overline{)56}$

㉚ $9\overline{)81}$

㉛ $8\overline{)32}$

Match the division sentences on the toys with the quotients that the children are holding.   Write the representing letters in the spaces.

㉜ | | | |

㉝ | | | |

㉞ | | | |

A $16 \div 2$

B $3\overline{)27}$

C $72 \div 8$

D $72 \div 9$

E $6\overline{)18}$

F $9\overline{)27}$

G $15 \div 5$

H $4\overline{)32}$

I $24 \div 8$

J $18 \div 2$

K $45 \div 5$

L $3\overline{)24}$

ISBN: 978-1-897164-13-6

Solve the problems. Show your work.

㉟ 9 children shared a box of 54 chocolates equally among them. How many chocolates did each child get?

_____ ÷ _____ = _____

Each child got _____ chocolates.

㊱ Sally bought 8 sketch books for $56. How much did each sketch book cost?

_____ ÷ _____ = _____

Each sketch book cost $ _____ .

㊲ The school music room has 45 seats arranged in rows of 9. How many rows of seats are there in the music room?

_____ ÷ _____ = _____

There are _____ rows of seats in the music room.

Just for Fun

Help Sally use the number cards to form the following numbers. You need not use all the cards each time.

0   1   3

6   9

① A 2-digit number closest to 100

② A 3-digit number closest to 100

③ The number closest to 1000

④ The number closest to 500

ISBN: 978-1-897164-13-6

14 Division with Remainders

Divide 30 pencils equally among 7 children.
How many pencils does each child have?
How many pencils are left over?

30 ÷ 7
= 4 with 2 left over
= 4R2

```
     4 R2
7 ) 3 0
    2 8
    ───
      2
```

Each child has 4 pencils.
2 pencils are left over.

HINTS:

- Use multiplication facts to do division.

  e.g. 30 ÷ 7 = ?

  Think: 7 x 4 = 28

            7 x 5 = 35

  7 multiplied by 4 is closest to but not greater than 30.

  so
  ```
       4  ←── quotient
  7 ) 3 0  ←── align the numbers on
      2 8      the right hand side
      ───
        2  ←── 30 – 28 = 2 left over
  ```

  Write : 30 ÷ 7 = 4R2   or

  quotient ↗ ↑

  ```
       4 R 2
  7 ) 3 0
      2 8
      ───
        2  ←── remainder
  ```

Circle and write a division sentence to match each picture.

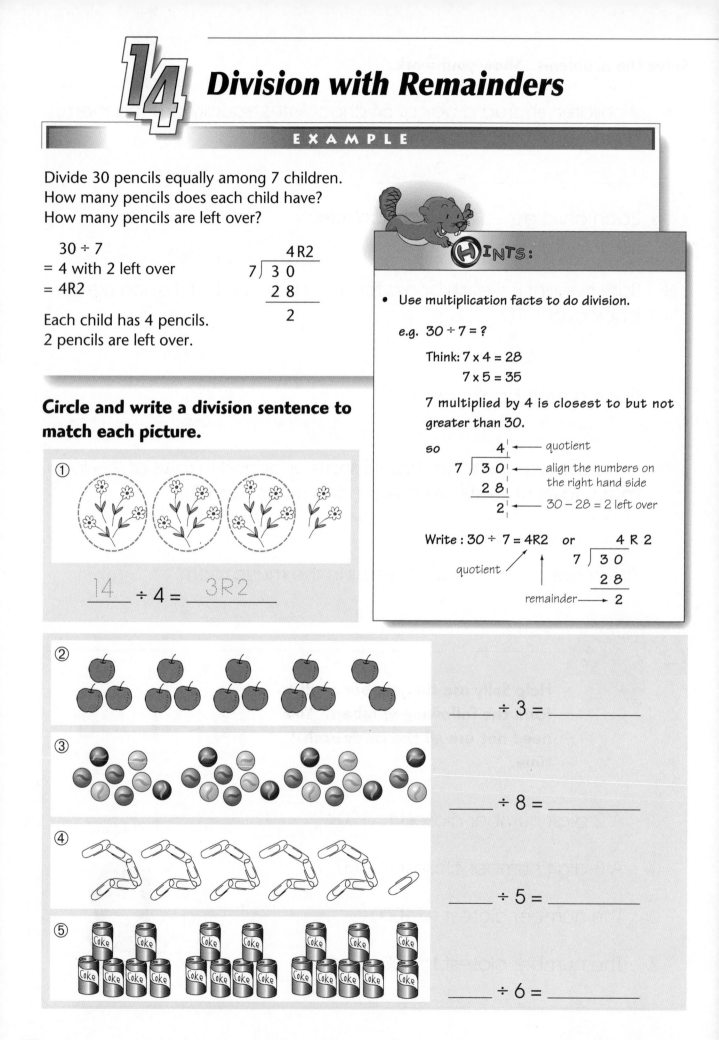

① ___14___ ÷ 4 = ___3R2___

② _____ ÷ 3 = _____

③ _____ ÷ 8 = _____

④ _____ ÷ 5 = _____

⑤ _____ ÷ 6 = _____

ISBN: 978-1-897164-13-6

Do the division.

⑥ $25 \div 4 =$ _____ R _____

⑦ $40 \div 7 =$ _____ R _____

⑧ $80 \div 9 =$ _____

⑨ $26 \div 8 =$ _____

⑩ $35 \div 4 =$ _____

⑪ $27 \div 5 =$ _____

⑫ $44 \div 7 =$ _____

⑬ $41 \div 8 =$ _____

⑭ $17 \div 2 =$ _____

⑮ $51 \div 9 =$ _____

⑯ $39 \div 5 =$ _____

⑰ $22 \div 3 =$ _____

⑱ $9 \overline{)2\ 5}$

⑲ $3 \overline{)1\ 9}$

⑳ $5 \overline{)4\ 6}$

㉑ $6 \overline{)5\ 5}$

㉒ $7 \overline{)5\ 2}$

㉓ $4 \overline{)3\ 8}$

㉔ $8 \overline{)7\ 9}$

㉕ $6 \overline{)3\ 9}$

㉖ $3 \overline{)1\ 9}$

ISBN: 978-1-897164-13-6

Fill in the boxes in ㊷ with letters representing the division sentences with 1 left over. Write the letters in sequence and help Tom find the key to open his box.

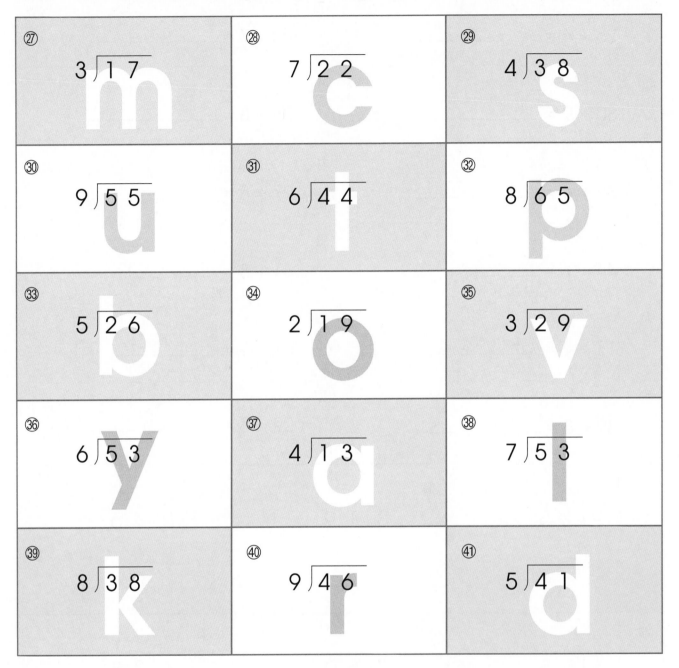

㉗ 3 ⟌ 1 7   m

㉘ 7 ⟌ 2 2   c

㉙ 4 ⟌ 3 8   s

㉚ 9 ⟌ 5 5   u

㉛ 6 ⟌ 4 4   i

㉜ 8 ⟌ 6 5   p

㉝ 5 ⟌ 2 6   b

㉞ 2 ⟌ 1 9   o

㉟ 3 ⟌ 2 9   v

㊱ 6 ⟌ 5 3   y

㊲ 4 ⟌ 1 3   a

㊳ 7 ⟌ 5 3   t

㊴ 8 ⟌ 3 8   k

㊵ 9 ⟌ 4 6   r

㊶ 5 ⟌ 4 1   d

㊷   The key is in the ⬚⬚⬚⬚⬚⬚⬚⬚⬚ .

ISBN: 978-1-897164-13-6

Solve the problems. Show your work.

㊸ 20 cakes on the table are arranged in rows of 6. How many rows of cakes are there on the table? How many cakes are left over?

_____ = _____

There are _____ row of cakes on the table. _____ cakes are left over.

㊹ 12 hot dogs are shared among 5 children. How many hot dogs does each child get? How many hot dogs are left over?

_____ = _____

Each child gets _____ hot dogs. _____ hot dogs are left over.

㊺ 89 books are put in a cupboard with 9 shelves. How many books are there on each shelf? How many books are left over?

_____ = _____

There are _____ books on each shelf. _____ books are left over.

Just for Fun

Help Tom use the number cards to form the following numbers. Write down all possible combinations.

① Numbers between 50 and 200

_____

② Even numbers between 300 and 600

_____

_____

③ Numbers between 800 and 1000

_____

| 0 | 3 | 5 |

| 8 | ? |

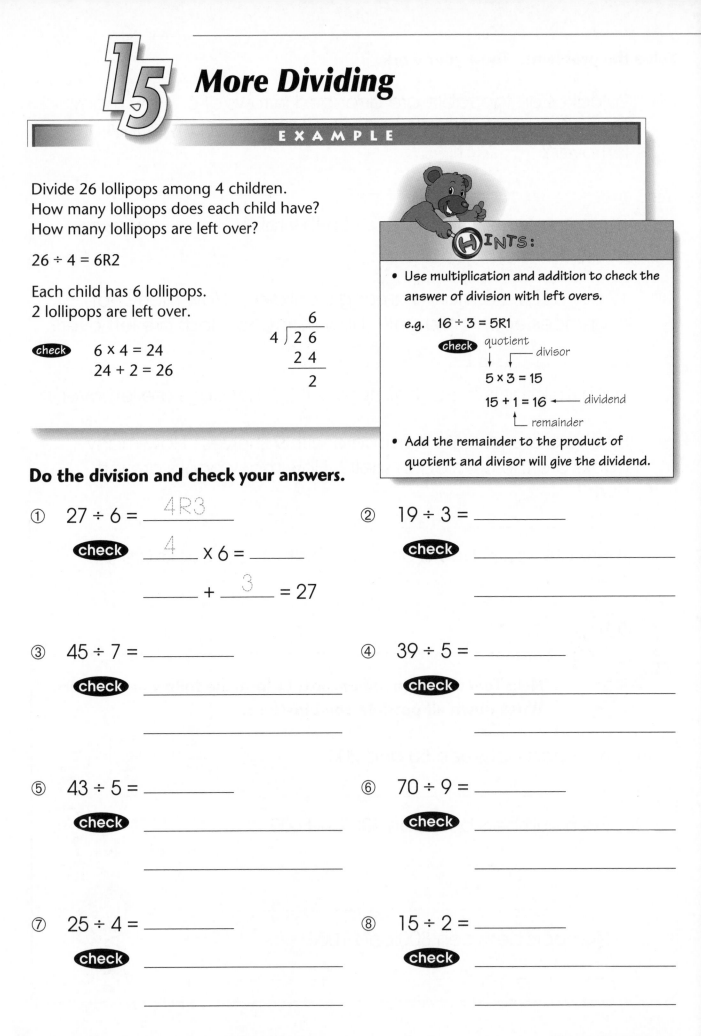

15 More Dividing

Divide 26 lollipops among 4 children.
How many lollipops does each child have?
How many lollipops are left over?

$26 \div 4 = 6R2$

Each child has 6 lollipops.
2 lollipops are left over.

check $6 \times 4 = 24$
$24 + 2 = 26$

$$\begin{array}{r} 6 \\ 4\overline{)2\ 6} \\ 2\ 4 \\ \hline 2 \end{array}$$

HINTS:

- Use multiplication and addition to check the answer of division with left overs.

  e.g. $16 \div 3 = 5R1$

  check   quotient
          $5 \times 3 = 15$ divisor
          $15 + 1 = 16$ ← dividend
                         └ remainder

- Add the remainder to the product of quotient and divisor will give the dividend.

Do the division and check your answers.

① $27 \div 6 =$ __4R3__

     check   __4__ $\times 6 =$ _____

         _____ $+$ __3__ $= 27$

② $19 \div 3 =$ _____

     check   _____

        _____

③ $45 \div 7 =$ _____

     check   _____

        _____

④ $39 \div 5 =$ _____

     check   _____

        _____

⑤ $43 \div 5 =$ _____

     check   _____

        _____

⑥ $70 \div 9 =$ _____

     check   _____

        _____

⑦ $25 \div 4 =$ _____

     check   _____

        _____

⑧ $15 \div 2 =$ _____

     check   _____

        _____

Do the division.

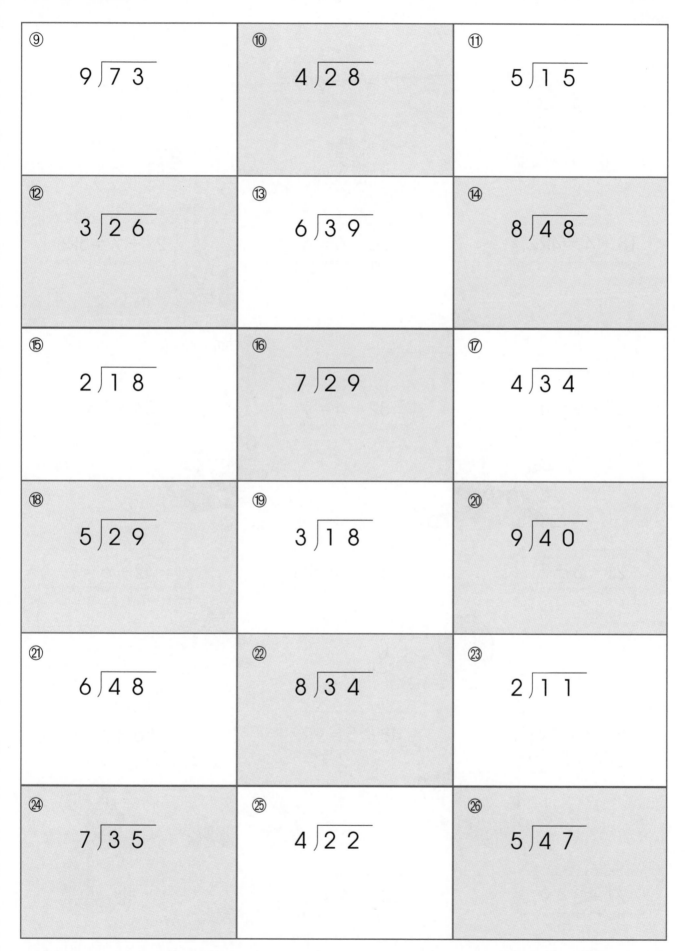

⑨ 9)73

⑩ 4)28

⑪ 5)15

⑫ 3)26

⑬ 6)39

⑭ 8)48

⑮ 2)18

⑯ 7)29

⑰ 4)34

⑱ 5)29

⑲ 3)18

⑳ 9)40

㉑ 6)48

㉒ 8)34

㉓ 2)11

㉔ 7)35

㉕ 4)22

㉖ 5)47

ISBN: 978-1-897164-13-6

Help Little Bear go to his mother following the path of correct answers. Draw the path.

27

11 ÷ 5 = 2R2

54 ÷ 9 = 7

18 ÷ 4 = 4R2

36 ÷ 6 = 6

27 ÷ 7 = 3R6

27 ÷ 9 = 4

32 ÷ 4 = 9

54 ÷ 9 = 6

21 ÷ 3 = 7

13 ÷ 2 = 6R1

42 ÷ 6 = 7

35 ÷ 8 = 4R3

48 ÷ 5 = 9R2

56 ÷ 7 = 9

27 ÷ 3 = 9

45 ÷ 9 = 5

ISBN: 978-1-897164-13-6

Answer the questions. Write the division sentence and put a ✓ in the box if there are remainders.

㉘   Divide 24 candies equally among 8 children.

㉙   46 cookies are shared among 5 children.

㉚   Put 30 stickers in rows of 6.

㉛   Divide 56 baseball cards among 8 children.

㉜   Arrange 27 chairs in rows of 9.

㉝   Fill 26 bottles in 4 six-pack cartons.

㉞   Tie 38 pencils into bunches of 7 pencils.

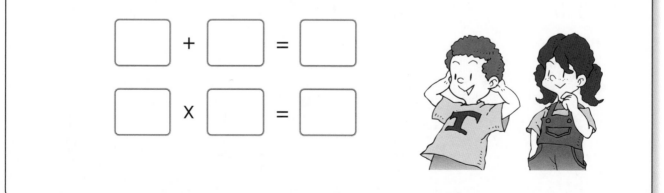

Write 1 to 6 in the boxes to make the addition sentence and multiplication sentence true. You cannot use any numbers twice.

☐ + ☐ = ☐

☐ x ☐ = ☐

ISBN: 978-1-897164-13-6

16 More Multiplying and Dividing

1. Arrange 35 stamps in rows of 5. How many rows are there?

    $35 \div 5 = 7$

    There are 7 rows.

2. There are 5 rows of stamps with 7 stamps in each row. How many stamps are there in all?

    $5 \times 7 = 35$

    There are 35 stamps in all.

HINTS:

- Read the problem carefully to see whether to use multiplication or division.

- Recall the fact families relating multiplication and division.

  e.g.

  $9 \times 8 = 72$ ⎤ changing the order
  $8 \times 9 = 72$ ⎦ of multiplication gives the same
  $72 \div 8 = 9$ product
  $72 \div 9 = 8$

Do the multiplication or division.

①
$$\begin{array}{r} 0 \\ \times\ 8 \\ \hline \end{array}$$

②
$$\begin{array}{r} 7 \\ \times\ 6 \\ \hline \end{array}$$

③ $7\overline{)5\,6}$

④ $4\overline{)3\,6}$

⑤ $3\overline{)1\,8}$

⑥ $6\overline{)4\,8}$

⑦ $5\overline{)3\,5}$

⑧ $9\overline{)6\,3}$

⑨ $2\overline{)1\,2}$

⑩ $8\overline{)7\,2}$

⑪
$$\begin{array}{r} 5 \\ \times\ 2 \\ \hline \end{array}$$

⑫
$$\begin{array}{r} 3 \\ \times\ 0 \\ \hline \end{array}$$

⑬
$$\begin{array}{r} 1\ 0 \\ \times\ 5 \\ \hline \end{array}$$

⑭
$$\begin{array}{r} 1 \\ \times\ 9 \\ \hline \end{array}$$

   ISBN: 978-1-897164-13-6

Write a family of facts for each picture.

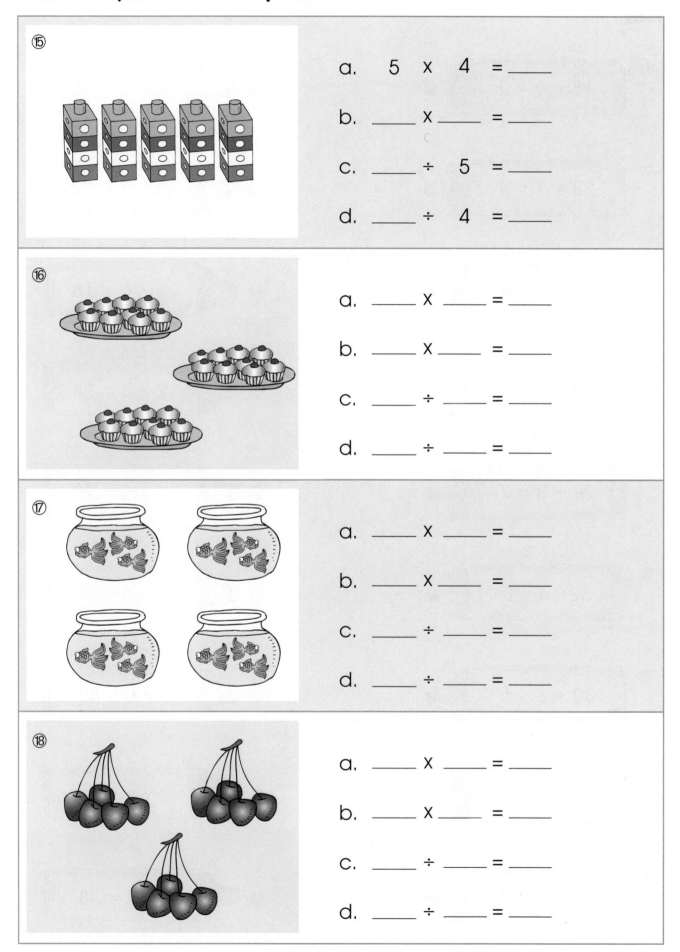

⑮

a. 5 x 4 = _____

b. _____ x _____ = _____

c. _____ ÷ 5 = _____

d. _____ ÷ 4 = _____

⑯

a. _____ x _____ = _____

b. _____ x _____ = _____

c. _____ ÷ _____ = _____

d. _____ ÷ _____ = _____

⑰

a. _____ x _____ = _____

b. _____ x _____ = _____

c. _____ ÷ _____ = _____

d. _____ ÷ _____ = _____

⑱

a. _____ x _____ = _____

b. _____ x _____ = _____

c. _____ ÷ _____ = _____

d. _____ ÷ _____ = _____

ISBN: 978-1-897164-13-6

Match the multiplication sentence and division sentence in the same family of facts.

⑲ $18 \div 6 = 3$ ●   ● A $7 \times 8 = 56$

⑳ $28 \div 7 = 4$ ●   ● B $3 \times 7 = 21$

㉑ $56 \div 7 = 8$ ●   ● C $3 \times 6 = 18$

㉒ $20 \div 4 = 5$ ●   ● D $7 \times 4 = 28$

㉓ $21 \div 3 = 7$ ●   ● E $4 \times 5 = 20$

㉔ $32 \div 4 = 8$ ●   ● F $6 \times 5 = 30$

㉕ $30 \div 6 = 5$ ●   ● G $9 \times 5 = 45$

㉖ $48 \div 8 = 6$ ●   ● H $4 \times 8 = 32$

㉗ $45 \div 5 = 9$ ●   ● I $6 \times 8 = 48$

ISBN: 978-1-897164-13-6

Solve the problems. Show your work.

㉘ Mom bought 3 pizzas for Sally's birthday party. Each pizza was then divided into 8 pieces. How many pieces of pizza were there in all?

_____ = _____

There were _____ pieces of pizza in all.

㉙ Mom divided the birthday cake into 12 pieces. The cake was shared among Sally and 5 friends. How many pieces of cake did each child have?

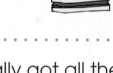

_____ = _____

Each child had _____ pieces of cake.

㉚ Mom made 4 different kinds of sandwiches. There were 8 sandwiches in each kind. How many sandwiches did Mom make in all?

_____ = _____

Mom made _____ sandwiches.

㉛ Five children shared equally a box of 28 lollipops. Sally got all the leftovers. How many lollipops did Sally get?

_____ = _____

Sally got _____ lollipops.

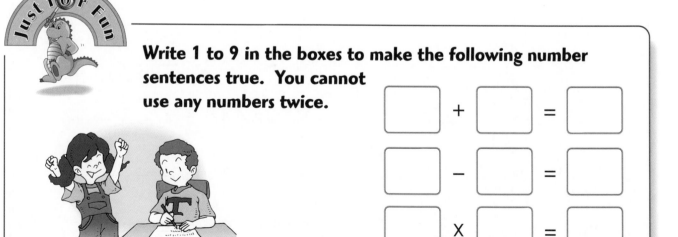

Just for Fun

Write 1 to 9 in the boxes to make the following number sentences true. You cannot use any numbers twice.

☐ + ☐ = ☐

☐ − ☐ = ☐

☐ X ☐ = ☐

Final Review

Fill in the missing numbers.

① 10 15 _____ 25 _____ _____ _____

② 18 _____ 36 45 _____ _____ _____

③ 18 16 _____ 12 _____ _____ _____

④ 36 32 _____ _____ 20 _____ _____

⑤ _____ 64 56 _____ 40 _____ _____

Find the answers.

⑥ 36 ÷ 9 = _____   ⑦ 45 ÷ 5 = _____   ⑧ 64 ÷ 8 = _____

⑨ 4 x 7 = _____   ⑩ 6 x 3 = _____   ⑪ 5 x 7 = _____

⑫ 72 ÷ 8 = _____   ⑬ 56 ÷ 7 = _____   ⑭ 54 ÷ 6 = _____

⑮ 3 x 8 = _____   ⑯ 5 x 4 = _____   ⑰ 10 x 2 = _____

⑱ 81 ÷ 9 = _____   ⑲ 40 ÷ 5 = _____   ⑳ 49 ÷ 7 = _____

㉑ 2 x 3 x 4 = _____   ㉒ 2 x 4 x 6 = _____

㉓ 1 x 3 x 5 = _____   ㉔ 0 x 4 x 8 = _____

㉕ 65 ÷ 9 = _____   ㉖ 40 ÷ 6 = _____

㉗ 25 ÷ 3 = _____   ㉘ 31 ÷ 4 = _____

ISBN: 978-1-897164-13-6

Do the multiplication and division.

㉙ $6\overline{)48}$	㉚ $5\overline{)35}$	㉛ $7\overline{)28}$	㉜ $2\overline{)18}$
㉝ $4\overline{)32}$	㉞ $3\overline{)18}$	㉟ $8\overline{)56}$	㊱ $9\overline{)36}$
㊲ 6×7	㊳ 8×2	㊴ 1×5	㊵ 9×9
㊶ 3×9	㊷ 4×9	㊸ 0×7	㊹ 5×6
㊺ $9\overline{)63}$	㊻ $2\overline{)14}$	㊼ $5\overline{)45}$	㊽ $3\overline{)24}$
㊾ $6\overline{)49}$	㊿ $4\overline{)33}$	(51) $8\overline{)45}$	(52) $7\overline{)56}$

ISBN: 978-1-897164-13-6

Write the fact families for each group of numbers.

(53)

⑨ ⑤ 45

_____ X _____ = _____

_____ X _____ = _____

_____ ÷ _____ = _____

_____ ÷ _____ = _____

(54)

⑧ ④ 32

_____ X _____ = _____

_____ X _____ = _____

_____ ÷ _____ = _____

_____ ÷ _____ = _____

Fill in the missing numbers.

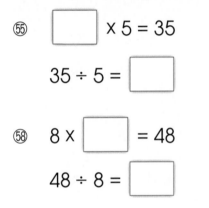
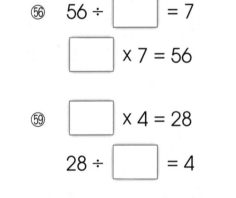
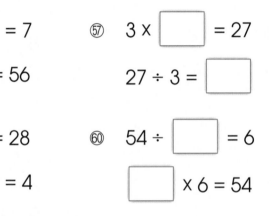

(55) ☐ x 5 = 35

35 ÷ 5 = ☐

(56) 56 ÷ ☐ = 7

☐ x 7 = 56

(57) 3 x ☐ = 27

27 ÷ 3 = ☐

(58) 8 x ☐ = 48

48 ÷ 8 = ☐

(59) ☐ x 4 = 28

28 ÷ ☐ = 4

(60) 54 ÷ ☐ = 6

☐ x 6 = 54

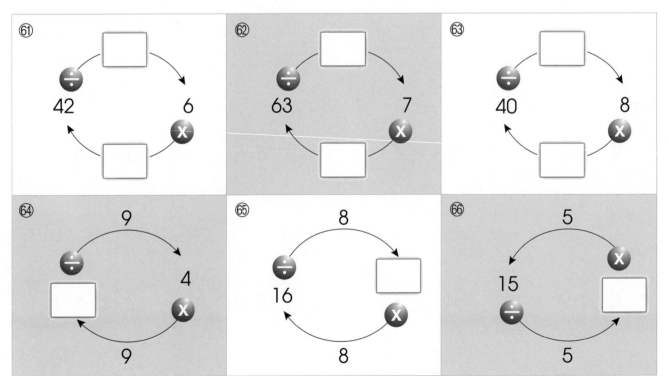

(61) ÷ 42   6 x ☐ ☐

(62) ÷ 63   7 x ☐ ☐

(63) ÷ 40   8 x ☐ ☐

(64) 9 ÷   4 x ☐ 9

(65) 8 ÷   16 x ☐ 8

(66) 5 x   15 ÷ ☐ 5

ISBN: 978-1-897164-13-6

Put the following cards in the right places.

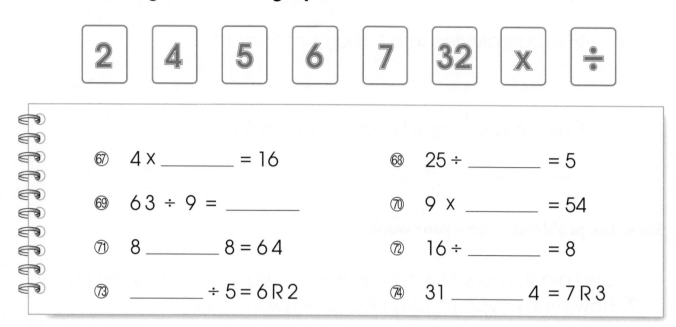

| 2 | 4 | 5 | 6 | 7 | 32 | x | ÷ |

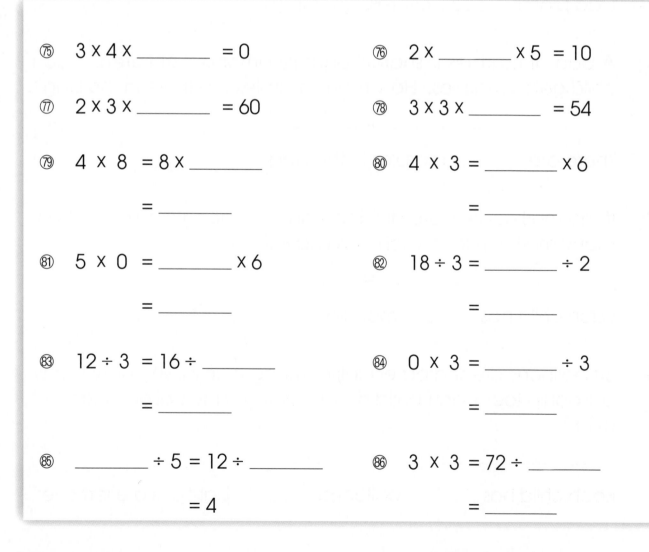

⑥⑦ $4 \times \rule{2cm}{0.4pt} = 16$ ⑥⑧ $25 \div \rule{2cm}{0.4pt} = 5$

⑥⑨ $63 \div 9 = \rule{2cm}{0.4pt}$ ⑦⓪ $9 \times \rule{2cm}{0.4pt} = 54$

⑦① $8 \rule{2cm}{0.4pt} 8 = 64$ ⑦② $16 \div \rule{2cm}{0.4pt} = 8$

⑦③ $\rule{2cm}{0.4pt} \div 5 = 6\,R\,2$ ⑦④ $31 \rule{2cm}{0.4pt} 4 = 7\,R\,3$

Fill in the blanks.

⑦⑤ $3 \times 4 \times \rule{2cm}{0.4pt} = 0$ ⑦⑥ $2 \times \rule{2cm}{0.4pt} \times 5 = 10$

⑦⑦ $2 \times 3 \times \rule{2cm}{0.4pt} = 60$ ⑦⑧ $3 \times 3 \times \rule{2cm}{0.4pt} = 54$

⑦⑨ $4 \times 8 = 8 \times \rule{2cm}{0.4pt}$ ⑧⓪ $4 \times 3 = \rule{2cm}{0.4pt} \times 6$

       $= \rule{1.5cm}{0.4pt}$ $= \rule{1.5cm}{0.4pt}$

⑧① $5 \times 0 = \rule{2cm}{0.4pt} \times 6$ ⑧② $18 \div 3 = \rule{2cm}{0.4pt} \div 2$

       $= \rule{1.5cm}{0.4pt}$ $= \rule{1.5cm}{0.4pt}$

⑧③ $12 \div 3 = 16 \div \rule{2cm}{0.4pt}$ ⑧④ $0 \times 3 = \rule{2cm}{0.4pt} \div 3$

       $= \rule{1.5cm}{0.4pt}$ $= \rule{1.5cm}{0.4pt}$

⑧⑤ $\rule{2cm}{0.4pt} \div 5 = 12 \div \rule{2cm}{0.4pt}$ ⑧⑥ $3 \times 3 = 72 \div \rule{2cm}{0.4pt}$

       $= 4$ $= \rule{1.5cm}{0.4pt}$

ISBN: 978-1-897164-13-6

Write a multiplication sentence and a division sentence for each statement.

⑧⑦ 48 scouts divided into 6 teams of 8 scouts

_____ X _____ = _____   _____ ÷ _____ = _____

⑧⑧ 5 sketch books at $7 each, totalling $35

_____ X _____ = _____   _____ ÷ _____ = _____

Solve the problems. Show your work.

⑧⑨ Dad plants a row of 8 cypress trees on each side of the driveway. How many cypress trees does Dad plant in all?

_____ = _____

Dad plants _____ cypress trees in all.

⑨⓪ A bag of marbles is shared equally among 9 children. Each child gets 4 marbles. How many marbles are there in the bag?

_____ = _____

There are _____ marbles in the bag.

⑨① If the marbles in ⑨⓪ are divided equally among 6 children, how many marbles does each child have?

_____ = _____

Each child has _____ marbles.

⑨② 34 balloons are shared equally among 4 children. How many balloons does each child have? How many balloons are left over?

_____ = _____

Each child has _____ balloons. _____ balloons are left over.

ISBN: 978-1-897164-13-6

Overview

In Section II, children practised multiplication and division. They also used fact families to explore the relationship between multiplication and division. In this section, these skills are built upon to solve problems.

Measurement applications include perimeter, area, capacity, time and temperature.

Children investigate the attributes of 3-D figures such as prisms and pyramids, and 2-D figures such as rhombuses and parallelograms. They are also expected to identify patterns and transformations, such as reflection, translation and rotation.

Data management involves reading circle graphs and bar graphs. Fractions and probability are included.

Review

Uncle Jack has a grocery store. Help him record the measurement of the sign of his store and answer the questions.

← 1m →

1m

B & C Grocery Store

① The length of the sign is _____ m.

② The width of the sign is _____ m.

③ The perimeter of the sign is _____ m.

④ The area of the sign is _____ square metres.

Look at the opening hours of Uncle Jack's store. Answer the questions.

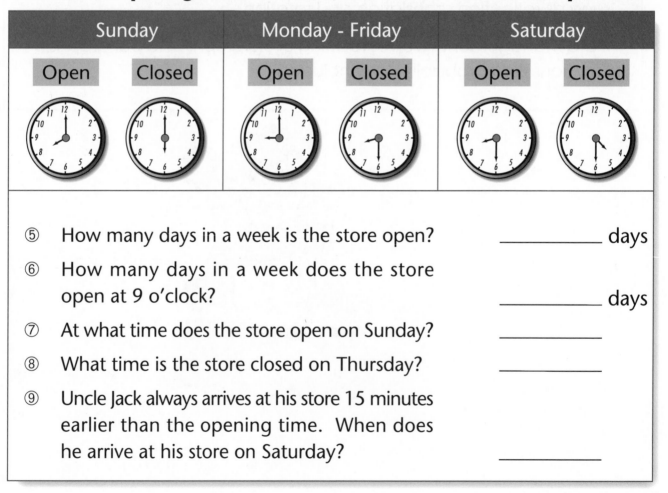

⑤ How many days in a week is the store open? _____ days

⑥ How many days in a week does the store open at 9 o'clock? _____ days

⑦ At what time does the store open on Sunday? _____

⑧ What time is the store closed on Thursday? _____

⑨ Uncle Jack always arrives at his store 15 minutes earlier than the opening time. When does he arrive at his store on Saturday? _____

ISBN: 978-1-897164-13-6

There is a lucky draw in Uncle Jack's store. Follow the patterns and help Uncle Jack label the raffle tickets. Then circle the correct words and write the numbers to complete the pattern rules.

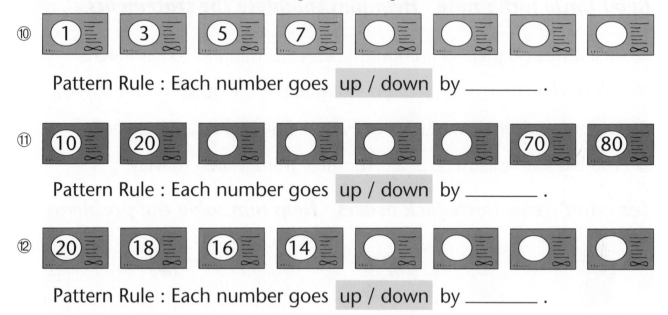

⑩

Pattern Rule : Each number goes up / down by _____ .

⑪

Pattern Rule : Each number goes up / down by _____ .

⑫

Pattern Rule : Each number goes up / down by _____ .

Look at the prizes for the customers. Count and write the number of prizes in the boxes. Then name the shapes.

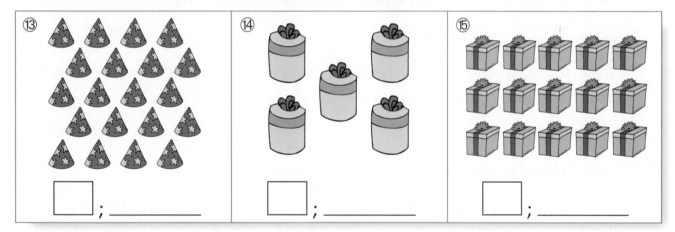

⑬ _____ ; _____

⑭ _____ ; _____

⑮ _____ ; _____

Look at the prizes above. Circle the correct word for the chances of getting a prize.

⑯ The chance of getting a 🎁   Often   Sometimes   Never

⑰ The chance of getting a 🎉   Often   Sometimes   Never

⑱ The chance of getting a 🎁   Often   Sometimes   Never

⑲ The chance of getting a 🎁 is greater / smaller than getting a 🎁 .

ISBN: 978-1-897164-13-6

Review

Read Uncle Jack's note. Help him complete the statements.

⑳ Take three quarters of an hour or _____ minutes to eat lunch.

㉑ Take half an hour or _____ minutes to put the goods on the shelves.

㉒ Order goods from the supplier every 14 days or _____ weeks.

㉓ The big sale will last _____ months, from March to May.

See what items Uncle Jack orders. Help him solve the problems.

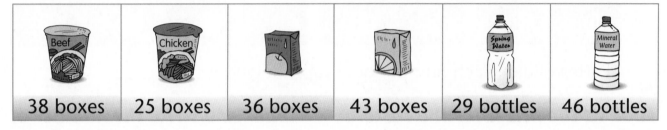

Beef	Chicken			Spring Water	Mineral Water
38 boxes	25 boxes	36 boxes	43 boxes	29 bottles	46 bottles

㉔ How many boxes of cup noodles does Uncle Jack order?

_____ = _____   _____ boxes

㉕ How many more boxes of beef flavoured cup noodles does Uncle Jack order than the chicken flavoured ones?

_____ = _____   _____ more boxes

㉖ How many boxes of juice does Uncle Jack order?

_____ = _____   _____ boxes

㉗ How many more boxes of orange juice does Uncle Jack order than apple juice?

_____ = _____   _____ more boxes

㉘ How many bottles of water does Uncle Jack order?

_____ = _____   _____ bottles

㉙ How many more bottles of mineral water does Uncle Jack order than spring water?

_____ = _____   _____ more bottles

 ISBN: 978-1-897164-13-6

Uncle Jack asks his customers about their favourite brand of crackers. Look at his tally chart and help him colour the graph. Then answer the questions.

Mega's Choice	St. Jimmy	T & G	Fairmount	Co Co
ℍℍ ‖	ℍℍ ℍℍ ‖	ℍℍ ‖	‖‖	ℍℍ ℍℍ

㉚

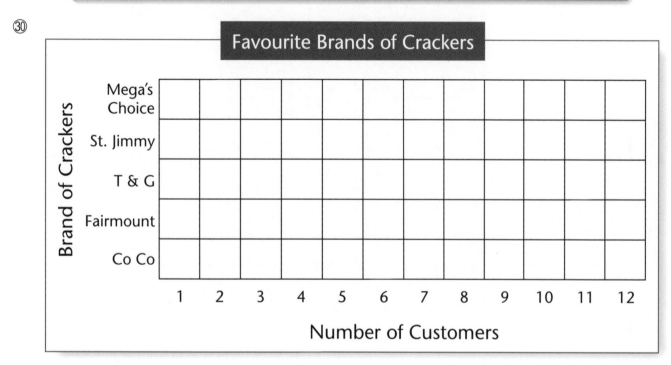

㉛ What is the title of the graph?

_____

㉜ How many brands of crackers are there? _____ brands

㉝ How many customers chose T & G? _____ customers

㉞ If 3 men chose Mega's Choice, how many women chose Mega's Choice? _____ women

㉟ How many more customers chose Co Co than T & G? _____ more

㊱ Which brand did most customers choose? _____

㊲ How many customers did Uncle Jack ask? _____ customers

ISBN: 978-1-897164-13-6

1 Numbers to 100

Albert draws a 100-chart for his friend, Bill the alien. Help Bill write the missing numbers in words to complete the chart.

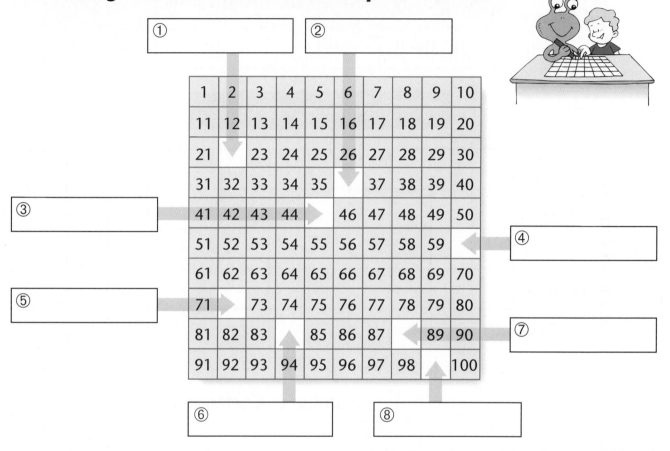

See how Bill places his spaceships on the number lines. Help him fill in the missing numbers.

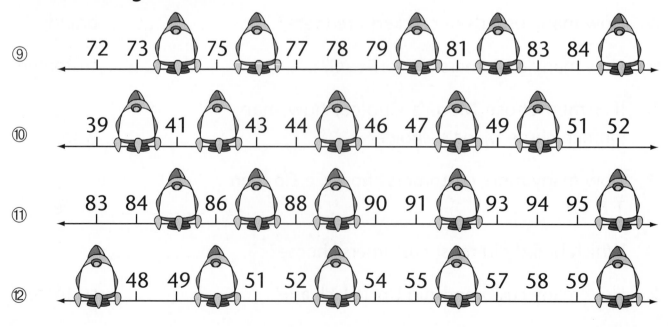

Write the missing numbers and answer the questions.

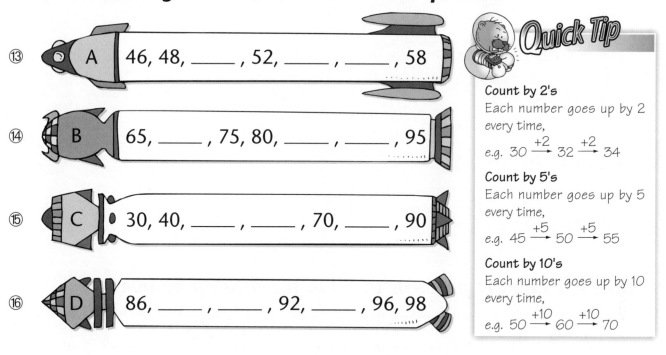

⑬ A 46, 48, _____, 52, _____, _____, 58

⑭ B 65, _____, 75, 80, _____, _____, 95

⑮ C 30, 40, _____, _____, 70, _____, 90

⑯ D 86, _____, _____, 92, _____, 96, 98

Quick Tip

Count by 2's
Each number goes up by 2 every time,
e.g. 30 $\xrightarrow{+2}$ 32 $\xrightarrow{+2}$ 34

Count by 5's
Each number goes up by 5 every time,
e.g. 45 $\xrightarrow{+5}$ 50 $\xrightarrow{+5}$ 55

Count by 10's
Each number goes up by 10 every time,
e.g. 50 $\xrightarrow{+10}$ 60 $\xrightarrow{+10}$ 70

⑰ Which number should go after 58 in spaceship A? _____

⑱ Which number should go after 95 in spaceship B? _____

⑲ Which number should go before 30 in spaceship C? _____

⑳ Which number should go before 86 in spaceship D? _____

Count backward to write the missing numbers.

㉑ 95, 90, _____, _____, _____, _____, _____, 60

㉒ 38, 36, _____, _____, _____, _____, _____, 24

㉓ 80, 70, _____, _____, _____, _____, _____, 10

㉔ 75, 70, _____, _____, _____, _____, _____, 40

㉕ 66, 64, _____, _____, _____, _____, _____, 52

㉖ 52, 50, _____, _____, _____, _____, _____, 38

㉗ 40, 35, _____, _____, _____, _____, _____, 5

Write the numbers in order from least to greatest on the planets.

㉘ 24 , 19 , 53 , 64

㉙ 30 , 55 , 81 , 70

㉚ 62 , 73 , 70 , 51

㉛ 36 , 48 , 13 , 25

Follow the number patterns to fill in the missing numbers.

㉜ 2, 4, 8, 14, ___, ___ , 44, 58, ___, ___

㉝ 4, 24, 5, 25, _6_, 26 , 7, _27_, _8_, _28_

㉞ 7, 7, 14, 8, 8, 16, 9, _9_ , 18, _10_, _10_ , 20

㉟ 10 , 1 , 9 , 10 , 2 , 8 , 10 , _3_ , 7, _10_ , 4 , 6

Use the numbers on the stars to answer the questions.

16   52   36   80   50   67   63

㊱ Which numbers are greater than forty-five?   _____

㊲ Which numbers are even?   _____

㊳ Which number is 10 more than seventy?   _____

㊴ Which numbers have 6 in the tens column?   _____

㊵ Which number comes right after 51?   _____

㊶ Which numbers are between 10 and 40?   _____

ISBN: 978-1-897164-13-6

100 aliens are lining up outside the spaceship. Look at the picture and solve the problems.

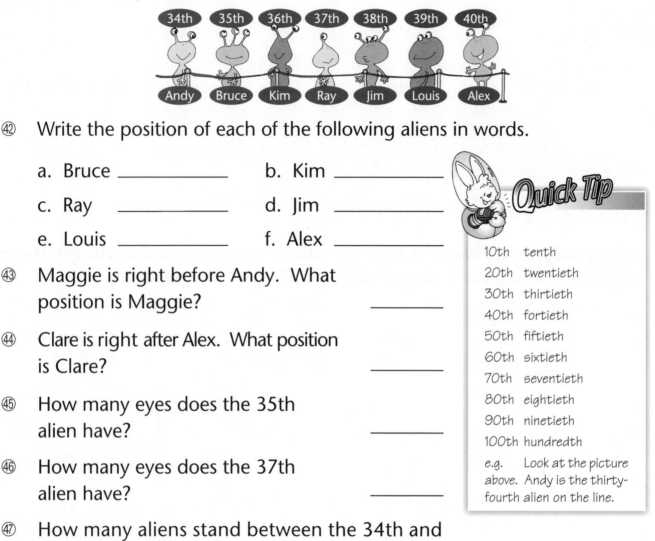

㊷ Write the position of each of the following aliens in words.

a. Bruce _____

b. Kim _____

c. Ray _____

d. Jim _____

e. Louis _____

f. Alex _____

Quick Tip

10th	tenth
20th	twentieth
30th	thirtieth
40th	fortieth
50th	fiftieth
60th	sixtieth
70th	seventieth
80th	eightieth
90th	ninetieth
100th	hundredth

e.g. Look at the picture above. Andy is the thirty-fourth alien on the line.

㊸ Maggie is right before Andy. What position is Maggie? _____

㊹ Clare is right after Alex. What position is Clare? _____

㊺ How many eyes does the 35th alien have? _____

㊻ How many eyes does the 37th alien have? _____

㊼ How many aliens stand between the 34th and the 39th aliens? _____

㊽ If Jim and Louis leave the line, what is the new position of Alex? _____

MIND BOGGLER

Look at the picture above. Answer the questions.

① How many aliens are standing before Bruce? _____

② Every 10th aliens in the line gets a prize. Who in the picture can get a prize? _____

2 Addition and Subtraction

Examples

① 16 + 29 =

Add the ones.

①— Carry 1
1**6** to the
+ 2**9** tens.
5

Add the tens.

①
1 6
+ 2 9
4 5

16 + 29 = 45

② 32 – 17 =

Subtract the ones.

2 12 —Borrow
3̶ 2̶ 1 from
– 1 7 the tens.
5

Subtract the tens.

2 12
3̶ 2̶
– 1 7
1 5

32 – 17 = 15

Add or subtract. Then write in order the letters representing the questions with 55 as the answer in ⑰ and find out what Charles says.

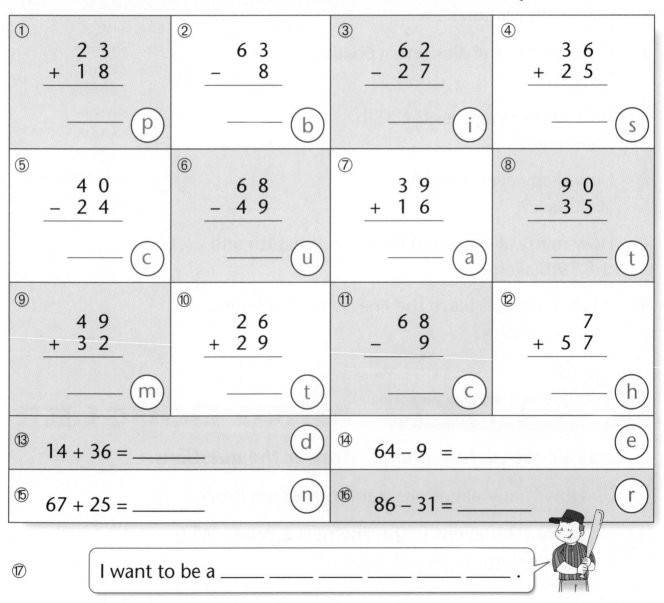

①
```
  2 3
+ 1 8
-----
```
___ (p)

②
```
  6 3
–   8
-----
```
___ (b)

③
```
  6 2
– 2 7
-----
```
___ (i)

④
```
  3 6
+ 2 5
-----
```
___ (s)

⑤
```
  4 0
– 2 4
-----
```
___ (c)

⑥
```
  6 8
– 4 9
-----
```
___ (u)

⑦
```
  3 9
+ 1 6
-----
```
___ (a)

⑧
```
  9 0
– 3 5
-----
```
___ (t)

⑨
```
  4 9
+ 3 2
-----
```
___ (m)

⑩
```
  2 6
+ 2 9
-----
```
___ (t)

⑪
```
  6 8
–   9
-----
```
___ (c)

⑫
```
    7
+ 5 7
-----
```
___ (h)

⑬ 14 + 36 = _____ (d)

⑭ 64 – 9 = _____ (e)

⑮ 67 + 25 = _____ (n)

⑯ 86 – 31 = _____ (r)

⑰ I want to be a ____ ____ ____ ____ ____ .

ISBN: 978-1-897164-13-6

Add or subtract. Then check your answers.

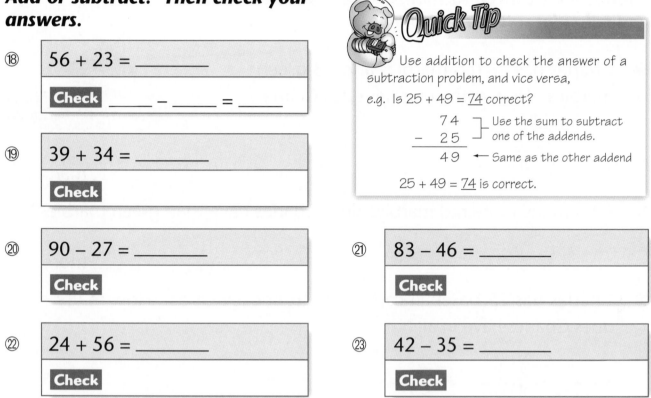

⑱ 56 + 23 = _____

Check _____ − _____ = _____

⑲ 39 + 34 = _____

Check

⑳ 90 − 27 = _____

Check

㉑ 83 − 46 = _____

Check

㉒ 24 + 56 = _____

Check

㉓ 42 − 35 = _____

Check

Quick Tip

Use addition to check the answer of a subtraction problem, and vice versa,

e.g. Is 25 + 49 = 74 correct?

$$\begin{array}{r} 7\,4 \\ -\ 2\,5 \\ \hline 4\,9 \end{array}$$ ⎤ Use the sum to subtract one of the addends.

4 9 ← Same as the other addend

25 + 49 = 74 is correct.

Use the given number sentences to find the missing numbers.

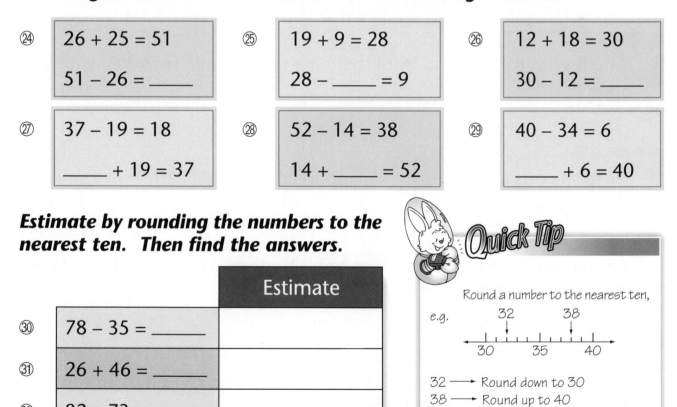

㉔ 26 + 25 = 51

51 − 26 = _____

㉕ 19 + 9 = 28

28 − _____ = 9

㉖ 12 + 18 = 30

30 − 12 = _____

㉗ 37 − 19 = 18

_____ + 19 = 37

㉘ 52 − 14 = 38

14 + _____ = 52

㉙ 40 − 34 = 6

_____ + 6 = 40

Estimate by rounding the numbers to the nearest ten. Then find the answers.

	Estimate
㉚ 78 − 35 = _____	
㉛ 26 + 46 = _____	
㉜ 82 − 73 = _____	
㉝ 40 − 25 = _____	

Quick Tip

Round a number to the nearest ten,

e.g. 32   38

30   35   40

32 ⟶ Round down to 30
38 ⟶ Round up to 40
35 ⟶ Round up to 40

A number halfway between 2 numbers should be rounded up.

ISBN: 978-1-897164-13-6

Charles likes collecting things. Read what he collects and help him solve the problems.

㉞ Charles has 46 red marbles and 38 green marbles. How many marbles does Charles have in all?

_____ ◯ _____ = _____   _____ marbles

㉟ How many more red marbles does Charles have than green marbles?

_____ ◯ _____ = _____   _____ more

㊱ Charles has 25 baseball cards and 36 hockey cards. How many cards does Charles have in all?

_____ ◯ _____ = _____   _____ cards

㊲ How many more hockey cards does Charles have than baseball cards?

_____ ◯ _____ = _____   _____ more

㊳ Charles has 85 toy cars; 36 of them are sports cars. How many are not sports cars?

_____ ◯ _____ = _____   _____

㊴ 17 sports cars are red. How many sports cars are not red?

_____ ◯ _____ = _____   _____ sport cars

㊵ Charles wants to give 16 toy cars to his brother. How many toy cars will Charles have left?

_____ ◯ _____ = _____   _____ toy cars

㊶ Charles's brother, Tim, has 39 toy cars. If Charles gives him 16 toy cars, how many toy cars will Tim have in all?

_____ ◯ _____ = _____   _____ toy cars

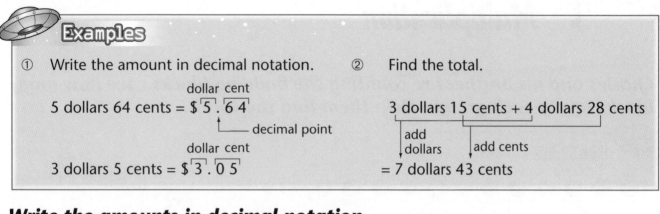

① Write the amount in decimal notation.

dollar cent

5 dollars 64 cents = $ 5 . 6 4

decimal point

dollar cent

3 dollars 5 cents = $ 3 . 0 5

② Find the total.

3 dollars 15 cents + 4 dollars 28 cents

add dollars add cents

= 7 dollars 43 cents

Write the amounts in decimal notation.

㊷ 4 dollars 16 cents = $ _____   ㊸ 1 dollar 45 cents = $ _____

㊹ 10 dollars 30 cents = $ _____   ㊺ 6 dollars 28 cents = $ _____

㊻ 8 dollars 9 cents = $ _____   ㊼ 7 dollars 6 cents = $ _____

Write the costs of the toys in decimal notation. Then solve the problems and write the answers in decimal notation.

㊽ $ _____   ㊾ $ _____   ㊿ $ _____

�51 Charles buys a dartboard and a toy car. How much
     does he need to pay? $ _____

�52 Joyce buys a toy car and a top. How much does she
     need to pay? $ _____

�53 Larry buys 2 tops. How much does he need to pay? $ _____

MIND BOGGLER

Look at the pictures above. Answer Charles's questions.

I want to buy a dartboard, a toy car, and a top for
my brother. How much do I need to pay?

Charles needs to pay $ _____ .

Quick Tip

Don't forget
$1 = 100 cents

3 Multiplication

Charles and his brother are counting the building blocks. See how many blocks are in each group. Help them find the totals.

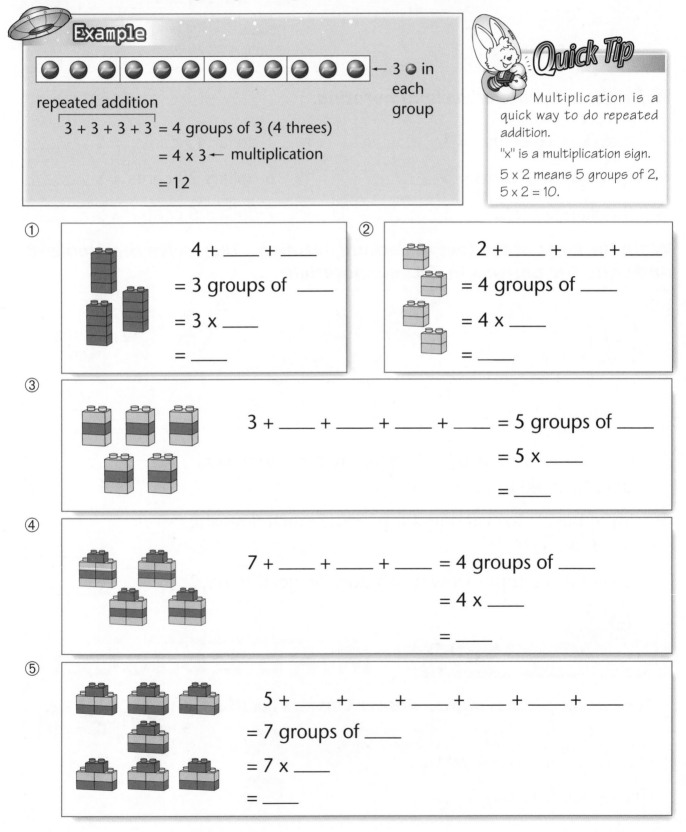

Example

●●● ●●● ●●● ●●● ← 3 ● in each group

repeated addition

3 + 3 + 3 + 3 = 4 groups of 3 (4 threes)

= 4 x 3 ← multiplication

= 12

Quick Tip

Multiplication is a quick way to do repeated addition.

"x" is a multiplication sign.

5 x 2 means 5 groups of 2, 5 x 2 = 10.

① 4 + ___ + ___

= 3 groups of ___

= 3 x ___

= ___

② 2 + ___ + ___ + ___

= 4 groups of ___

= 4 x ___

= ___

③ 3 + ___ + ___ + ___ + ___ = 5 groups of ___

= 5 x ___

= ___

④ 7 + ___ + ___ + ___ = 4 groups of ___

= 4 x ___

= ___

⑤ 5 + ___ + ___ + ___ + ___ + ___ + ___

= 7 groups of ___

= 7 x ___

= ___

ISBN: 978-1-897164-13-6

Fill in the blanks with numbers.

⑥ 5 + 5 + 5 + 5 + 5 + 5   = ____ groups of ____ = ____ x ____ = _____

⑦ 6 + 6 + 6 + 6 + 6 + 6 + 6   = ____ groups of ____ = ____ x ____ = _____

⑧ 8 + 8 + 8 + 8 + 8   = ____ groups of ____ = ____ x ____ = _____

⑨ 9 + 9 + 9 + 9 + 9 + 9   = ____ groups of ____ = ____ x ____ = _____

⑩ 4 + 4 + 4 + 4 + 4 + 4 + 4   = ____ groups of ____ = ____ x ____ = _____

⑪ 2 + 2 + 2 + 2   = ____ groups of ____ = ____ x ____ = _____

⑫ 3 + 3 + 3 + 3 + 3   = ____ groups of ____ = ____ x ____ = _____

Charles puts his marbles into groups. Help him write a multiplication sentence and find the total for each picture.

⑬
7 groups of _____ = _____ x _____
= _____

⑭
4 groups of _____ = _____ x _____
= _____

⑮
3 groups of _____ = _____ x _____
= _____

⑯
6 groups of _____ = _____ x _____
= _____

⑰
5 groups of _____ = _____ x _____
= _____

ISBN: 978-1-897164-13-6

Use the groups of shapes to find the answers.

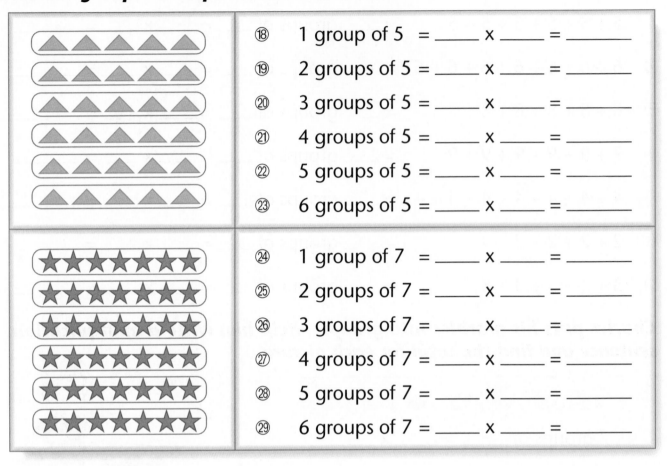

⑱ 1 group of 5 = _____ x _____ = _____

⑲ 2 groups of 5 = _____ x _____ = _____

⑳ 3 groups of 5 = _____ x _____ = _____

㉑ 4 groups of 5 = _____ x _____ = _____

㉒ 5 groups of 5 = _____ x _____ = _____

㉓ 6 groups of 5 = _____ x _____ = _____

㉔ 1 group of 7 = _____ x _____ = _____

㉕ 2 groups of 7 = _____ x _____ = _____

㉖ 3 groups of 7 = _____ x _____ = _____

㉗ 4 groups of 7 = _____ x _____ = _____

㉘ 5 groups of 7 = _____ x _____ = _____

㉙ 6 groups of 7 = _____ x _____ = _____

Find the products.

㉚
$$\begin{array}{r} 4 \\ \times \quad 2 \\ \hline \end{array}$$
_____

㉛
$$\begin{array}{r} 5 \\ \times \quad 2 \\ \hline \end{array}$$
_____

㉜
$$\begin{array}{r} 6 \\ \times \quad 4 \\ \hline \end{array}$$
_____

㉝
$$\begin{array}{r} 8 \\ \times \quad 2 \\ \hline \end{array}$$
_____

㉞
$$\begin{array}{r} 7 \\ \times \quad 3 \\ \hline \end{array}$$
_____

㉟
$$\begin{array}{r} 7 \\ \times \quad 5 \\ \hline \end{array}$$
_____

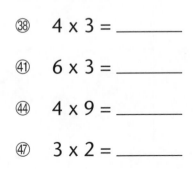

Quick Tip

In a multiplication sentence, the numbers that multiply are called factors, and the answer is called product.

$$\begin{array}{r} 4 \\ \times \quad 5 \\ \hline 2\,0 \end{array}$$
← factors
4 x 5 = 20
← product

㊱ 8 x 6 = _____

㊲ 3 x 3 = _____

㊳ 4 x 3 = _____

㊴ 5 x 5 = _____

㊵ 7 x 2 = _____

㊶ 6 x 3 = _____

㊷ 4 x 7 = _____

㊸ 9 x 3 = _____

㊹ 4 x 9 = _____

㊺ 6 x 2 = _____

㊻ 5 x 7 = _____

㊼ 3 x 2 = _____

ISBN: 978-1-897164-13-6

Look what Charles and his mother want to buy. Solve the problems.

㊽ Charles's mom wants to buy 3 packs of batteries. How many batteries are there in all?

There are _____ batteries in all.

_____ x _____

㊾ She wants to buy 9 packs of juice. How many boxes of juice are there in all?

There are _____ boxes of juice in all.

_____ x _____

㊿ Charles wants 2 boxes of carrot muffins. How many carrot muffins does Charles want?

Charles wants _____ carrot muffins.

_____ x _____

51 Charles's brother, Tim, wants 3 boxes of blueberry muffins. How many blueberry muffins does Tim want?

Tim wants _____ blueberry muffins.

_____ x _____

52 Charles's mom buys 5 boxes of frozen pizza. How many pizzas does she buy in all?

She buys _____ pizzas in all.

_____ x _____

MIND BOGGLER

Use a calculator to find the products.

① 12 x 5 = _____   ←Press 1 2 x 5 = .

② 35 x 7 = _____   ←Press 3 5 x 7 = .

③ 24 x 6 = _____   ←Press 2 4 x 6 = .

ISBN: 978-1-897164-13-6

4 Measurement I

Read Tommy's note. Help him fill in the blanks with mm, cm, m, or km.

Quick Tip

Units of measure
(from greatest to smallest):
km - kilometre
m - metre
cm - centimetre
mm - millimetre

① The length of Uncle John's farm is about 3 _____ .

② The length of my shoe is about 20 _____ .

③ The width of the classroom door is about 60 _____ .

④ The length of my pencil is about 14 _____ .

⑤ The thickness of a quarter is about 3 _____ .

⑥ The distance from Toronto to Montreal is about 500 _____ .

⑦ The distance between the dining table and the couch is about 4 _____ .

Estimate the length of each line. Then measure and record the actual measurement in mm.

⑧ **A** ————————————————

Estimate : _____ mm   Actual length : _____ mm

⑨ **B** ——————————————

Estimate : _____ mm   Actual length : _____ mm

⑩ **C** ——————————

Estimate : _____ mm   Actual length : _____ mm

Look at the lines above. Answer the questions.

⑪ How much longer is A than C?   _____ mm

⑫ Which is the longest line?   Line _____

ISBN: 978-1-897164-13-6

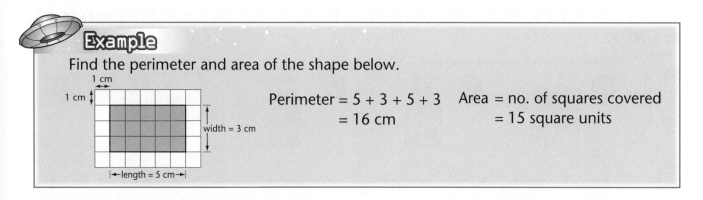

Example

Find the perimeter and area of the shape below.

Perimeter = 5 + 3 + 5 + 3
= 16 cm

Area = no. of squares covered
= 15 square units

Look at the shapes that Tommy cut. Find the perimeters and areas. Then solve the problems.

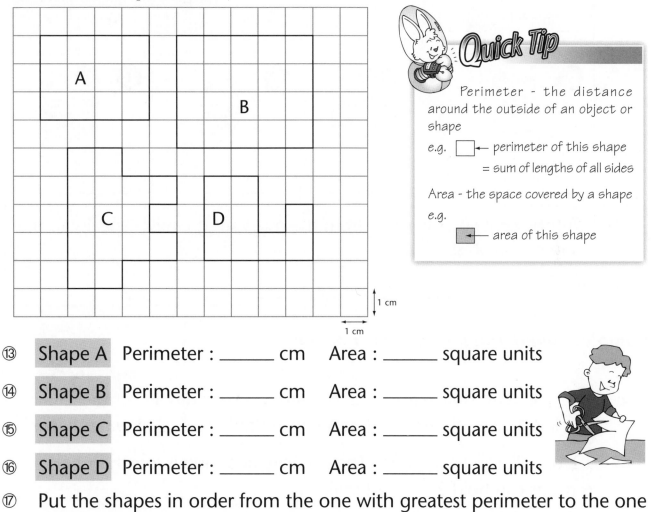

Quick Tip

Perimeter - the distance around the outside of an object or shape

e.g. ⬜ ← perimeter of this shape

= sum of lengths of all sides

Area - the space covered by a shape

e.g.

⬛ ← area of this shape

⑬ Shape A Perimeter : _____ cm Area : _____ square units

⑭ Shape B Perimeter : _____ cm Area : _____ square units

⑮ Shape C Perimeter : _____ cm Area : _____ square units

⑯ Shape D Perimeter : _____ cm Area : _____ square units

⑰ Put the shapes in order from the one with greatest perimeter to the one with smallest.

_____ , _____ , _____ , _____

⑱ Put the shapes in order from the one with greatest area to the one with smallest.

_____ , _____ , _____ , _____

Look at Tommy's containers. Record the capacities and put the containers in order.

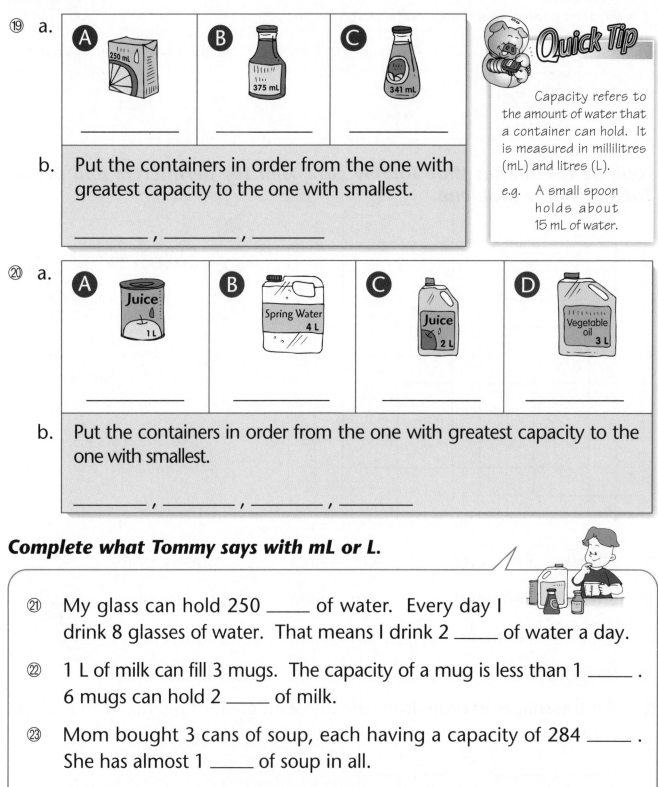

⑲ a.

A 250 mL _____

B 375 mL _____

C 341 mL _____

Quick Tip

Capacity refers to the amount of water that a container can hold. It is measured in millilitres (mL) and litres (L).

e.g. A small spoon holds about 15 mL of water.

b. Put the containers in order from the one with greatest capacity to the one with smallest.

_____ , _____ , _____

⑳ a.

A Juice 1 L _____

B Spring Water 4 L _____

C Juice 2 L _____

D Vegetable oil 3 L _____

b. Put the containers in order from the one with greatest capacity to the one with smallest.

_____ , _____ , _____ , _____

Complete what Tommy says with mL or L.

㉑ My glass can hold 250 _____ of water. Every day I drink 8 glasses of water. That means I drink 2 _____ of water a day.

㉒ 1 L of milk can fill 3 mugs. The capacity of a mug is less than 1 _____ . 6 mugs can hold 2 _____ of milk.

㉓ Mom bought 3 cans of soup, each having a capacity of 284 _____ . She has almost 1 _____ of soup in all.

㉔ The capacity of the bottle is smaller than that of a can. If a 2-L carton of milk can fill 4 bottles, it will take more than 2 _____ of milk to fill 4 cans.

Tommy weighs the things with a scale. Help him record the weights and put the things in order.

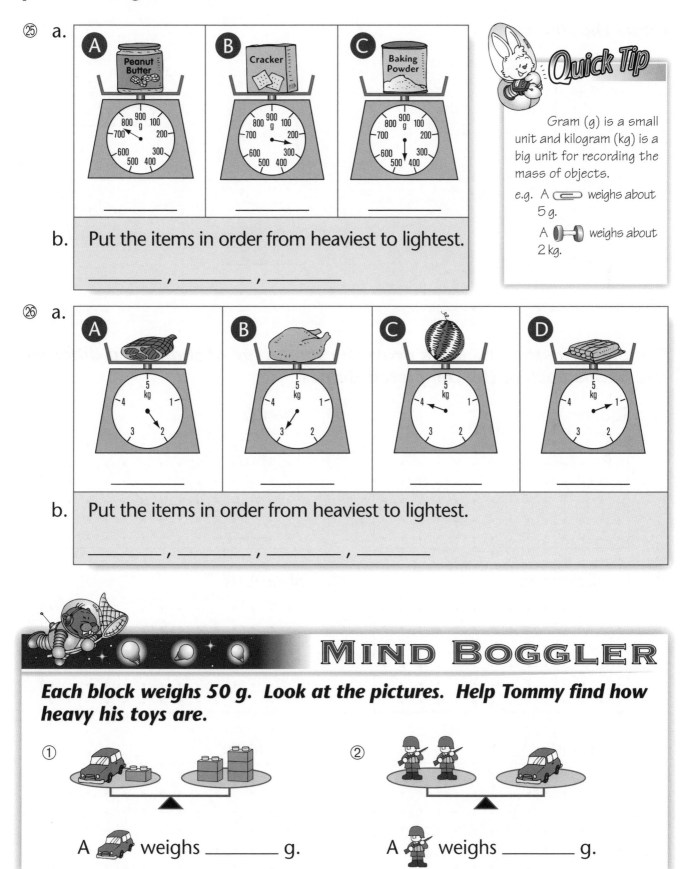

㉕ a.

A   Peanut Butter

B   Cracker

C   Baking Powder

b. | Put the items in order from heaviest to lightest.

_____ , _____ , _____

Quick Tip

Gram (g) is a small unit and kilogram (kg) is a big unit for recording the mass of objects.

e.g. A ⟨⟩ weighs about 5 g.

A ⟨⟩ weighs about 2 kg.

㉖ a.

A

B

C

D

b. | Put the items in order from heaviest to lightest.

_____ , _____ , _____ , _____

MIND BOGGLER

Each block weighs 50 g. Look at the pictures. Help Tommy find how heavy his toys are.

①   A 🚗 weighs _____ g.

②   A 🪖 weighs _____ g.

Name the shapes.

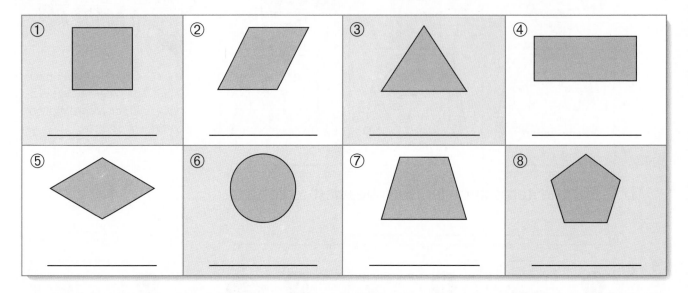

① ② ③ ④

⑤ ⑥ ⑦ ⑧

Complete the shapes. Then draw the same type of shape in a different size beside each of the completed shapes.

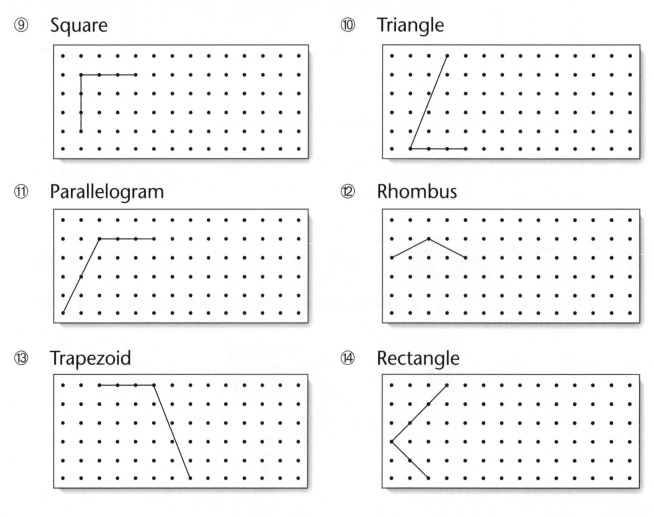

⑨ Square

⑩ Triangle

⑪ Parallelogram

⑫ Rhombus

⑬ Trapezoid

⑭ Rectangle

ISBN: 978-1-897164-13-6

Write the number of sides and vertices in each shape. Then decide whether or not the dotted line is a line of symmetry for the shape. Write 'Yes' or 'No'.

⑮ Number of sides							
⑯ Number of vertices							
⑰ Line of symmetry							

Put a check mark ✔ in the circles if the statements are correct; otherwise, put a cross ✘.

⑱ All squares have lines of symmetry. ◯

⑲ All triangles have lines of symmetry. ◯

⑳ A parallelogram has 3 vertices. ◯

㉑ A trapezoid has 4 sides. ◯

㉒ A rhombus has 4 equal sides. ◯

Draw all the lines of symmetry for the following shapes.

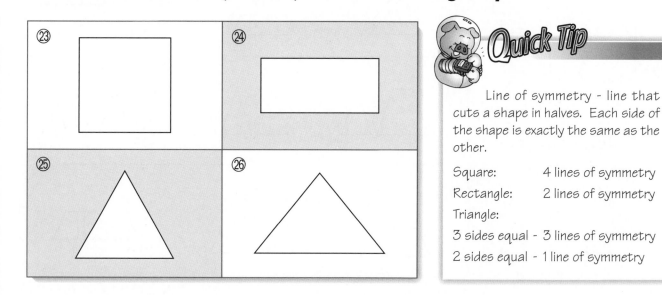

Quick Tip

Line of symmetry - line that cuts a shape in halves. Each side of the shape is exactly the same as the other.

Square: 4 lines of symmetry
Rectangle: 2 lines of symmetry
Triangle:
3 sides equal - 3 lines of symmetry
2 sides equal - 1 line of symmetry

ISBN: 978-1-897164-13-6

Look at the diagrams. Count and write the number of each shape.

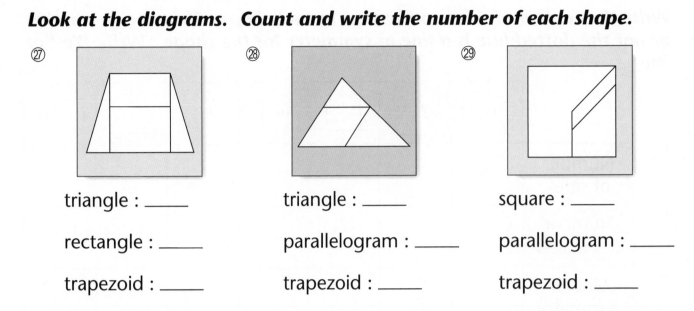

㉗

triangle : ＿＿

rectangle : ＿＿

trapezoid : ＿＿

㉘

triangle : ＿＿

parallelogram : ＿＿

trapezoid : ＿＿

㉙

square : ＿＿

parallelogram : ＿＿

trapezoid : ＿＿

See how Tommy folds and cuts his paper. Check ✔ the correct letters to show what shapes he can get.

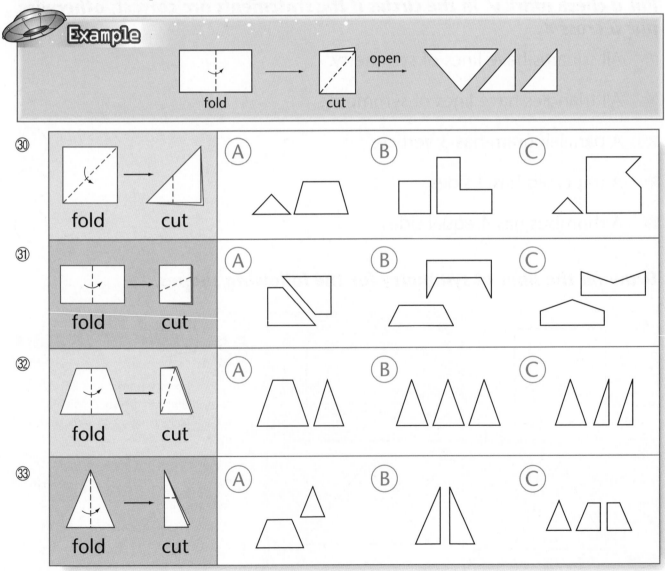

Example

fold   cut   open

㉚ fold   cut   Ⓐ   Ⓑ   Ⓒ

㉛ fold   cut   Ⓐ   Ⓑ   Ⓒ

㉜ fold   cut   Ⓐ   Ⓑ   Ⓒ

㉝ fold   cut   Ⓐ   Ⓑ   Ⓒ

ISBN: 978-1-897164-13-6

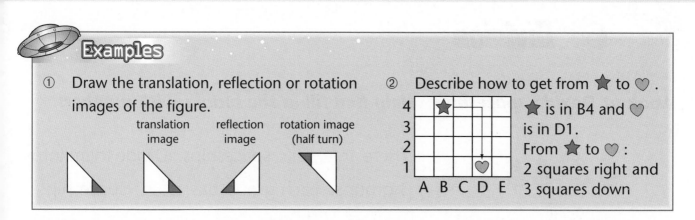

① Draw the translation, reflection or rotation images of the figure.

translation image   reflection image   rotation image (half turn)

② Describe how to get from ★ to ♡.

★ is in B4 and ♡ is in D1.
From ★ to ♡ :
2 squares right and 3 squares down

Read what Tommy says. Help him draw the shapes on the grid. Then fill in the blanks and circle the correct words.

▭ is in A3. I flip it and put its reflection image in B6.

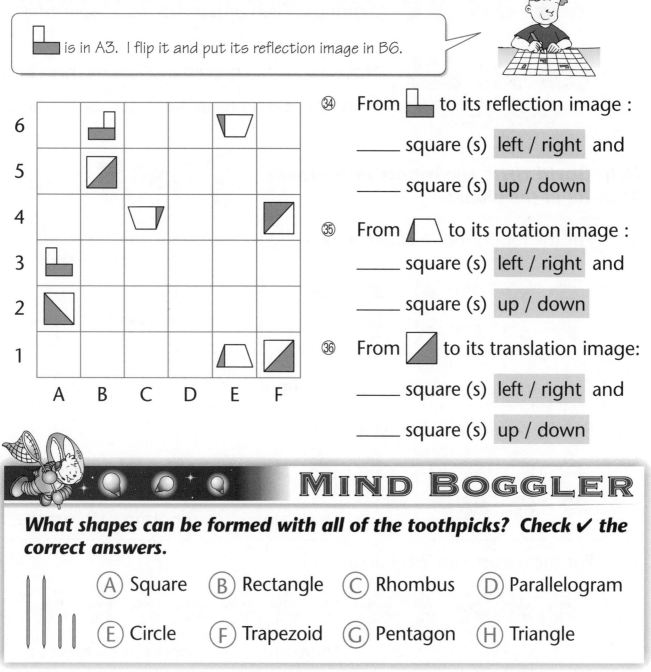

㉞ From ▭ to its reflection image :

_____ square (s) left / right and

_____ square (s) up / down

㉟ From ◿ to its rotation image :

_____ square (s) left / right and

_____ square (s) up / down

㊱ From ◪ to its translation image:

_____ square (s) left / right and

_____ square (s) up / down

MIND BOGGLER

What shapes can be formed with all of the toothpicks? Check ✔ the correct answers.

(A) Square   (B) Rectangle   (C) Rhombus   (D) Parallelogram

(E) Circle   (F) Trapezoid   (G) Pentagon   (H) Triangle

6 Division

Look at David's spaceships. Help him fill in the blanks with numbers.

① There are _____ spaceships. Divide them into 3 groups. Each group has _____ spaceships.

② There are _____ spaceships. Divide them into 3 groups. Each group has _____ spaceships.

③ There are _____ spaceships. Divide them into 5 groups. Each group has _____ spaceships.

Help David circle the robots into groups. Then fill in the blanks.

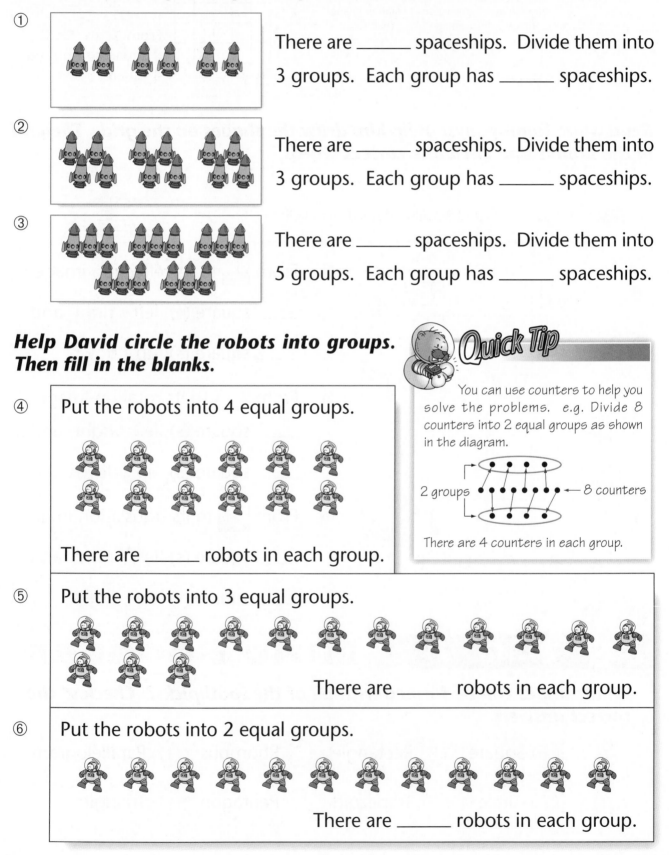

Quick Tip

You can use counters to help you solve the problems. e.g. Divide 8 counters into 2 equal groups as shown in the diagram.

2 groups ← 8 counters

There are 4 counters in each group.

④ Put the robots into 4 equal groups.

There are _____ robots in each group.

⑤ Put the robots into 3 equal groups.

There are _____ robots in each group.

⑥ Put the robots into 2 equal groups.

There are _____ robots in each group.

   ISBN: 978-1-897164-13-6

David's brother, Kenneth, wants to divide his rockets equally into groups. Help him circle the rockets and write the answers in the boxes.

⑦ 3 rockets are in each group. How many groups are there?

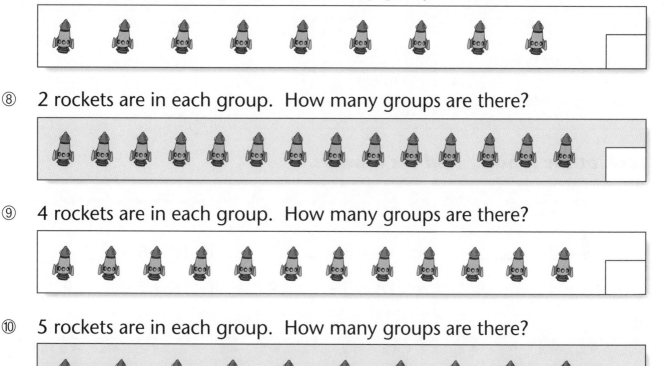

⑧ 2 rockets are in each group. How many groups are there?

⑨ 4 rockets are in each group. How many groups are there?

⑩ 5 rockets are in each group. How many groups are there?

Help Kenneth circle the spaceships into groups and find out how many spaceships are left.

⑪ 3 spaceships are in each group.

There are _____ groups.
_____ spaceships are left.

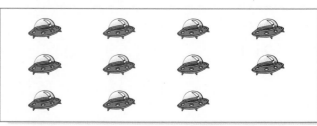

⑫ 4 spaceships are in each group.

There are _____ groups.
_____ spaceships are left.

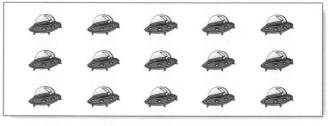

⑬ 5 spaceships are in each group.

There are _____ groups.
_____ spaceships are left.

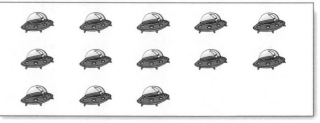

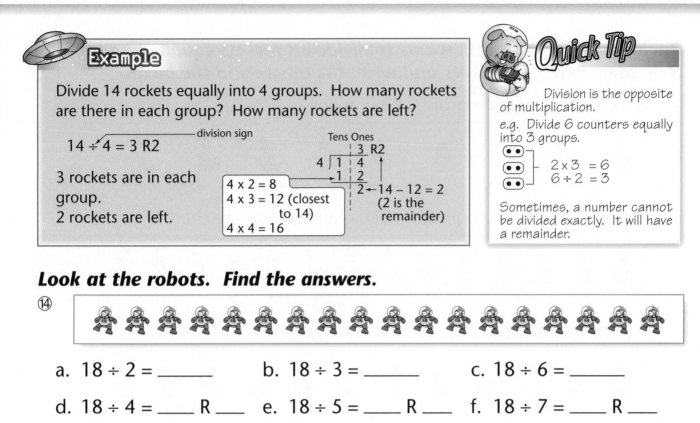

Example

Divide 14 rockets equally into 4 groups. How many rockets are there in each group? How many rockets are left?

$14 \div 4 = 3 \text{ R2}$ — division sign

3 rockets are in each group.
2 rockets are left.

Tens Ones

    3 R2
4) 1 4
    1 2
      2 ← 14 − 12 = 2
        (2 is the remainder)

4 x 2 = 8
4 x 3 = 12 (closest to 14)
4 x 4 = 16

Quick Tip

Division is the opposite of multiplication.

e.g. Divide 6 counters equally into 3 groups.

2 x 3 = 6
6 ÷ 2 = 3

Sometimes, a number cannot be divided exactly. It will have a remainder.

Look at the robots. Find the answers.

⑭

a. $18 \div 2 =$ _____   b. $18 \div 3 =$ _____   c. $18 \div 6 =$ _____

d. $18 \div 4 =$ ___ R ___   e. $18 \div 5 =$ ___ R ___   f. $18 \div 7 =$ ___ R ___

⑮

a. $15 \div 2 =$ ___ R ___   b. $15 \div 3 =$ _____   c. $15 \div 4 =$ ___ R ___

d. $15 \div 5 =$ _____   e. $15 \div 6 =$ ___ R ___   f. $15 \div 7 =$ ___ R ___

Do the division.

⑯ $2 \overline{)14}$	⑰ $3 \overline{)20}$	⑱ $5 \overline{)42}$	⑲ $7 \overline{)32}$
⑳ $5 \overline{)25}$	㉑ $6 \overline{)24}$	㉒ $4 \overline{)30}$	㉓ $8 \overline{)39}$

㉔ $40 \div 5 =$ _____	㉕ $31 \div 9 =$ _____	㉖ $26 \div 3 =$ _____
㉗ $19 \div 2 =$ _____	㉘ $20 \div 6 =$ _____	㉙ $11 \div 7 =$ _____
㉚ $23 \div 4 =$ _____	㉛ $15 \div 8 =$ _____	㉜ $22 \div 9 =$ _____

David and Kenneth are playing with their toys. Help them solve the problems.

㉝ The children put 24 astronauts into 3 spaceships. How many astronauts are in each spaceship?

______ ÷ ______ = ______

______ astronauts are in each spaceship.

㉞ Kenneth puts 26 spaceships on 8 planets. How many spaceships are on each planet? How many spaceships are left?

______ ÷ ______ = ______

______ spaceships are on each planet; ______ spaceships are left.

㉟ David puts 20 rockets into 9 boxes. How many rockets are in each box? How many rockets are left?

______ ÷ ______ = ______

______ rockets are in each box; ______ rockets are left.

㊱ Kenneth has 38 robots. He puts every 7 robots into a box. How many boxes does he need? How many robots are left?

______ ÷ ______ = ______

He needs ______ boxes; ______ robots are left.

㊲ There are 5 robots in 1 pack. David buys 30 robots. How many packs of robots does David buy?

______ ÷ ______ = ______

David buys ______ packs of robots.

MIND BOGGLER

Help David solve the problems.

I divide 20 green robots and 15 red robots into groups. If there are 3 green robots and 2 red robots in each group, how many groups can I get? How many robots are left?

David can get ______ groups; ______ robots are left.

Data Management

Read the graph showing the number of customers that went to Uncle Ben's fast food shop last week. Answer the questions.

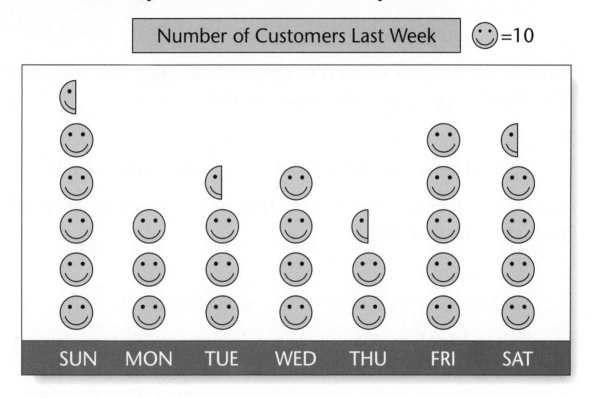

① What is the title of this graph?

_____

② How many customers are represented by a 🙂? _____ customers

③ How many customers were there on Wednesday? _____ customers

④ How many customers were there on Saturday? _____ customers

⑤ How many more customers were there on Sunday than Tuesday? _____ more

⑥ If 27 customers were men on Wednesday, how many customers were women? _____ women

⑦ Which day had the most customers? _____

⑧ Which day had the fewest customers? _____

⑨ On Friday, each customer bought 2 cans of pop. How many cans of pop were sold that day? _____ cans

ISBN: 978-1-897164-13-6

Look at the graph on P.150 again. Complete the table and colour the graph to show the information.

⑩

Day	SUN	MON	TUE	WED	THU	FRI	SAT
Number of Customers							

⑪

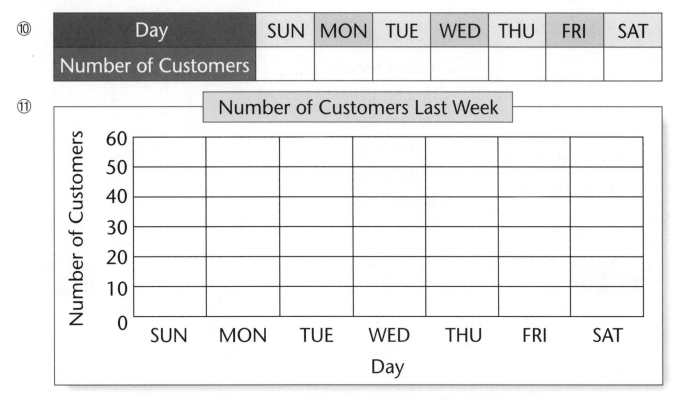

Read the food items sold last week. Help Uncle Ben label the circle graph and answer the questions.

Food	Pita	Sandwich	Pizza	Hamburger
Number of Items Sold	30	180	90	60

⑫ <u>Food Items Sold Last Week</u>

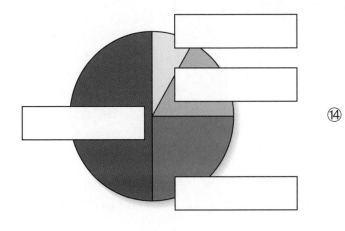

⑬ How many kinds of food are sold by Uncle Ben? What are they?

_____ kinds; _____

_____

⑭ If 26 hamburgers with cheese were sold, how many hamburgers sold were without cheese?

_____ hamburgers sold were without cheese.

ISBN: 978-1-897164-13-6

Customers can choose different pitas and sandwiches. Write the choices in the diagram and answer the questions.

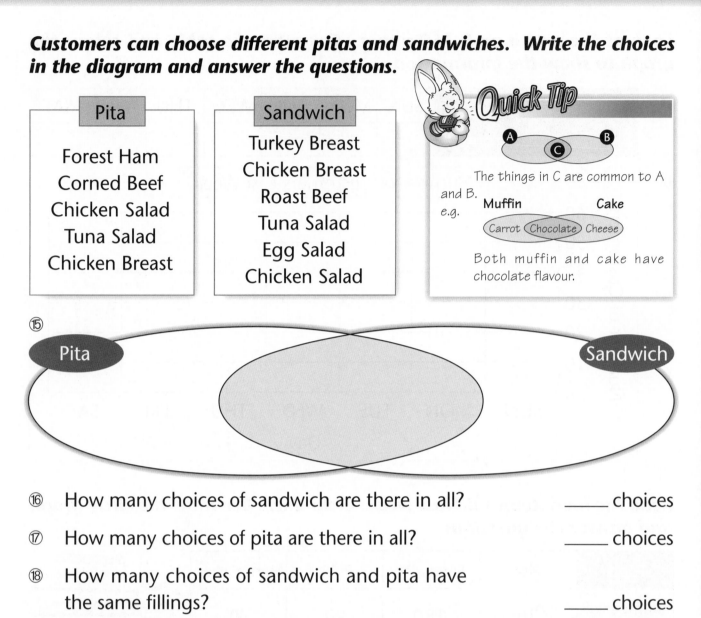

Pita
Forest Ham
Corned Beef
Chicken Salad
Tuna Salad
Chicken Breast

Sandwich
Turkey Breast
Chicken Breast
Roast Beef
Tuna Salad
Egg Salad
Chicken Salad

⑮

Pita   Sandwich

⑯ How many choices of sandwich are there in all? _____ choices

⑰ How many choices of pita are there in all? _____ choices

⑱ How many choices of sandwich and pita have the same fillings? _____ choices

Uncle Ben shows the sale of pitas yesterday with a circle graph. Yesterday, he sold 10 chicken salad pitas. Read the graph and complete the table. Then answer the questions.

⑲

	Number of Pitas Sold
Chicken Salad	
Chicken Breast	
Forest Ham	
Tuna Salad	

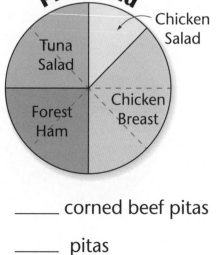

Pitas Sold

⑳ How many corned beef pitas were sold? _____ corned beef pitas

㉑ How many pitas were sold in all? _____ pitas

ISBN: 978-1-897164-13-6

Each combo has 2 slices of pizza and 1 can of pop. Read the table and make a bar graph to show the number of combos sold last week. Answer the questions.

	SUN	MON	TUE	WED	THU	FRI	SAT
Number of Combos Sold	30	20	15	10	20	25	30

㉒

10
5
0

Day

㉓ How many slices of pizza were sold on Friday? _____ slices

㉔ How many combos were sold during weekdays? _____ combos

㉕ If each combo costs $5, how much did Uncle Ben get on Tuesday? $ _____

㉖ How many cans of pop were sold with combos last week? _____ cans

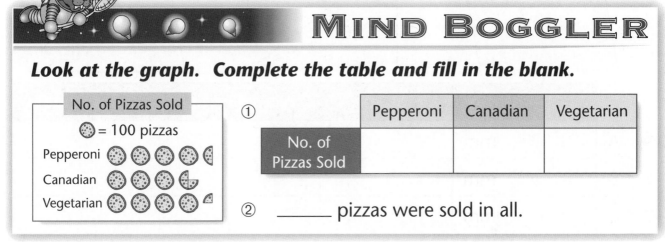

MIND BOGGLER

Look at the graph. Complete the table and fill in the blank.

No. of Pizzas Sold

🍕 = 100 pizzas

Pepperoni 🍕🍕🍕🍕◖
Canadian 🍕🍕🍕◔
Vegetarian 🍕🍕🍕🍕◢

①

	Pepperoni	Canadian	Vegetarian
No. of Pizzas Sold			

② _____ pizzas were sold in all.

Progress Test

Fill in the missing numbers.

① 100 , 95 , ____ , 85 , 80 , ____ , ____ , 65 , 60 , ____

② 100 , 90 , 80 , ____ , ____ , 50 , ____ , 30 , 20 , 10

③ 46 , 48 , 50 , ____ , 54 , ____ , ____ , ____ , 62 , 64

④ 94 , 92 , ____ , ____ , 86 , ____ , 82 , 80 , ____ , 76

Add or subtract. Then write the answers in words.

⑤
```
    6 2
  + 2 9
  _____
```
_____

⑥
```
    7 3
  - 4 5
  _____
```
_____

⑦
```
    6 5
  - 4 6
  _____
```
_____

⑧
```
    5 9
  + 1 8
  _____
```
_____

⑨ 60 – 15 = ____

⑩ 23 – 17 = ____

⑪ 55 + 37 = ____

⑫ 41 + 16 = ____

⑬ 72 – 18 = ____

⑭ 16 + 48 = ____

Measure the length of the dotted line in each shape and fill in the blanks.

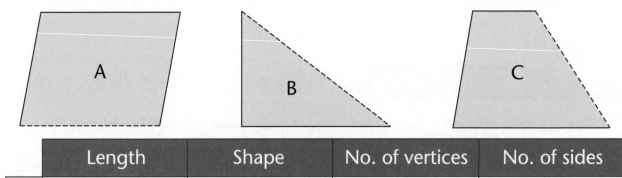

	Length	Shape	No. of vertices	No. of sides
⑮ A	mm			
⑯ B	mm			
⑰ C	mm			

ISBN: 978-1-897164-13-6

Look at the empty containers. Complete the table and answer the questions.

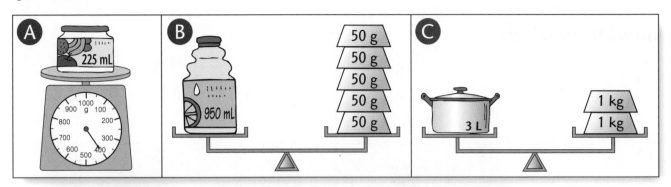

Container	A	B	C
⑱ Capacity			
⑲ Weight			

⑳ Which container has the greatest capacity? _____

㉑ Which container is the lightest? _____

Look at the pictures. Complete the number sentences.

㉒

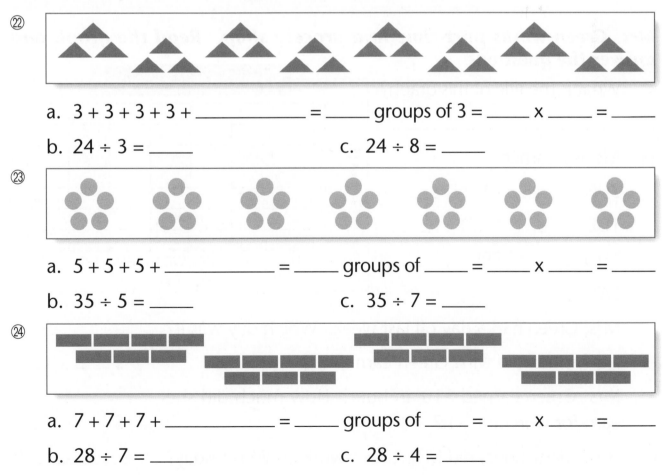

a. 3 + 3 + 3 + 3 + _____ = _____ groups of 3 = _____ x _____ = _____

b. 24 ÷ 3 = _____   c. 24 ÷ 8 = _____

㉓

a. 5 + 5 + 5 + _____ = _____ groups of _____ = _____ x _____ = _____

b. 35 ÷ 5 = _____   c. 35 ÷ 7 = _____

㉔

a. 7 + 7 + 7 + _____ = _____ groups of _____ = _____ x _____ = _____

b. 28 ÷ 7 = _____   c. 28 ÷ 4 = _____

ISBN: 978-1-897164-13-6

Multiply or divide.

㉕ $\begin{array}{r} 7 \\ \times\ 4 \\ \hline \end{array}$	㉖ $\begin{array}{r} 6 \\ \times\ 5 \\ \hline \end{array}$	㉗ $5\overline{)40}$	㉘ $6\overline{)42}$
㉙ $7\overline{)35}$	㉚ $9\overline{)25}$	㉛ $\begin{array}{r} 3 \\ \times\ 9 \\ \hline \end{array}$	㉜ $\begin{array}{r} 4 \\ \times\ 8 \\ \hline \end{array}$

㉝ $6 \times 4\ =$ _____	㉞ $14 \div 6 =$ _____
㉟ $26 \div 8 =$ _____	㊱ $9 \times 5\ =$ _____
㊲ $7 \times 3\ =$ _____	㊳ $2 \times 9\ =$ _____
㊴ $32 \div 4 =$ _____	㊵ $20 \div 7 =$ _____
㊶ $39 \div 8 =$ _____	㊷ $5 \times 4\ =$ _____

Mrs. Green works part-time in a grocery shop. Read the graph and answer the questions.

㊸ What is the title of this graph?

_____

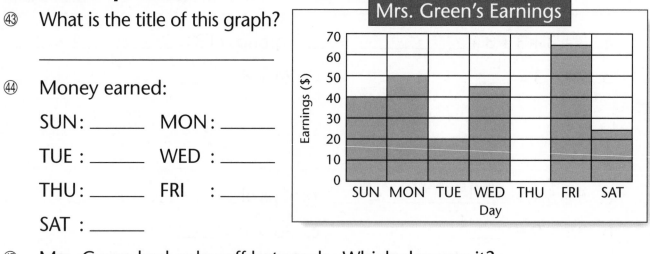

㊹ Money earned:

SUN: _____   MON : _____

TUE : _____   WED : _____

THU: _____   FRI : _____

SAT : _____

㊺ Mrs. Green had a day off last week. Which day was it? _____

㊻ How much did Mrs. Green earn in all? $ _____

㊼ Mrs. Green earned $10 an hour. How much did she earn for working $\frac{1}{2}$ h? $ _____

㊽ How many hours did Mrs. Green work on Wednesday? _____ h

   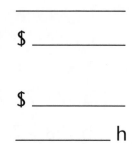 ISBN: 978-1-897164-13-6

Solve the problem.

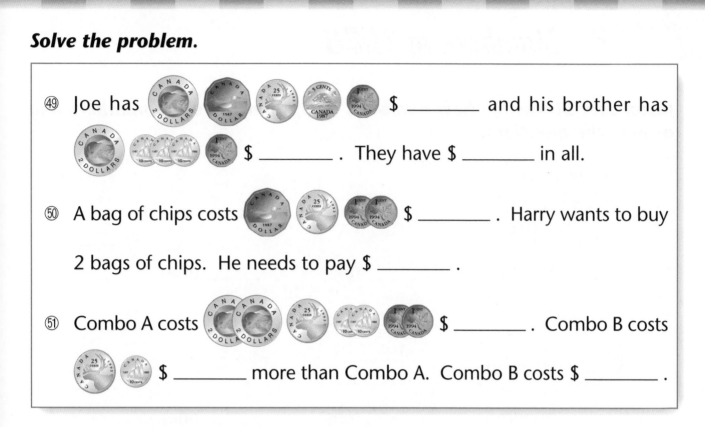

49 Joe has [coins] $ _____ and his brother has [coins] $ _____ . They have $ _____ in all.

50 A bag of chips costs [coins] $ _____ . Harry wants to buy 2 bags of chips. He needs to pay $ _____ .

51 Combo A costs [coins] $ _____ . Combo B costs [coins] $ _____ more than Combo A. Combo B costs $ _____ .

52 May had 43 coins. She spent 15 coins for snacks. She has _____ coins left.

53 There are 46 bags ketchup flavoured chips and 39 bags barbecue flavoured chips on the shelf. There are _____ bags of chips in all.

54 David shares 14 chocolate bars equally with his brother. Each person gets _____ chocolate bars.

55 Every day Joe saves 5¢. He saves _____ ¢ one week.

56 Eva has 20 necklaces. She puts every 6 necklaces into a jewellery box. She needs _____ jewellery boxes, with _____ necklaces left.

57 There are 8 crackers in 1 bag. Mrs. Stein buys 4 bags of crackers. She buys _____ crackers in all.

58 Each bag of crackers costs $3. Mrs. Stein pays $ _____ for 4 bags of crackers.

59 Mrs. Stein puts the crackers bought in 58 into 5 containers. Each container holds _____ crackers, with _____ crackers left.

ISBN: 978-1-897164-13-6

Jason uses blocks to show numbers. Help him write the numbers and answer the questions.

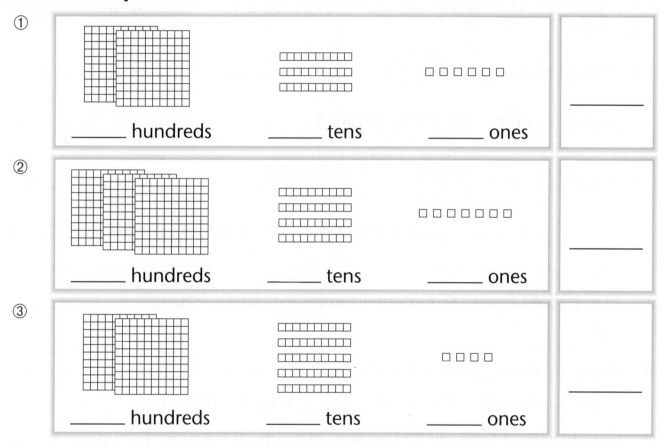

① _____ hundreds _____ tens _____ ones _____

② _____ hundreds _____ tens _____ ones _____

③ _____ hundreds _____ tens _____ ones _____

④ Which numbers are smaller than 300? _____

⑤ Which number is 100 greater than 247? _____

⑥ Which number is 10 greater than 226? _____

⑦ Which number is the greatest? _____

⑧ Which number has 4 in the ones place? _____

Write the numbers that the arrows are pointing at.

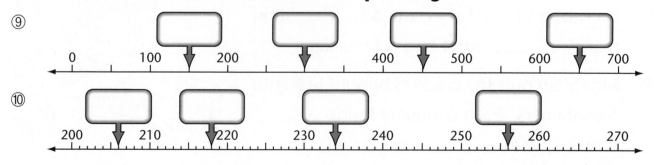

⑨

⑩

See how Jason counts. Help him fill in the missing numbers.

⑪ Count by 2's.

   a. 108 , _____ , _____ , _____ , _____ , _____

   b. 624 , _____ , _____ , _____ , _____ , _____

⑫ Count by 5's.

   a. 250 , _____ , _____ , _____ , _____ , _____ , _____

   b. 650 , _____ , _____ , _____ , _____ , _____ , _____

⑬ Count by 10's.

   a. 420 , _____ , _____ , _____ , _____ , _____ , _____

   b. 830 , _____ , _____ , _____ , _____ , _____ , _____

⑭ Count by 100's.

   a. 200 , _____ , _____ , _____ , _____ , _____ , _____

   b. 301 , _____ , _____ , _____ , _____ , _____ , _____

⑮ Count by 25's.

   a. 25 , _____ , _____ , _____ , _____ , _____ , _____ , _____

   b. 625 , _____ , _____ , _____ , _____ , _____ , _____ , _____

Help Jason count backward by 100's from 1000 and Helen by 50's from 800 to find their toys. Colour the numbers.

⑯ Colour Jason's route yellow.   ⑰ Colour Helen's route red.

950	800	750	600	300	350	300	200
1000	900	800	700	600	400	250	200
900	650	600	550	500	450	400	300
700	700	550	400	400	300	200	100
800	750	700	450	350	200	300	100

ISBN: 978-1-897164-13-6

Look at the 3 cards each child picked. Help them form all the possible 3-digit numbers with the cards. Then put the numbers in order.

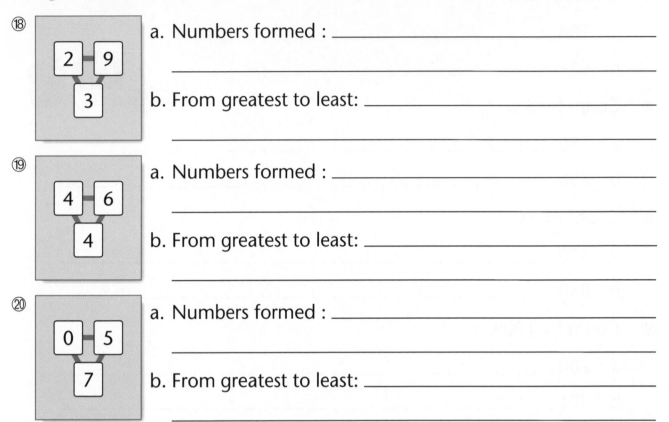

⑱
a. Numbers formed : _____

_____

b. From greatest to least: _____

_____

⑲
a. Numbers formed : _____

_____

b. From greatest to least: _____

_____

⑳
a. Numbers formed : _____

_____

b. From greatest to least: _____

_____

Jason and his neighbours use number cards to show their house numbers. Look at their house numbers and answer the questions.

Jason 3 0 9   Helen 2 5 8   Tim 2 3 6   Mabel 2 5 9

㉑ If Mabel counts by 50's from her house, can she reach Jason's house? _____

㉒ If Jason counts backward by 10's from his house, can he reach Mabel's house? _____

㉓ If Tim counts by 10's from his house, can he reach Helen's house? _____

㉔ If Helen counts by 2's from her house 5 times, she can reach Mandy's house. What is Mandy's house number? _____

㉕ If Mabel counts backward by 10's from her house 4 times, she can reach Aunt Mary's house. What is Aunt Mary's house number? _____

  ISBN: 978-1-897164-13-6

Write each child's score and solve the problems.

Jason — Hundreds, Tens, Ones
Helen — Hundreds, Tens, Ones
Tim — Hundreds, Tens, Ones
Mabel — Hundreds, Tens, Ones

Hundreds Tens Ones

Quick Tip

Comparing 3-digit numbers:
1st Compare the hundreds digit.
2nd Compare the tens digit.
3rd Compare the ones digit.

㉖

	Jason	Helen	Tim	Mabel
Score				

㉗ Use arrows to show the children's scores.

Jason

0   100   200   300   400   500   600   700
↓ (Jason near 500)

㉘ Who got the highest score? _____

㉙ Who got the lowest score? _____

㉚ If Helen threw 2 more rings and both rings caught the 'Hundreds' pole, what would her score be? Did she win? _____ _____

㉛ Jason wants to score 582 points. What is the least number of rings he needs to do that? _____

MIND BOGGLER

Look at the table in ㉖. Help Mabel and Tim solve the problems.

① If Mabel trades 200 points for a gift, how many points will she have left? _____ points

② Tim needs 400 points to trade a toy car. How many more points does he need? _____ points

ISBN: 978-1-897164-13-6

9 Measurement II

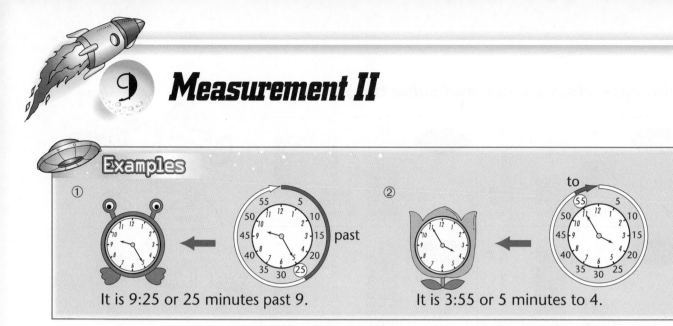
Help Uncle Louis record the times or draw the clock hands. Then find out how long he took to finish each job.

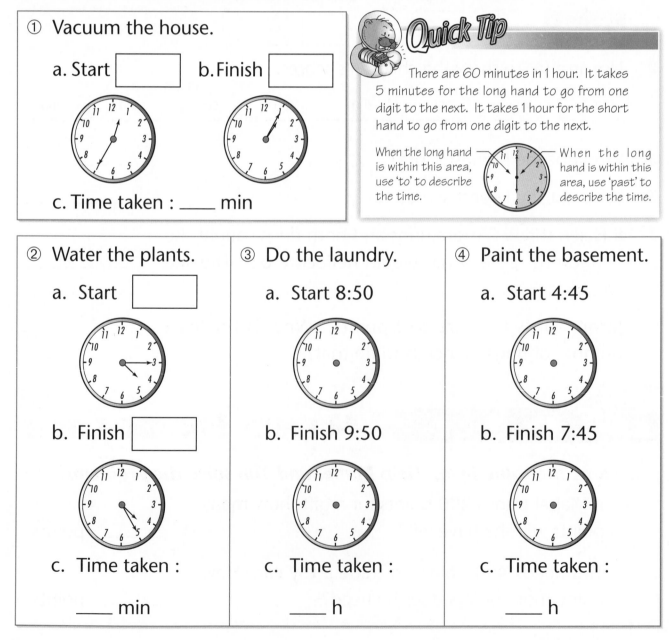

① Vacuum the house.

   a. Start [ ]　　b. Finish [ ]

   c. Time taken : ____ min

Quick Tip

There are 60 minutes in 1 hour. It takes 5 minutes for the long hand to go from one digit to the next. It takes 1 hour for the short hand to go from one digit to the next.

When the long hand is within this area, use 'to' to describe the time.

When the long hand is within this area, use 'past' to describe the time.

② Water the plants.

   a. Start [ ]

   b. Finish [ ]

   c. Time taken :

   ____ min

③ Do the laundry.

   a. Start 8:50

   b. Finish 9:50

   c. Time taken :

   ____ h

④ Paint the basement.

   a. Start 4:45

   b. Finish 7:45

   c. Time taken :

   ____ h

ISBN: 978-1-897164-13-6

Look at Uncle Louis's plan for 2003. Help him solve the problems.

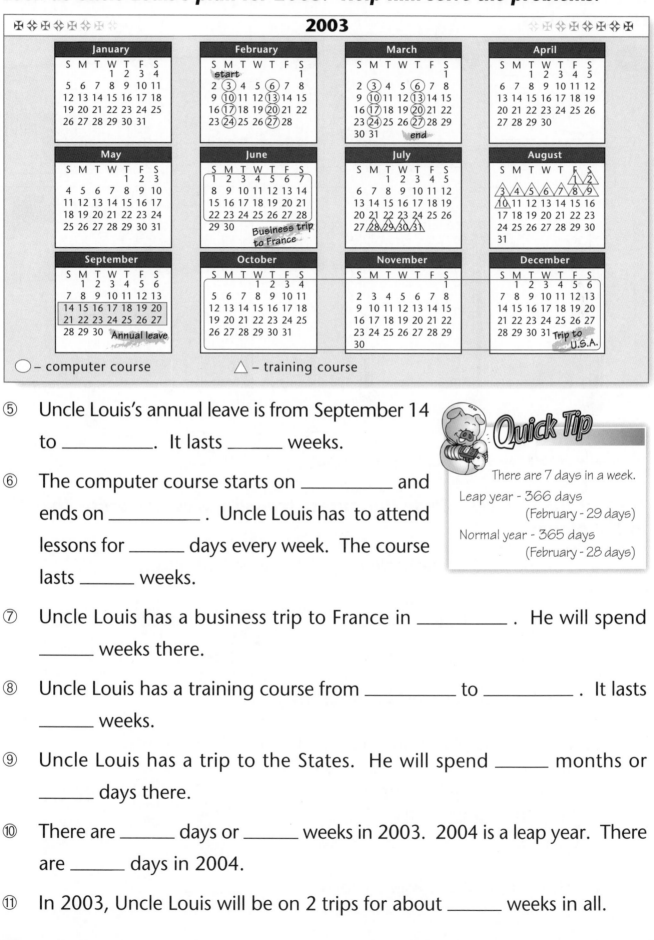

⑤ Uncle Louis's annual leave is from September 14 to _____ . It lasts _____ weeks.

⑥ The computer course starts on _____ and ends on _____ . Uncle Louis has to attend lessons for _____ days every week. The course lasts _____ weeks.

Quick Tip

There are 7 days in a week.

Leap year - 366 days
    (February - 29 days)

Normal year - 365 days
    (February - 28 days)

⑦ Uncle Louis has a business trip to France in _____ . He will spend _____ weeks there.

⑧ Uncle Louis has a training course from _____ to _____ . It lasts _____ weeks.

⑨ Uncle Louis has a trip to the States. He will spend _____ months or _____ days there.

⑩ There are _____ days or _____ weeks in 2003. 2004 is a leap year. There are _____ days in 2004.

⑪ In 2003, Uncle Louis will be on 2 trips for about _____ weeks in all.

ISBN: 978-1-897164-13-6

Record the temperatures. Then match the pictures with the correct thermometers.

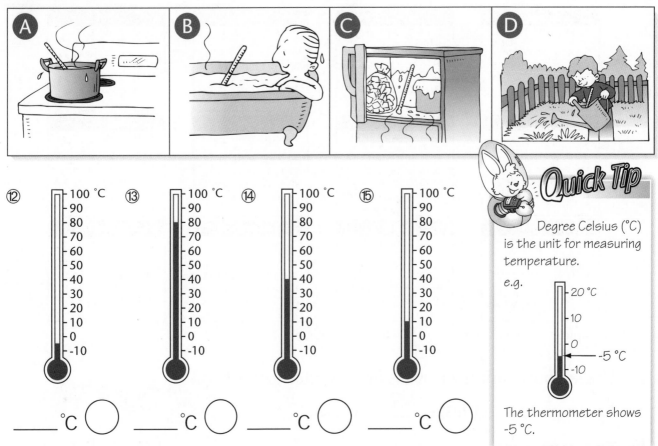

Quick Tip

Degree Celsius (°C) is the unit for measuring temperature.

e.g.

The thermometer shows -5 °C.

⑫ ____°C ◯   ⑬ ____°C ◯   ⑭ ____°C ◯   ⑮ ____°C ◯

Look at the pictures. Circle the correct temperatures or words. Then fill in the blanks.

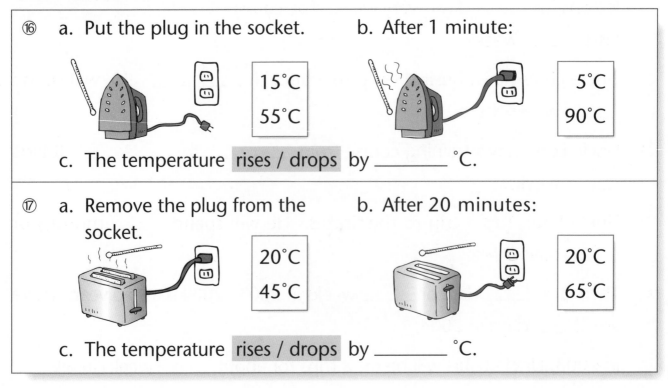

⑯ a. Put the plug in the socket.   b. After 1 minute:

15°C   5°C
55°C   90°C

c. The temperature rises / drops by _____ °C.

⑰ a. Remove the plug from the socket.   b. After 20 minutes:

20°C   20°C
45°C   65°C

c. The temperature rises / drops by _____ °C.

ISBN: 978-1-897164-13-6

Uncle Louis wants to trade his money. Fill in the blanks with numbers.

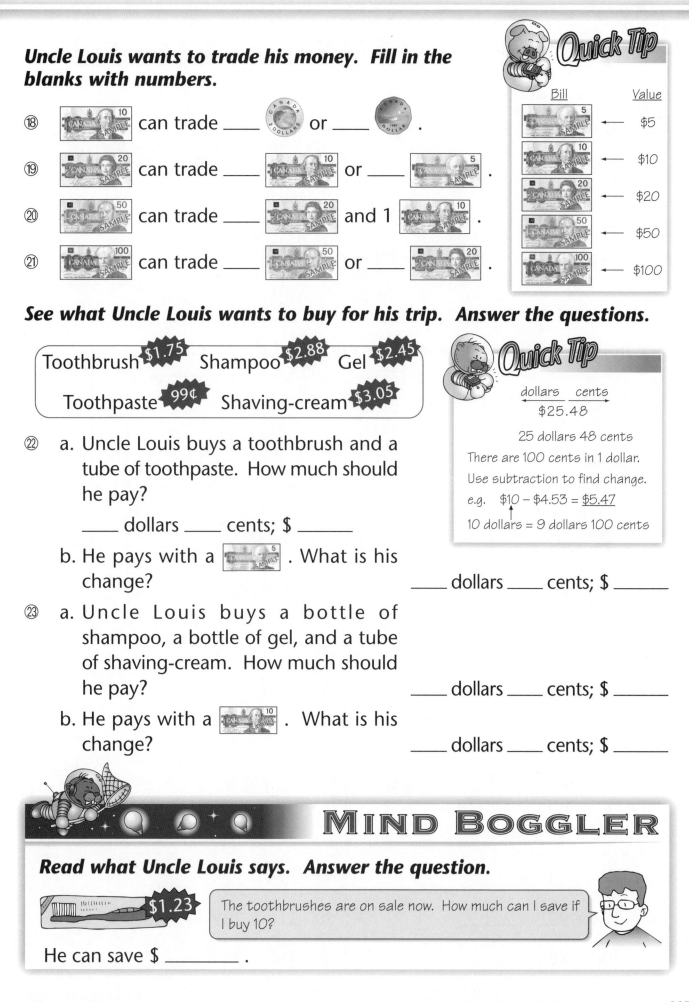

⑱ [$10 bill] can trade ____ [$2 coin] or ____ [$1 coin] .

⑲ [$20 bill] can trade ____ [$10 bill] or ____ [$5 bill] .

⑳ [$50 bill] can trade ____ [$20 bill] and 1 [$10 bill] .

㉑ [$100 bill] can trade ____ [$50 bill] or ____ [$20 bill] .

Quick Tip

Bill		Value
[$5 bill]	←	$5
[$10 bill]	←	$10
[$20 bill]	←	$20
[$50 bill]	←	$50
[$100 bill]	←	$100

See what Uncle Louis wants to buy for his trip. Answer the questions.

Toothbrush $1.75   Shampoo $2.88   Gel $2.45

Toothpaste 99¢   Shaving-cream $3.05

Quick Tip

dollars | cents
← $25.48 →

25 dollars 48 cents

There are 100 cents in 1 dollar.

Use subtraction to find change.

e.g. $10 − $4.53 = $5.47

10 dollars = 9 dollars 100 cents

㉒ a. Uncle Louis buys a toothbrush and a tube of toothpaste. How much should he pay?

____ dollars ____ cents; $ _____

b. He pays with a [$5 bill] . What is his change?

____ dollars ____ cents; $ _____

㉓ a. Uncle Louis buys a bottle of shampoo, a bottle of gel, and a tube of shaving-cream. How much should he pay?

____ dollars ____ cents; $ _____

b. He pays with a [$10 bill] . What is his change?

____ dollars ____ cents; $ _____

MIND BOGGLER

Read what Uncle Louis says. Answer the question.

[toothbrush] $1.23

The toothbrushes are on sale now. How much can I save if I buy 10?

He can save $ _____ .

ISBN: 978-1-897164-13-6

10 *More about Addition and Subtraction*

Example

$234 + 79 = ?$

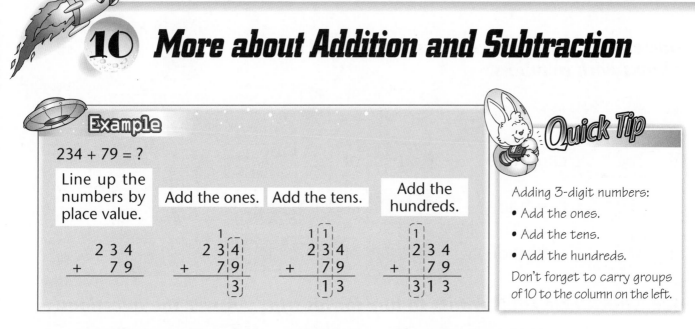

Quick Tip

Adding 3-digit numbers:
- Add the ones.
- Add the tens.
- Add the hundreds.

Don't forget to carry groups of 10 to the column on the left.

See how many pills are in each group. Find the total.

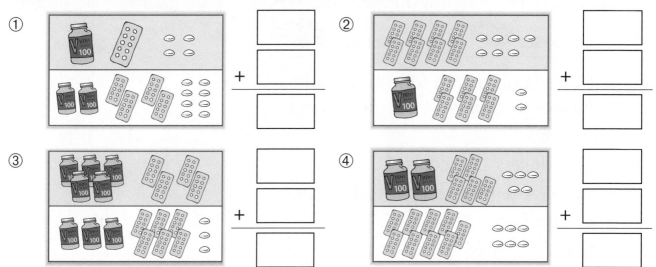

① ②

③ ④

Add.

⑤ $\begin{array}{r} 246 \\ +\ 133 \\ \hline \end{array}$	⑥ $\begin{array}{r} 175 \\ +\ 263 \\ \hline \end{array}$	⑦ $\begin{array}{r} 408 \\ +\ 339 \\ \hline \end{array}$	⑧ $\begin{array}{r} 343 \\ +\ 288 \\ \hline \end{array}$
⑨ $\begin{array}{r} 94 \\ +\ 347 \\ \hline \end{array}$	⑩ $\begin{array}{r} 294 \\ +\ 66 \\ \hline \end{array}$	⑪ $\begin{array}{r} 159 \\ +\ 326 \\ \hline \end{array}$	⑫ $\begin{array}{r} 405 \\ +\ 76 \\ \hline \end{array}$

⑬ $87 + 533$ = _____	⑭ $175 + 125$ = _____
⑮ $274 + 99$ = _____	⑯ $318 + 289$ = _____
⑰ $506 + 284$ = _____	⑱ $456 + 85$ = _____

ISBN: 978-1-897164-13-6

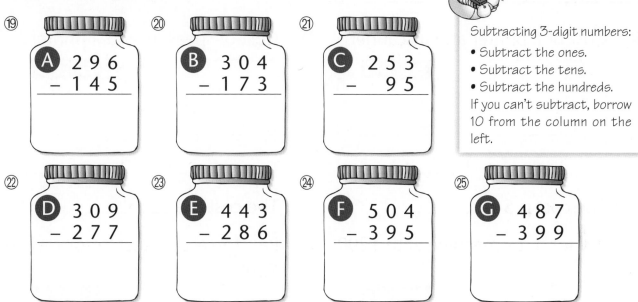

Example

513 – 279 = ?

Line up the numbers by place value.	Subtract the ones.	Subtract the tens.	Subtract the hundreds.
5 1 3 – 2 7 9	0 13 5 X̶ 3 – 2 7 9 4	4 10 5̶ X̶ 3 – 2 7 9 3 4	4 5̶ 1 3 – 2 7 9 2 3 4

Find the number of pills in each bottle. Then answer the questions.

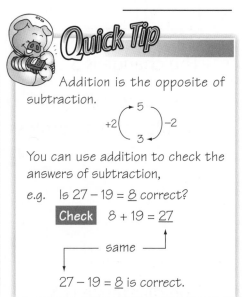

Quick Tip

Subtracting 3-digit numbers:
• Subtract the ones.
• Subtract the tens.
• Subtract the hundreds.
If you can't subtract, borrow 10 from the column on the left.

⑲ A 2 9 6
   – 1 4 5

⑳ B 3 0 4
   – 1 7 3

㉑ C 2 5 3
     – 9 5

㉒ D 3 0 9
   – 2 7 7

㉓ E 4 4 3
   – 2 8 6

㉔ F 5 0 4
   – 3 9 5

㉕ G 4 8 7
   – 3 9 9

㉖ Which bottles contain more than 120 pills? _____

㉗ Which bottle contains the fewest pills? _____

Subtract and check the answers.

	Check
㉘ 591 – 376 = _____	
㉙ 254 – 119 = _____	
㉚ 672 – 88 = _____	
㉛ 403 – 268 = _____	
㉜ 429 – 146 = _____	
㉝ 234 – 158 = _____	

Quick Tip

Addition is the opposite of subtraction.

+2 (5 / 3) –2

You can use addition to check the answers of subtraction,

e.g. Is 27 – 19 = 8 correct?

Check 8 + 19 = 27

—— same ——

27 – 19 = 8 is correct.

COMPLETE MATHSMART (GRADE 3)

Estimate by rounding the amount to the nearest ten. Then find the actual amount.

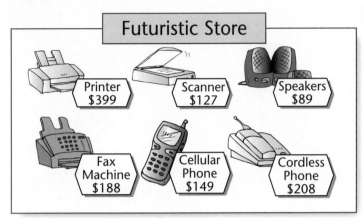

Futuristic Store

Printer $399
Scanner $127
Speakers $89
Fax Machine $188
Cellular Phone $149
Cordless Phone $208

Quick Tip

Rounding number to the nearest 10:

• Look at the digit in the ones column.

• If the digit is 5 or greater than 5, the number should be rounded up. Otherwise, it should be rounded down,

e.g.   273 —round down→ 270

276 —round up→ 280

③④ Cost of a printer and a scanner

```
   ____
+  ____
```

Estimate
```
   ____
+  ____
```

The cost is $ _____ .

③⑤ Cost of speakers and a printer

```
   ____
+  ____
```

Estimate
```
   ____
+  ____
```

The cost is $ _____ .

③⑥ Pay for a fax machine with $200

```
   ____
-  ____
```

Estimate
```
   ____
-  ____
```

The change is $ _____ .

③⑦ Pay for a cordless phone with $300

```
   ____
-  ____
```

Estimate
```
   ____
-  ____
```

The change is $ _____ .

③⑧ The price difference between a cellular and a cordless phone

```
   ____
-  ____
```

Estimate
```
   ____
-  ____
```

The difference is $ _____ .

③⑨ Cost of speakers and a fax machine

```
   ____
+  ____
```

Estimate
```
   ____
+  ____
```

The cost is $ _____ .

ISBN: 978-1-897164-13-6

Solve the problems.

④ There are 656 g of grapes in a basket. The total weight of the basket and the grapes is 982 g. What is the weight of the basket?

_____ = _____

_____ g

④ Two packets of bird seeds weigh 863 g. If one packet weighs 288 g, what is the weight of the other packet?

_____ = _____

_____ g

④ Sue is 126 cm tall. Sheila is 38 cm taller than Sue. How tall is Sheila?

_____ = _____

_____ cm

④ The capacity of a glass is 225 mL. If Betty drinks 2 glasses of orange juice, how much orange juice does she drink?

_____ = _____

_____ mL

④ There are 923 children at a book fair. 475 of them are girls. How many boys are at the book fair?

_____ = _____

_____ boys

④ Uncle Ray bought 2 boxes of plums, each containing 295 plums. How many plums did Uncle Ray buy in all?

_____ = _____

_____ plums

④ Mrs. Kennedy baked 109 chocolate cookies and 216 butter cookies. How many cookies did she bake in all?

_____ = _____

_____ cookies

MIND BOGGLER

Jason spilled some ink on his work. Help him find out the numbers under the blots.

① 2 ⬛ 6
+ ⬛ 6 ⬛
----
4 2 5

② ⬛ 3 ⬛
− 1 ⬛ 8
----
4 7 5

③ 5 ⬛ 1
− ⬛ 6 ⬛
----
2 3 7

11 Geometry II

Join the dots to complete the prisms and write their names. Then complete the table and answer the questions.

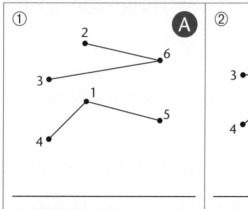

① **A**

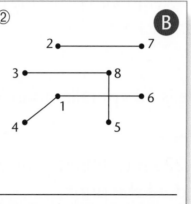

② **B**

_____

_____

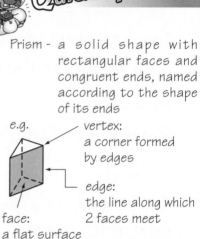
	Solid	Number of vertices	Number of edges	Number of faces	Number of rectangular faces	Number of triangular faces
③	A					
④	B					

⑤ Are their ends congruent? _____

⑥ Can they slide on all faces? _____

Complete the sentences.

⑦ 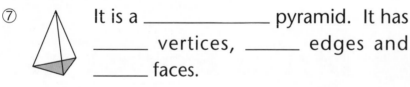 It is a _____ pyramid. It has _____ vertices, _____ edges and _____ faces.

⑧ It is a _____ pyramid. It has _____ vertices, _____ edges and _____ faces.

⑨ It is a _____ pyramid. It has _____ vertices, _____ edges and _____ faces.

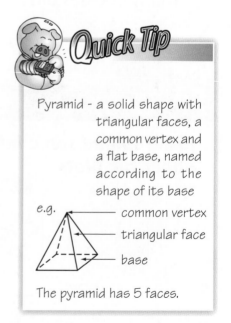

Jacky wants to make a rectangular prism. Help him colour the net and answer the question.

⑩ Colour each pair of congruent faces with the same colour.

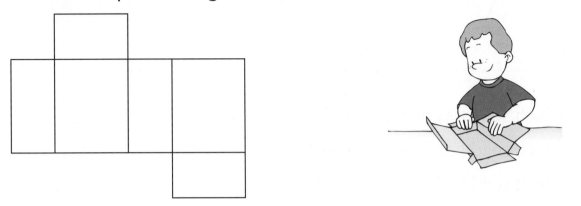

⑪ How many pairs of congruent faces are there? _____ pairs

Look at the nets below. Put a check mark ✔ in the circle if the net can form a rectangular prism. Otherwise, put a cross ✗.

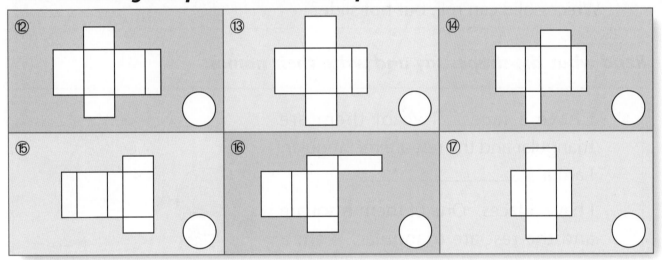

⑫   ⑬   ⑭

⑮   ⑯   ⑰

There are pictures on the rectangular prisms. Help Jacky draw them on the nets.

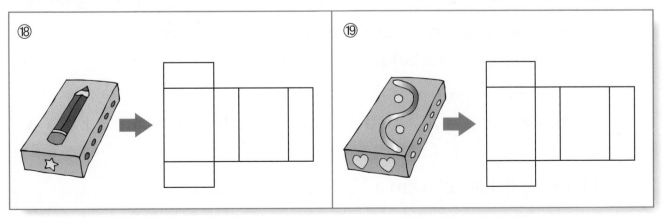

⑱   ⑲

ISBN: 978-1-897164-13-6

Name the solids and answer the questions.

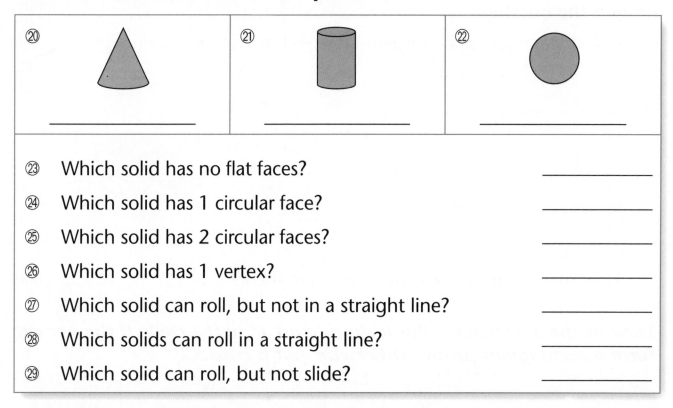

20 _____

21 _____

22 _____

23 Which solid has no flat faces? _____

24 Which solid has 1 circular face? _____

25 Which solid has 2 circular faces? _____

26 Which solid has 1 vertex? _____

27 Which solid can roll, but not in a straight line? _____

28 Which solids can roll in a straight line? _____

29 Which solid can roll, but not slide? _____

Read what the shapes say and write their names.

30 I have 5 faces. Two of them are triangular and the rest are rectangular. I am a _____ .

31 I have 5 faces. One of them is square and the rest are triangular. I am a _____ .

32 I have 1 circular face. I can slide. I am a _____ .

33 I have 6 faces, 8 vertices and 8 edges. All of my faces are rectangular. I am a _____ .

34 I have 6 faces. All of them are exactly the same. I am a _____ .

35 I have no flat faces. I am a _____ .

ISBN: 978-1-897164-13-6

Colour all the faces of each solid that you can see.

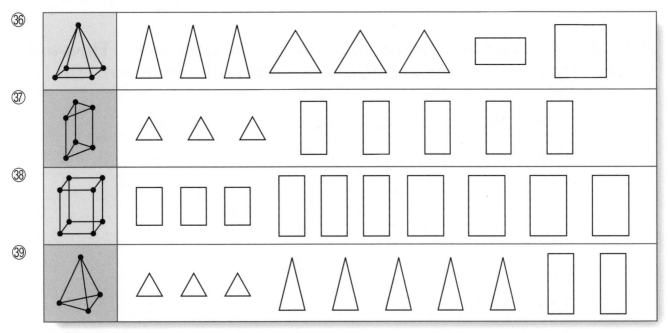

Answer the questions. Write the letters.

A square pyramid   **B** cone   **C** sphere

D rectangular prism   **E** triangular prism   **F** cylinder

G triangular pyramid   **H** rectangular pyramid

40 Which solids have rectangular faces?   _____

41 Which solids have triangular faces?   _____

42 Which solids have circular faces?   _____

43 Which solids have 5 faces?   _____

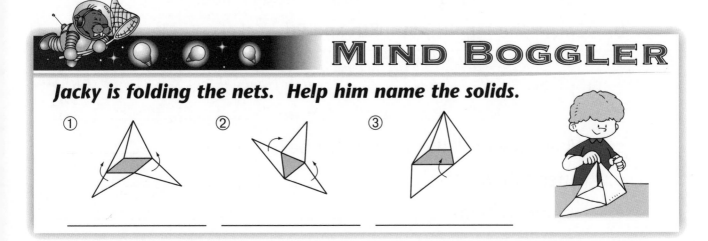

MIND BOGGLER

Jacky is folding the nets. Help him name the solids.

① _____   ② _____   ③ _____

ISBN: 978-1-897164-13-6

12 Patterning

Help Elaine colour her stickers and answer the questions. Then use a letter pattern and a number pattern to show each colour pattern.

① a. Colour the 1st, 3rd, 5th, 7th and 9th stickers yellow.

b. Colour the 2nd, 4th, 6th and 8th stickers red.

| 1st | 2nd | 3rd | 4th | 5th | 6th | 7th | 8th | 9th | 10th |

c. What colour will the 10th sticker be? _____

d. Letter pattern : __ __ __ __ __ __ __ __ __ __

e. Number pattern : __ __ __ __ __ __ __ __ __ __

---

② a. Colour the 1st, 2nd, 4th, 5th, 7th and 8th stickers orange.

b. Colour the 3rd, 6th and 9th stickers green.

| 1st | 2nd | 3rd | 4th | 5th | 6th | 7th | 8th | 9th | 10th |

c. What colour will the 10th sticker be? _____

d. Letter pattern : __ __ __ __ __ __ __ __ __ __

e. Number pattern : __ __ __ __ __ __ __ __ __ __

---

③ a. Colour the 2nd, 3rd, 6th and 7th stickers blue.

b. Colour the 1st, 4th, 5th, 8th and 9th stickers purple.

| 1st | 2nd | 3rd | 4th | 5th | 6th | 7th | 8th | 9th | 10th |

c. What colour will the 10th sticker be? _____

d. Letter pattern : __ __ __ __ __ __ __ __ __ __

e. Number pattern : __ __ __ __ __ __ __ __ __ __

ISBN: 978-1-897164-13-6

See how the attributes change in each pattern. Write the pattern rules with the help of the words given.

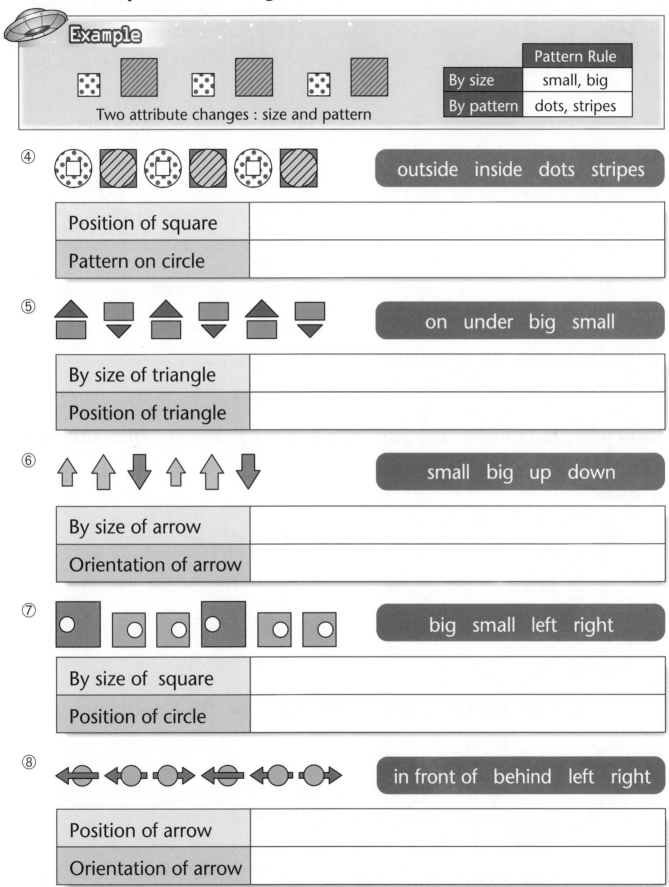

Example

Two attribute changes : size and pattern

	Pattern Rule
By size	small, big
By pattern	dots, stripes

④ outside   inside   dots   stripes

Position of square	
Pattern on circle	

⑤ on   under   big   small

By size of triangle	
Position of triangle	

⑥ small   big   up   down

By size of arrow	
Orientation of arrow	

⑦ big   small   left   right

By size of square	
Position of circle	

⑧ in front of   behind   left   right

Position of arrow	
Orientation of arrow	

Look at the 100-chart. Fill in the blanks and circle the correct words.

⑨ a. The circled numbers are : _____

_____

_____

_____

1	2	3	④	5	6	7	⑧	9	10
11	⑫	13	14	15	⑯	17	18	19	⑳
21	22	23	㉔	25	26	27	㉘	29	30
31	㉜	33	34	35	㊱	37	38	39	㊵
41	42	43	㊹	45	46	47	㊽	49	50
51	㊿	53	54	55	56	57	58	59	60
61	62	63	64	65	66	67	68	69	70
71	72	73	74	75	76	77	78	79	80
81	82	83	84	85	86	87	88	89	90
91	92	93	94	95	96	97	98	99	100

b. Each number increases / decreases

by _____ each time.

⑩ a. The shaded numbers are : _____

_____

_____

_____

b. Each number increases / decreases by _____ each time.

⑪ a. The circled and shaded numbers are : _____

b. Each number increases / decreases by _____ each time.

Read what the children say and complete the patterns. Then circle the correct numbers or words.

⑫ Starting at 20, add 5 to each number.

a. 20 , _____ , _____ , _____ , _____

b. Each number increases / decreases by 5 / 10 each time.

⑬ Starting at 10, subtract 4 and then add 3 to each number.

a. 10 , _____ , _____ , _____ , _____

b. Each number increases / decreases by 1 / 7 each time.

⑭ Multiply the whole numbers from 1 to 10 by 2.

a.

	1	2	3	4	5	6	7	8	9	10
x 2										

b. Each product ends in 0 / 1 , 2 / 3 , 4 / 5 , 6 / 7 , or 8 / 9 .

ISBN: 978-1-897164-13-6

See how Dennis arranges his marbles. Draw the marbles in the next 2 rows and circle the correct words.

⑮

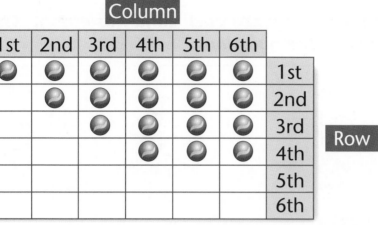

Column

	1st	2nd	3rd	4th	5th	6th	
	●	●	●	●	●	●	1st
		●	●	●	●	●	2nd
			●	●	●	●	3rd
				●	●	●	4th
							5th
							6th

Row

⑯ The marbles in the columns increase / decrease by 1 / 2 each time.

⑰ The marbles in the rows increase / decrease by 1 / 2 each time.

Look at the marbles above. Complete the tables.

⑱

Column	1st	2nd	3rd	4th	5th	6th
Number of marbles	1					

⑲

Row	1st	2nd	3rd	4th	5th	6th
Number of marbles	6					

⑳

	first column	first 2 columns	first 3 columns	first 4 columns	first 5 columns	all 6 columns
Number of marbles in all	1					

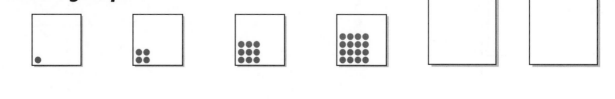

MIND BOGGLER

Write the number of marbles you need for each group and draw the next 2 groups.

___   ___   ___   ___   ___   ___

ISBN: 978-1-897164-13-6

13 Fractions

The shaded parts show how much pizza each child has eaten. Check ✔ the correct letters and answer the questions.

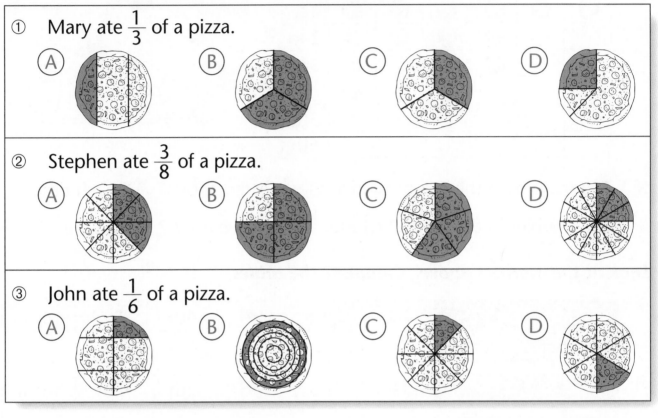

① Mary ate $\frac{1}{3}$ of a pizza.

Ⓐ Ⓑ Ⓒ Ⓓ

② Stephen ate $\frac{3}{8}$ of a pizza.

Ⓐ Ⓑ Ⓒ Ⓓ

③ John ate $\frac{1}{6}$ of a pizza.

Ⓐ Ⓑ Ⓒ Ⓓ

④ Who ate more pizza, Mary or John? _____

⑤ Who ate more pizza, Stephen or John? _____

Colour the figures to show the fractions. Then put the fractions in order.

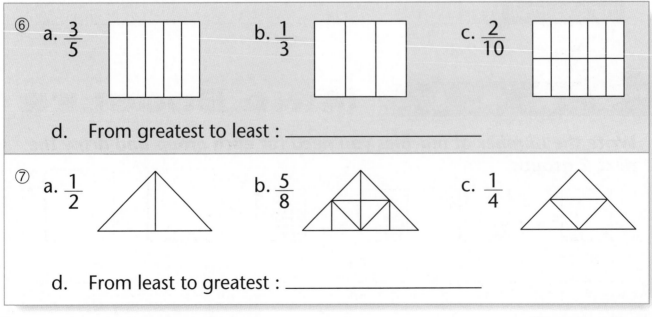

⑥ a. $\frac{3}{5}$ b. $\frac{1}{3}$ c. $\frac{2}{10}$

d. From greatest to least : _____

⑦ a. $\frac{1}{2}$ b. $\frac{5}{8}$ c. $\frac{1}{4}$

d. From least to greatest : _____

ISBN: 978-1-897164-13-6

See how Mrs. Duncan puts her things in groups. Fill in the blanks with numbers or fractions.

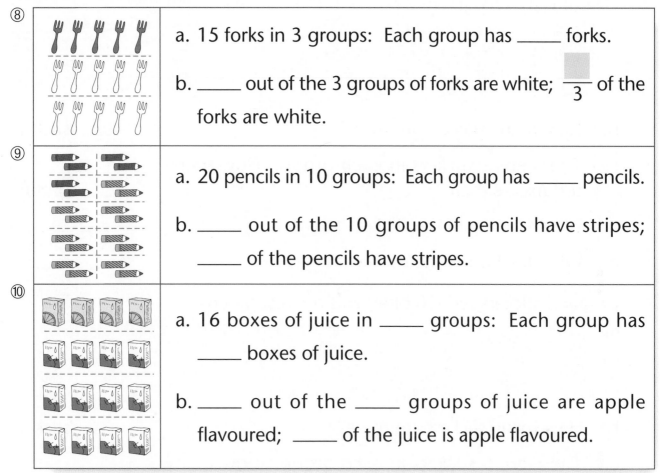

⑧
a. 15 forks in 3 groups: Each group has _____ forks.

b. _____ out of the 3 groups of forks are white; $\frac{\square}{3}$ of the forks are white.

⑨
a. 20 pencils in 10 groups: Each group has _____ pencils.

b. _____ out of the 10 groups of pencils have stripes; _____ of the pencils have stripes.

⑩
a. 16 boxes of juice in _____ groups: Each group has _____ boxes of juice.

b. _____ out of the _____ groups of juice are apple flavoured; _____ of the juice is apple flavoured.

Look at the shapes and write fractions to complete each sentence.

⑪
a. _____ of the shapes are triangles.

b. _____ of the shapes are circles.

⑫
a. _____ of the shapes are squares.

b. _____ of the shapes are stars.

⑬
a. _____ of the shapes are hearts.

b. _____ of the shapes are rectangles.

ISBN: 978-1-897164-13-6

Colour the stickers and answer the questions.

⑭ Colour 6 stickers green, 2 red, and the rest yellow.

a.
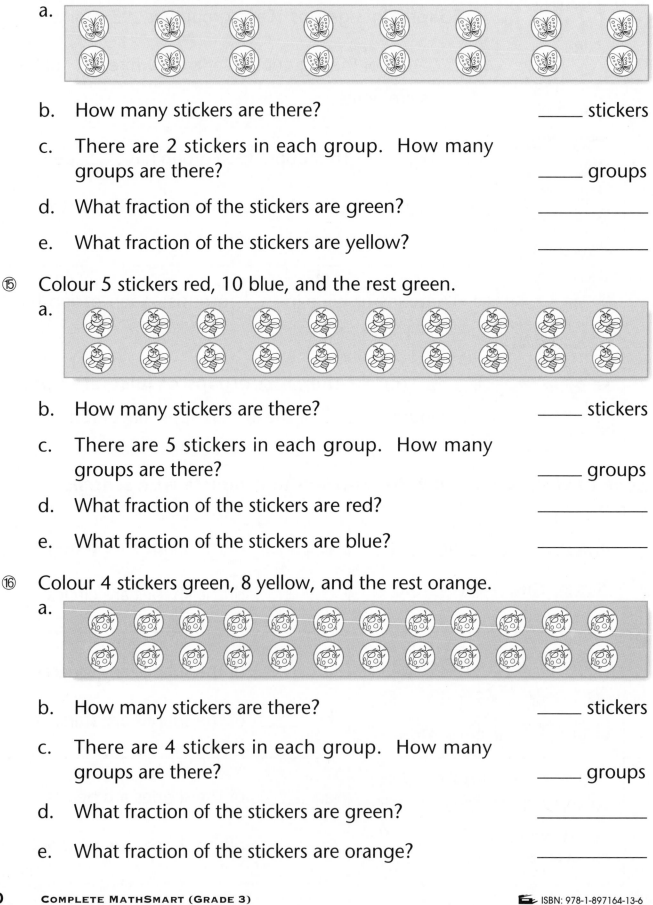

b. How many stickers are there? _____ stickers

c. There are 2 stickers in each group. How many groups are there? _____ groups

d. What fraction of the stickers are green? _____

e. What fraction of the stickers are yellow? _____

⑮ Colour 5 stickers red, 10 blue, and the rest green.

a.

b. How many stickers are there? _____ stickers

c. There are 5 stickers in each group. How many groups are there? _____ groups

d. What fraction of the stickers are red? _____

e. What fraction of the stickers are blue? _____

⑯ Colour 4 stickers green, 8 yellow, and the rest orange.

a.

b. How many stickers are there? _____ stickers

c. There are 4 stickers in each group. How many groups are there? _____ groups

d. What fraction of the stickers are green? _____

e. What fraction of the stickers are orange? _____

ISBN: 978-1-897164-13-6

Use fractions to show the pizzas in each group.

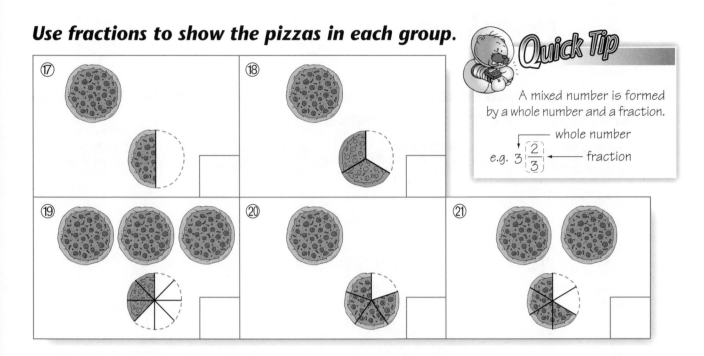

Quick Tip

A mixed number is formed by a whole number and a fraction.

e.g. $3\dfrac{2}{3}$ — whole number, — fraction

Molly folds the paper strips along the dotted lines. Help her use fractions to show how long each shaded part is. Write the letters in the circles.

A $\dfrac{1}{3}$ of the paper strip

B $\dfrac{1}{4}$ of the paper strip

C $\dfrac{1}{2}$ of the paper strip

D $\dfrac{1}{5}$ of the paper strip

㉒ ◯

㉓ ◯

㉔ ◯

㉕ ◯

MIND BOGGLER

Help Mrs. Ducan find the reduced prices.

① The sale price is half of its ticket price.

$ 80

Reduced price : $ _____

② The sale price is a quarter of the ticket price.

$ 88

Reduced price : $ _____

14 Probability

Read what the children say. Choose from the words below to describe the chances for the events to happen.

impossible   unlikely   likely   certain

① I am 105 cm tall. Next year, I will be taller than 105 cm.

_____

② I am so hungry I think I can eat 2 slices of pizza.

_____

③ I like animals. I will keep a dinosaur in my backyard one day.

_____

④ I got 55 out of 100 on the Math test. I think I am the best in class.

_____

⑤ There are 4 red jellybeans in a jar containing 200 jellybeans. If I pick 1 jellybean from the jar, I will get a red one.

_____

⑥ I like snow. I will see snow in winter.

_____

⑦ I spin the spinner once.

a. The arrow lands on 🍦 .   _____

b. The arrow lands on 🍟 .   _____

c. The arrow lands on 🍭 .   _____

    ISBN: 978-1-897164-13-6

Uncle Tom lets his customers pick 1 ball from the box and get the food for free. Complete the tables and answer the questions.

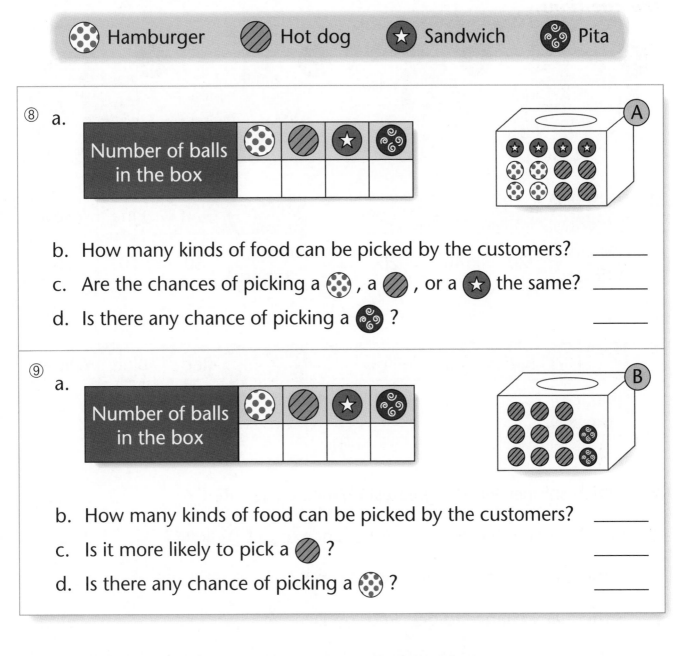

Hamburger   Hot dog   Sandwich   Pita

⑧ a.

Number of balls in the box	🔵	🔵	⭐	🔵

b. How many kinds of food can be picked by the customers? _____

c. Are the chances of picking a 🔵 , a 🔵 , or a ⭐ the same? _____

d. Is there any chance of picking a 🔵 ? _____

⑨ a.

Number of balls in the box	🔵	🔵	⭐	🔵

b. How many kinds of food can be picked by the customers? _____

c. Is it more likely to pick a 🔵 ? _____

d. Is there any chance of picking a 🔵 ? _____

Look at the above boxes and answer the questions.

⑩ Mrs. Gibbon likes sandwiches. Which box should she choose?   Box _____

⑪ Aunt Mary likes hot dogs. Which box should she choose?   Box _____

⑫ Jim likes pitas. Which box should he choose?   Box _____

⑬ Patrick does not like sandwiches. Which box should he choose?   Box _____

Lucy makes 4 spinners and spins each spinner 80 times. Help her match the spinners with the tables. Write the letters in the circles and answer the questions.

A — Blue, Yellow, Red

B — Yellow, Blue, Red

C — Red, Yellow, Blue

D — Red, Yellow, Blue

⑭
Land on	Red	Blue	Yellow
No. of times	20	40	20

⑮
Land on	Red	Blue	Yellow
No. of times	60	10	10

⑯
Land on	Red	Blue	Yellow
No. of times	26	27	27

⑰
Land on	Red	Blue	Yellow
No. of times	20	21	39

⑱ Which spinner has the greatest chance to get 'Red'? _____

⑲ Which spinner has the greatest chance to get 'Yellow'? _____

⑳ Is there any chance to get 'White' on B? _____

㉑ Is there any chance to get 'Red' on D? _____

㉒ Is the chance of getting 'Blue' the same as 'Yellow' on A? _____

㉓ Is the chance of getting 'Blue' the same as 'Yellow' on D? _____

㉔ Lucy says that if she spins B 160 times, the number of times the arrow lands on 'Blue' is about 80. Is she correct? _____

㉕ If Lucy spins C 90 times, how many times do you think she gets 'Red'? _____

ISBN: 978-1-897164-13-6

Janet has 6 cards with the numbers 1, 2, or 3. Each time she shuffles the cards and picks one. Here are the numbers she has got after picking 30 times. Complete the tally chart and answer the questions.

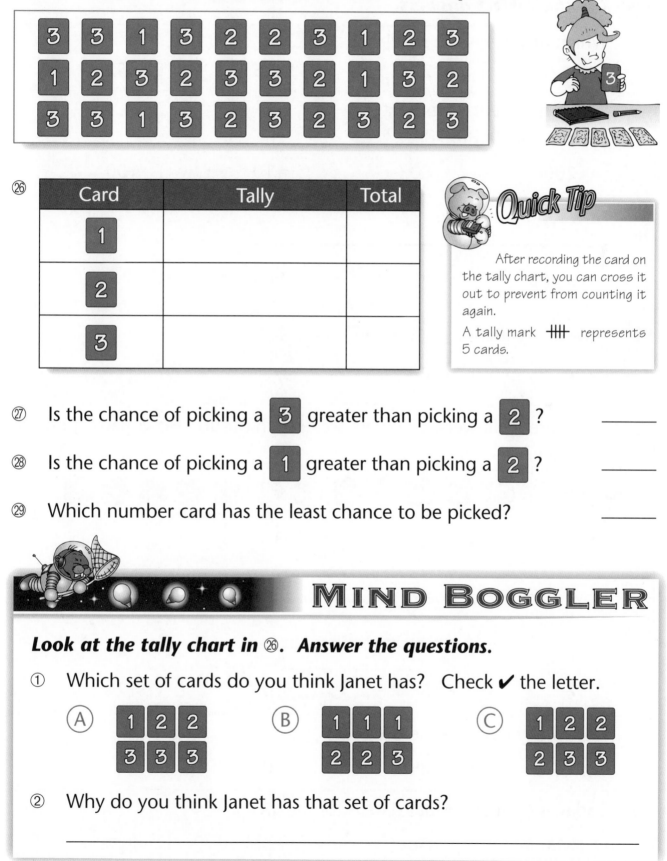

3	3	1	3	2	2	3	1	2	3
1	2	3	2	3	3	2	1	3	2
3	3	1	3	2	3	2	3	2	3

㉖

Card	Tally	Total
1		
2		
3		

Quick Tip

After recording the card on the tally chart, you can cross it out to prevent from counting it again.

A tally mark ⟍⟍⟍⟋ represents 5 cards.

㉗ Is the chance of picking a **3** greater than picking a **2** ? _____

㉘ Is the chance of picking a **1** greater than picking a **2** ? _____

㉙ Which number card has the least chance to be picked? _____

MIND BOGGLER

Look at the tally chart in ㉖. Answer the questions.

① Which set of cards do you think Janet has? Check ✔ the letter.

Ⓐ 1 2 2 / 3 3 3

Ⓑ 1 1 1 / 2 2 3

Ⓒ 1 2 2 / 2 3 3

② Why do you think Janet has that set of cards?

_____

ISBN: 978-1-897164-13-6

Check ✔ the correct answers.

① Which number is the smallest?

(A) 524   (B) 245   (C) 425   (D) 452

② Which number comes next?
40, 50, 60, 70, 80, 90, _____

(A) 200   (B) 80   (C) 110   (D) 100

③ How long is the line?

_____

(A) 9 cm   (B) 85 mm   (C) 98 mm   (D) 8 cm

④ How many triangles are there?

(A) 5   (B) 6   (C) 7   (D) 8

⑤ There are 15 flowers. 5 flowers are in each group. How many groups are there?

(A) 1   (B) 2   (C) 3   (D) 4

⑥ How many edges does a rectangular prism have?

(A) 6   (B) 8   (C) 10   (D) 12

⑦ How many days are there in July?

(A) 28   (B) 29   (C) 30   (D) 31

⑧ Today is April 30. What date is tomorrow?

(A) May 1   (B) April 31   (C) April 30   (D) June 1

ISBN: 978-1-897164-13-6

⑨ What number is the arrow pointing at?

400   500   600   700

(A) 450   (B) 550   (C) 570   (D) 530

⑩ How much does Peter have?

(A) $6.42   (B) $5.52   (C) $5.42   (D) $6.52

⑪ Each basket has 8 plums. How many plums are in 3 baskets?

(A) 16   (B) 24   (C) 18   (D) 20

⑫ What fraction of the shape is shaded?

(A) $\frac{4}{6}$ (B) $\frac{8}{4}$ (C) $\frac{4}{8}$ (D) $\frac{4}{12}$

⑬ What fraction of the flowers are 🌷 ?

(A) $\frac{1}{3}$ (B) $\frac{1}{6}$ (C) $\frac{2}{3}$ (D) $\frac{3}{18}$

⑭ What is the sum of 265 and 179?

(A) 454   (B) 354   (C) 344   (D) 444

⑮ How many days are there in 6 weeks?

(A) 36   (B) 42.   (C) 30   (D) 48

⑯ What time is it?

(A) 8:04   (B) 9:20

(C) 8:20   (D) twenty minutes to nine

Final Test

Find the answers.

⑰ $\begin{array}{r} 5\ 2\ 4 \\ -\ 1\ 7\ 6 \end{array}$	⑱ $\begin{array}{r} 8\ 9 \\ +\ 4\ 5\ 5 \end{array}$	⑲ $\begin{array}{r} 2\ 0\ 3 \\ -\ \ \ 9\ 4 \end{array}$	⑳ $\begin{array}{r} 1\ 7\ 7 \\ +\ 2\ 8\ 9 \end{array}$
㉑ $\begin{array}{r} 7 \\ \times\ \ 5 \end{array}$	㉒ $6\overline{)40}$	㉓ $3\overline{)24}$	㉔ $\begin{array}{r} 6 \\ \times\ \ 9 \end{array}$

㉕ $148 + 236$ = _____	㉖ $500 - 319$ = _____
㉗ $439 - 388$ = _____	㉘ $294 + 357$ = _____
㉙ 2×8 = _____	㉚ 4×5 = _____
㉛ $36 \div 7$ = _____	㉜ $25 \div 6$ = _____

Fill in the missing numbers.

㉝ 92 , _____ , 88 , 86 , _____ , _____ , 80 , _____ , 76

㉞ 60 , 65 , _____ , _____ , 80 , _____ , 90 , _____

㉟ 403 , _____ , 405 , 406 , _____ , _____ , 409 , _____ , 411

Shade the thermometers to show the temperatures. Then put them in order from the highest reading to the lowest. Write the letters.

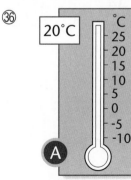
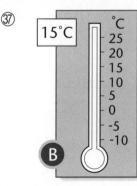
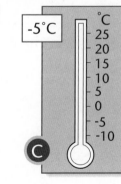
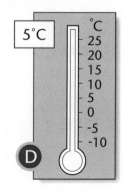

㊵ From the highest reading to the lowest : _____ , _____ , _____ , _____

ISBN: 978-1-897164-13-6

Solve the problems.

㊶ Lucy has 209 building blocks. Tim has 347 building blocks. How many building blocks do they have in all?

_____ = _____   _____ building blocks

㊷ How many more blocks does Tim have than Lucy?

_____ = _____   _____ more

㊸ Lucy has 3 groups of red blocks. Each group has 6 blocks. How many red blocks does Lucy have in all?

_____ = _____   _____ blocks

㊹ Tim divides 20 blocks equally into 4 groups. How many are there in each group?

_____ = _____   _____ blocks

㊺ Draw the next picture in each pattern.

a.

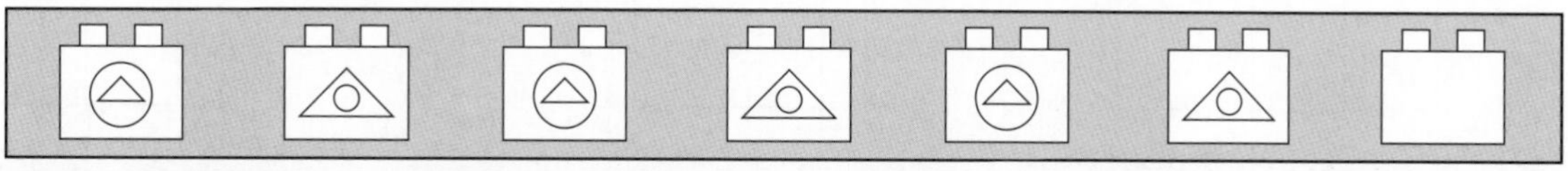

b.

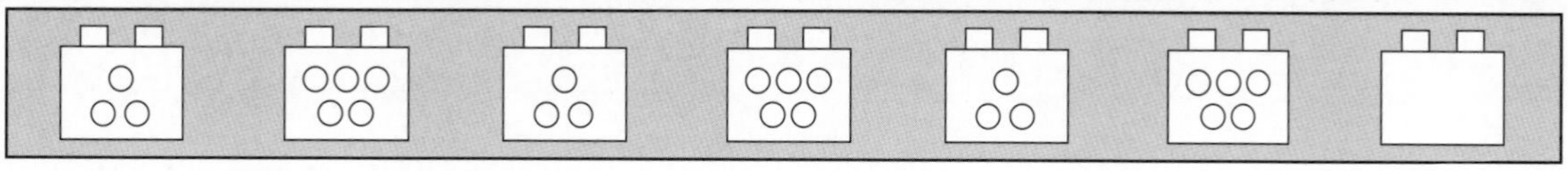

㊻ Colour $\frac{1}{3}$ of each group of blocks.

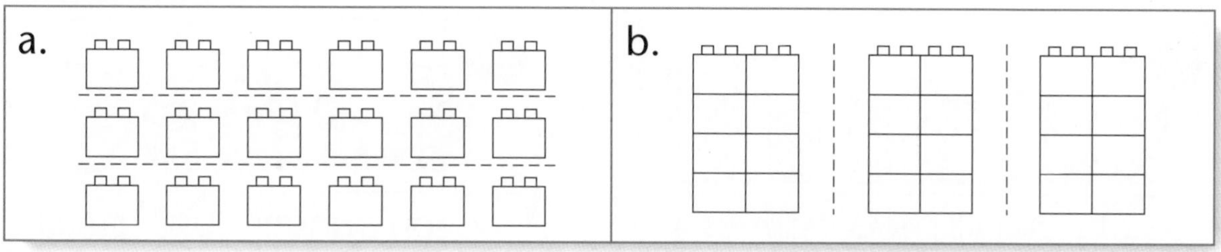

a.

b.

㊼ Find the area and perimeter of the label on the box.

a.   Area = _____ square units

b.   Perimeter = _____ cm

Uncle Paul is preparing gifts for his customers. He puts the gift into boxes of different shapes. Read the descriptions to find out what shapes the boxes are.

④⑧ It has 5 faces. One of the faces is rectangular and the rest are triangular. It has 5 vertices. _____

④⑨ It has 6 vertices, 9 edges, and 5 faces. Two of the faces are triangular and the rest are rectangular. _____

⑤⓪ It has 2 circular faces. It can roll or slide. _____

⑤① It has 6 faces. All of the faces are rectangular. _____

Look at the nets Uncle Paul cut to make gift boxes. Which of the nets below can form a rectangular prism? Check ✔ the letter.

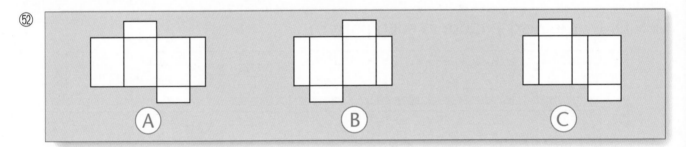

Look at the gift boxes and write the pattern rules with the help of the words given.

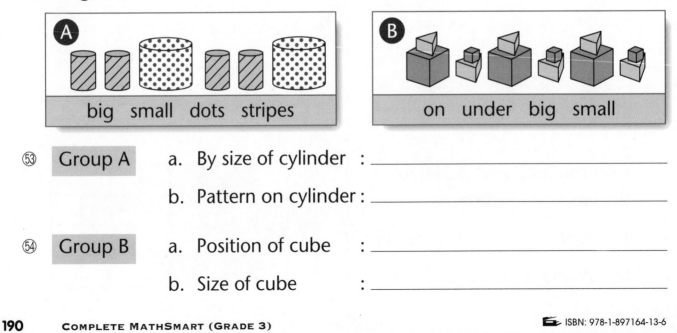

| A | big   small   dots   stripes |
| B | on   under   big   small |

⑤③ Group A   a. By size of cylinder : _____

b. Pattern on cylinder : _____

⑤④ Group B   a. Position of cube : _____

b. Size of cube : _____

ISBN: 978-1-897164-13-6

Record the gifts for Uncle Paul with a tally chart. Then answer the questions.

55

Gift	Tally	Total
🔺		
🔻		
🥁		
📦		

56 Is the chance of getting a 🥁 the same as that of getting a 🔻 ? _____

57 Is the chance of getting a 🔺 the same as that of getting a 📦 ? _____

58 Is there any chance for a customer to get a 🔺 ? _____

59 If 3 🔻 s have been given to the customers,

a. does a customer still have a chance to get a 🔻 ? _____

b. will the chance of getting a 🔻 be smaller or greater? _____

Look at the gifts above. Then answer the questions.

60 What fraction of the gifts are 🔺 ? _____

61 What fraction of the gifts are 🥁 ? _____

62 What fraction of the gifts are with dots? _____

63 What fraction of the gifts are with stripes? _____

64 Put every 2 gifts into a group.

a. How many groups are there? _____

b. How many groups of 📦 are there? _____

c. What fraction of the gifts are 📦 ? _____

Final Test

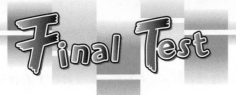

When did Uncle Paul open and close his store last Sunday? Write the times.

(65)

a. Open

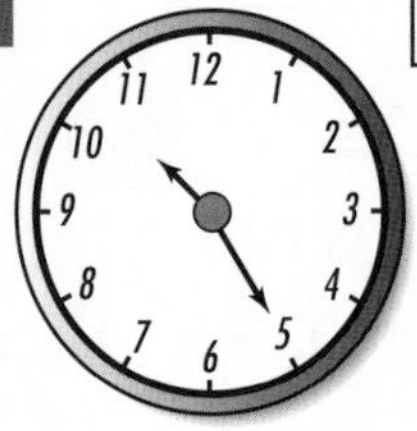

b. Closed

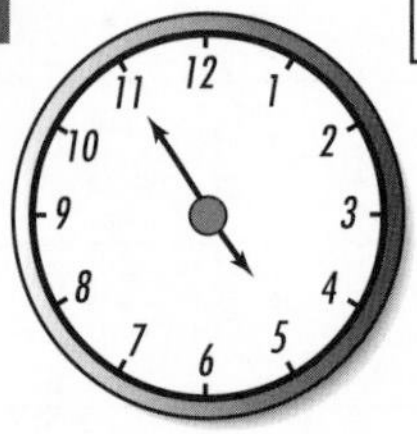

Use a bar graph to show how many customers visited Uncle Paul's store last week. Then answer the questions.

Day	SUN	MON	TUE	WED	THU	FRI	SAT
Number of Customers	80	55	40	30	60	75	70

(66)

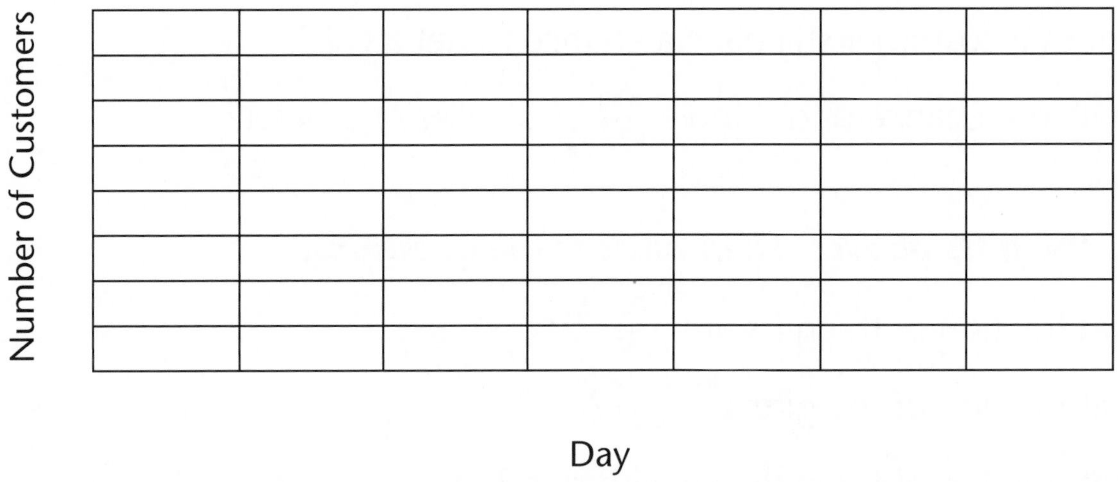

(67) Which day had the most customers? ____________

(68) How many customers were there last week? ____________

(69) If 49 customers were men on Friday, how many customers were women? ____________

(70) If every customer spent $10 on Tuesday, how much did Uncle Paul get that day? ____________

ISBN: 978-1-897164-13-6

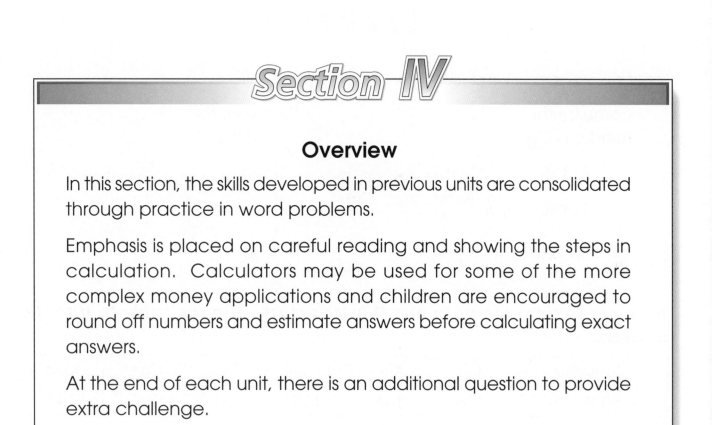

Section IV

Overview

In this section, the skills developed in previous units are consolidated through practice in word problems.

Emphasis is placed on careful reading and showing the steps in calculation. Calculators may be used for some of the more complex money applications and children are encouraged to round off numbers and estimate answers before calculating exact answers.

At the end of each unit, there is an additional question to provide extra challenge.

ISBN: 978-1-897164-13-6

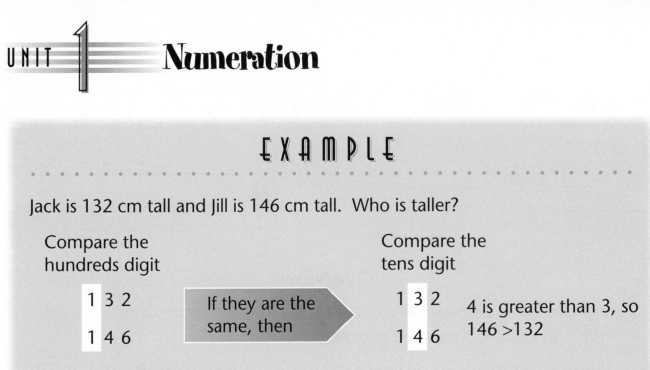

EXAMPLE

Jack is 132 cm tall and Jill is 146 cm tall. Who is taller?

Compare the
hundreds digit

1 3 2

1 4 6

If they are the same, then

Compare the
tens digit

1 3 2

1 4 6

4 is greater than 3, so
146 >132

Answer : Jill is taller than Jack.

Here are some students in Mrs Winter's class. Use the table to find the answers.

Student	Joe	Ann	Lesley	Paul	Gary	Joan
Height (cm)	134	145	120	130	125	144

① Write the names in order of height from the shortest to the tallest.

Answer : _____ , _____ , _____ , _____ , _____ ,

② If Lesley has grown 10 cm every year for the past 4 years, complete the table to show her height.

	1 year ago	2 years ago	3 years ago	4 years ago
Height (cm)				

③ How many centimetres would Paul have to grow to be as tall as Ann?

Answer :

④ What is the difference in height between the tallest student and the shortest student?

Answer :

ISBN: 978-1-897164-13-6

Mrs Winter's class is having a marble competition. Read the table and answer the questions.

Students	Joe	Ann	Lesley	Paul	Gary
Number of marbles	513	310	413	523	270

⑤ Write the names in order from the student that has the most marbles to the student that has the fewest.

Answer : _____

⑥ Who has 100 fewer marbles than Joe?

Answer : _____

⑦ Who has 40 more marbles than Gary?

Answer : _____

⑧ If you count up in 5's from the number of marbles Gary has, whose number will you get to first?

Answer : _____

⑨ Who can match another person's score by winning 10 marbles?

Answer : _____

CHALLENGE

If Gary is playing against Ann, how many marbles must Ann give to Gary for them to have the same number? Show your work and explain.

Answer : _____

Addition and Subtraction

EXAMPLE

A pond has 12 ducks on it. If 10 more fly in, how many ducks are there altogether?

Think :   'Add' words - more, altogether, join, in all

'Subtract' words - left, fewer, fly away

Write :   12 + 10 = 22

Answer :   There are 22 ducks altogether.

Use this picture of a farm to answer the questions.

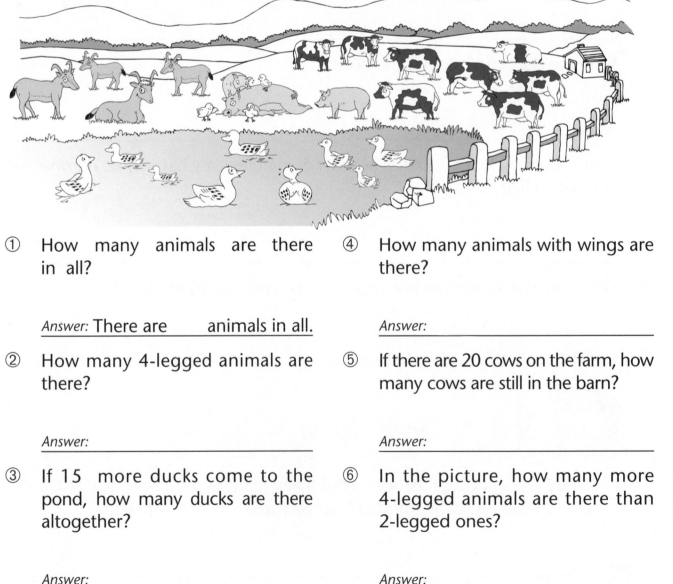

① How many animals are there in all?

Answer: There are _____ animals in all.

② How many 4-legged animals are there?

Answer: _____

③ If 15 more ducks come to the pond, how many ducks are there altogether?

Answer: _____

④ How many animals with wings are there?

Answer: _____

⑤ If there are 20 cows on the farm, how many cows are still in the barn?

Answer: _____

⑥ In the picture, how many more 4-legged animals are there than 2-legged ones?

Answer: _____

ISBN: 978-1-897164-13-6

Solve the problems. Show your work.

⑦ Peter has 39 goats. He wants to have 64 goats. How many more goats should he buy?

Answer: _____

⑧ Peter has 68 animals on his farm. He buys 23 more. How many animals does he have now?

Answer: _____

⑨ Peter has 24 ducks, 34 geese and 59 chickens. How many birds does he have?

Answer: _____

⑩ Peter sold 47 cows and 59 goats. How many cows and goats did Peter sell altogether?

Answer: _____

⑪ There are 196 gulls in Peter's field. 98 of them fly away but 105 more gulls arrive. How many gulls are there altogether?

Answer: _____

⑫ After 312 gulls have gone, there are 64 left. How many gulls were there at the start?

Answer: _____

⑬ There are 305 gulls but 84 of them fly away. How many gulls are left?

Answer: _____

⑭ There are 576 gulls, but 153 fly away. Then 283 more leave. How many gulls remain?

Answer: _____

⑮ 413 gulls are joined by 311 more. Then 136 more gulls come. How many gulls are there altogether?

Answer: _____

Steps for solving problems: ← **Read this first.**
1. **Write down the facts.**
2. **Decide what operations to use.**
3. **Calculate.**
4. **Write the answer.**

ISBN: 978-1-897164-13-6

Read the inventory of Peter's animals. Write the names of the animals.

Sheep 54	Pigs 58	Ducks 67
Goats 104	Cows 42	Chickens 121

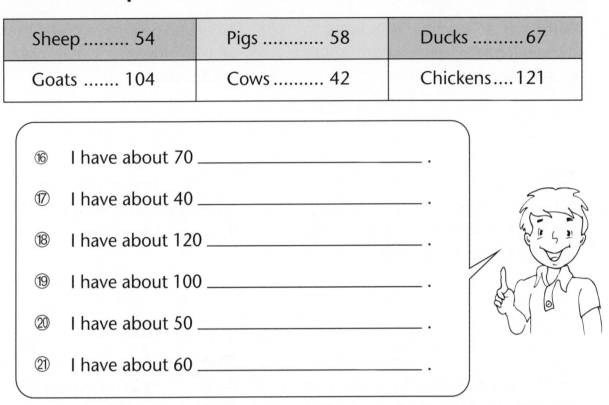

⑯ I have about 70 _____ .

⑰ I have about 40 _____ .

⑱ I have about 120 _____ .

⑲ I have about 100 _____ .

⑳ I have about 50 _____ .

㉑ I have about 60 _____ .

Look at Peter's fields and solve the problems. Show your work.

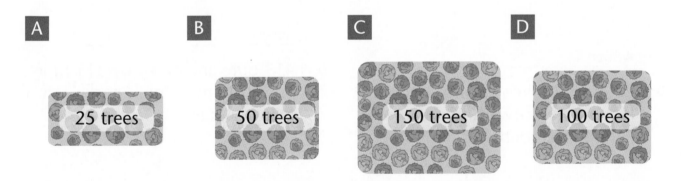

A 25 trees

B 50 trees

C 150 trees

D 100 trees

㉒ Peter wants to plant 48 apple trees in one of these fields. Which field should he use? Explain.

Answer: _____

㉓ If Peter plants 68 cherry trees in field C, how many more trees can he plant there afterwards?

Answer: _____

ISBN: 978-1-897164-13-6

㉔ If Peter plants 68 cherry plants in fields A and B, how many more trees can he plant there afterwards?

Answer: _____

㉕ Peter has 53 apple trees and 75 cherry trees. If he plants them in the same field, which field should he choose? Explain.

Answer: _____

㉖ How many more trees can Peter plant there?

Answer: _____

㉗ Peter has 91 peach trees in field D. If 36 of these are chopped down, how many more trees can he plant there?

Answer: _____

Peter has some ducks and some sheep on his farm. He counts 9 animals and 32 legs. How many ducks and sheep are there? Prove your answer with a picture.

```




```

Answer: _____

ISBN: 978-1-897164-13-6

UNIT 3 — **Multiplication**

There are 3 groups of 5 children at the camp. How many children are there altogether?

Think : Multiplication is repeated addition.

Write : $3 \times 5 = 15$ is $5 + 5 + 5 = 15$

Answer : There are 15 children altogether.

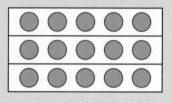

Follow Peter's method to complete the following table.

		Diagram	Multiplication sentence	Number of chips
①	5 cookies with 4 chocolate chips each	(5 cookies)	5×4	20
②	5 cookies with 6 chocolate chips each			
③	3 cookies with 4 chocolate chips each			
④	4 cookies with 7 chocolate chips each			
⑤	3 cookies with 5 chocolate chips each			
⑥	6 cookies with 2 chocolate chips each			

ISBN: 978-1-897164-13-6

Write a sentence to describe each picture. Then use multiplication to find how many fruits there are in all.

⑦

5 plates with _____ apples each.

$5 \times 3 =$ _____

There are _____ apples in all.

⑧

_____

_____

_____

⑨

_____

_____

_____

⑩

_____

_____

_____

⑪

_____

_____

_____

Solve the problems. Show your work.

⑫   If each box holds 8 apples, how many apples are there in 6 boxes?

Answer: _____

⑬   If each bag holds 7 oranges, how many oranges are there in 9 bags?

Answer: _____

Find how many snacks each group of children will get in all. Show your work.

1 🍽 for each person

Cookies

Crackers

Marshmallows

Brownies

Chicken nuggets

Candies

Cheese sticks

Pretzels

⑭ We like candies.

Answer : 3 children will get _____ candies in all.

⑮ We want crackers.

Answer : _____

⑯ We want chicken nuggets.

Answer : _____

⑰ We like cookies.

Answer : _____

⑱ We like cheese sticks.

Answer : _____

ISBN: 978-1-897164-13-6

⑲ We like brownies.

Answer : _____

⑳ We like marshmallows.

Answer : _____

㉑ We like pretzels.

Answer : _____

㉒ If each cookie has 6 chocolate chips, how many chips are there on a plate of cookies?

Answer : _____

㉓ If each cracker has 2 pieces of cheese, how many pieces are there on a plate of crackers?

Answer : _____

㉔ If each marshmallow weighs 5 grams, how many grams of marshmallows are there on a plate?

Answer : _____

㉕ If a candy costs 6¢, how much does a plate of candies cost?

Answer : _____

CHALLENGE

Terry put 2 nickels into his piggy bank on the first day, 4 nickels on the second day and 6 nickels on the third day. How many cents has Terry saved?

Answer: _____

EXAMPLE

Joe has 15 cupcakes at his party. If there are 5 children, how many cupcakes will each child get?

Think : How many groups of 5 are there in 15?

Write : 15 ÷ 5 = 3

Answer : Each child will get 3 cupcakes.

3 ← quotient

→ 5 ⟌ 1 5 ←

1 5 ┘ dividend

divisor

Circle each share of snacks. Then complete the division sentences and write the statements.

① Divide 10 cupcakes among 5 children. How many cupcakes will each child get?

10 ÷ 5 = _____

Answer: Each child will get _____ cupcakes.

② 3 boys share 12 cookies equally. How many cookies will each boy get?

12 ÷ _____ = _____

Answer: _____

③ Divide 20 candies into 5 groups. How many candies are there in each group?

_____ ÷ _____ = _____

Answer: _____

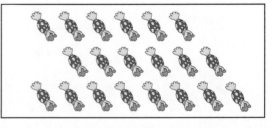

④ Divide 18 crackers among 6 children. How many crackers will each child get?

_____ ÷ _____ = _____

Answer: _____

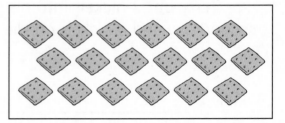

ISBN: 978-1-897164-13-6

Mrs Winter puts 24 doughnuts into baskets. Write the division sentences and statements.

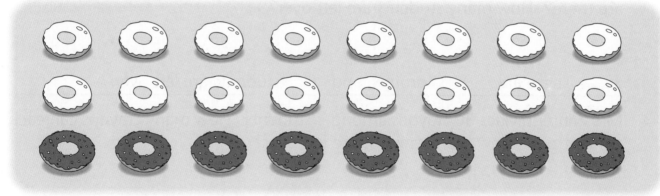

⑤ If Mrs Winter puts 3 doughnuts in each basket, how many baskets does she need?

Answer: She needs _____ baskets.

⑥ If Mrs Winter puts 4 doughnuts in each basket, how many baskets does she need ?

Answer: _____

⑦ If Mrs Winter puts 6 doughnuts in each basket, how many baskets does she need ?

Answer: _____

⑧ If Mrs Winter puts 8 doughnuts in each basket, how many baskets does she need ?

Answer: _____

⑨ There are 8 chocolate doughnuts and 16 honey doughnuts. Mrs Winter makes 2 groups with the same number of chocolate doughnuts and honey doughnuts in each group. How many chocolate doughnuts are there in each group?

Answer: _____

⑩ How many honey doughnuts are there in each group?

Answer: _____

⑪ Mrs Winter makes 4 groups with the same number of chocolate doughnuts and honey doughnuts in each group. How many chocolate doughnuts and honey doughnuts are there in each group?

Answer: _____

Solve the problems. Show your work.

⑫ Mrs Winter divides her class of 24 students into groups of 5. How many groups are there? How many students are left over?

Answer: There are _____ groups, and _____ students are left over.

⑬ Mrs Winter divides 30 crayons among 4 students. How many crayons can each student get? How many crayons are left over?

Answer: _____

⑭ Mrs Winter divides 48 markers among 9 students. How many markers can each student get? How many markers are left over?

Answer: _____

⑮ Mrs Winter divides 61 markers among 7 students. How many markers can each student get? How many markers are left over?

Answer: _____

⑯ Mrs Winter has 6 pencils and 8 rulers. If she wants each student to have 2 pencils and 1 ruler, how many students can she give them to?

Answer: _____

⑰ Mrs Winter has 19 erasers and 7 glue sticks. If she wants each student to have 2 erasers and 1 glue stick, how many students can she give them to?

Answer: _____

⑱ How many erasers and glue sticks are left over?

Answer: _____

   ISBN: 978-1-897164-13-6

Read the story and solve the problems.

Joe brought some cupcakes to school on his birthday. The cupcakes came in packages of 4 and 6.

⑲ How many small boxes would he need to hold 36 cupcakes?

Answer: _____

⑳ How many big boxes would he need to hold 36 cupcakes?

Answer: _____

㉑ How many small boxes would he need to hold 48 cupcakes?

Answer: _____

㉒ If Joe had 18 cupcakes, how many small boxes would he need?

Answer: _____

㉓ If Joe had 26 cupcakes, how many small boxes would he need?

Answer: _____

㉔ If Joe had 26 cupcakes, how many big boxes would he need?

Answer: _____

CHALLENGE

① How many small boxes would you buy to have 12 cupcakes? How much would you have to pay for them?

$3

$4

Answer: _____

② How many big boxes would you buy to have 12 cupcakes? How much would you have to pay for them?

Answer: _____

③ Which do you think is a better deal? Explain.

Answer: _____

ISBN: 978-1-897164-13-6

Fractions

EXAMPLE

Ann divided her pizza into 4 equal parts and ate 1 part. What fraction of Ann's pizza was eaten?

One out of four parts of the pizza was eaten.

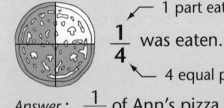

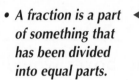 1 part eaten

$\dfrac{1}{4}$ was eaten.

4 equal parts

Answer : $\dfrac{1}{4}$ of Ann's pizza was eaten.

- *A fraction is a part of something that has been divided into equal parts.*

Read this first.

Write the numbers and fractions to complete the sentences. Then colour the eaten part of each pizza.

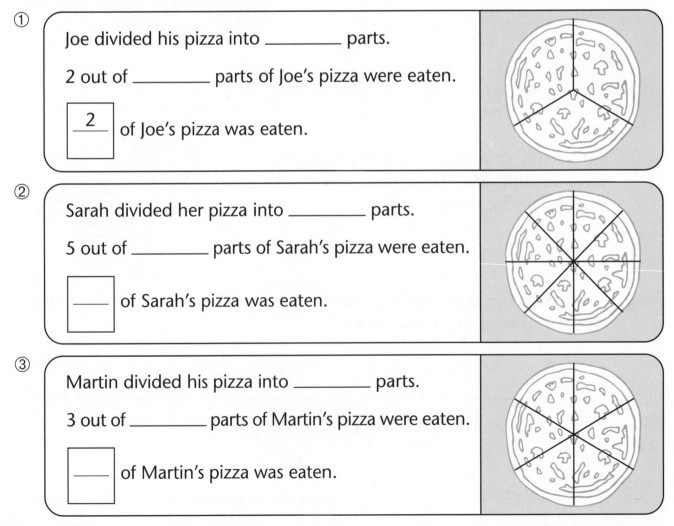

① Joe divided his pizza into _____ parts.

2 out of _____ parts of Joe's pizza were eaten.

$\dfrac{2}{}$ of Joe's pizza was eaten.

② Sarah divided her pizza into _____ parts.

5 out of _____ parts of Sarah's pizza were eaten.

$\dfrac{}{}$ of Sarah's pizza was eaten.

③ Martin divided his pizza into _____ parts.

3 out of _____ parts of Martin's pizza were eaten.

$\dfrac{}{}$ of Martin's pizza was eaten.

ISBN: 978-1-897164-13-6

Look at Ann's groceries. Write a statement to answer each question.

④   What fraction of the groceries are bags?

Answer: _____ of the groceries are bags.

⑤   What fraction of the groceries are cans?

Answer: _____

⑥   What fraction of the groceries are 🛍️ ?

Answer: _____

⑦   What fraction of the groceries are 🥫 ?

Answer: _____

⑧   What fraction of the bags are 👜 ?

Answer: _____

⑨   What fraction of the cans are 🥫 ?

Answer: _____

⑩   If Ann wanted $\frac{1}{2}$ of the groceries to be in bags, how many more bags would she need?

Answer: _____

⑪   If Ann wanted $\frac{1}{2}$ of the groceries to be in cans, how many cans would she take away?

Answer: _____

ISBN: 978-1-897164-13-6

Answer the questions. Then follow the answers to colour the string of beads.

⑫ 4 beads out of 6 are yellow. What fraction of the beads are yellow?

Answer: _____ of the beads are yellow.

⑬ 2 beads out of 6 are red. What fraction of the beads are red?

Answer: _____

⑭ Colour the beads.

number of parts
coloured

Read this first.

$$\frac{4}{6}$$ means 4 out of 6

number of parts
in all

---

⑮ 6 beads out of 12 are red. What fraction of the beads are red?

Answer: _____

⑯ 2 beads out of 12 are yellow. What fraction of the beads are yellow?

Answer: _____

⑰ 3 beads out of 12 are blue. What fraction of the beads are blue?

Answer: _____

⑱ 1 bead out of 12 is orange. What fraction of the beads are orange?

Answer: _____

⑲ Colour the beads.

ISBN: 978-1-897164-13-6

Read the table and answer the questions.

Flavour	Pop		Juice	
	Orange	Grape	Orange	Grape
Number of drinks	8	3	4	5

⑳ What fraction of the drinks are pop?

Answer: _____

㉑ What fraction of the drinks are juice?

Answer: _____

> • *First, find how many drinks Ann has bought in all.*
>
> **Read this first.**

㉒ What fraction of the juices are orange flavour?

Answer: _____

㉔ What fraction of the drinks are grape flavour?

Answer: _____

㉓ What fraction of the pops are orange flavour?

Answer: _____

㉕ What fraction of the drinks are orange flavour?

Answer: _____

CHALLENGE

Ann's Mom says, 'I have $\frac{1}{3}$, $\frac{1}{5}$ and $\frac{1}{4}$ of a pizza left'. Who should choose which piece?

① Rachel is very hungry. .... ☐ of a pizza.

② Ann is hungry. .... ☐ of a pizza.

③ John is not hungry. .... ☐ of a pizza.

EXAMPLE

Natasha bought a candy bar for $0.60. She used 3 coins to pay for the exact amount. Which coins did she use?

Think : Use the highest value of the coins possible. Try quarters and dimes.

Write : $0.25 + $0.25 + $0.10 = $0.60

Answer : Natasha used 2 quarters and 1 dime.

Each child paid the exact amount for the following items. Write the number sentences and statements.

① Joe used 2 coins to buy a balloon for $0.30. Which coins did he use?

Answer: Joe used _____ quarter(s) and _____ nickel(s).

② Katherine used 4 coins to buy an ice cream for $2.03. Which coins did she use?

Answer: _____

③ William used 4 coins to buy a bundle of flowers for $3.15. Which coins did he use?

Answer: _____

④ Ann used 6 coins to buy a box of chocolates for $1.81. Which coins did she use?

Answer: _____

⑤ Natasha used 5 coins to buy 2 hot dogs for $2.20 each. Which coins did she use?

• For question 5, find the total amount Natasha had to pay first. ← Read this first.

Answer: _____

ISBN: 978-1-897164-13-6

The chart shows the prices of food and drinks at a snack bar. Answer the children's questions. Show your work.

| Hamburger | $1.86 | Pizza | $2.75 | Pop | $0.95 |
| Hot dog | $1.68 | Fries | $1.04 | Milk | $1.28 |

⑥ Jane

How much do I need to pay for 1 hamburger and 1 milk?

Answer: Jane needs to pay $ _____ . _____

⑦ David

I am going to buy 1 hot dog and 1 pop. How much are they?

Answer: _____

⑧ Susan

How much do I need to pay for 2 pizzas and 1 hamburger?

Answer: _____

⑨ Tom

I paid $10.00 for 1 hot dog and 1 milk. What change did I get?

Answer: _____

⑩ Daisy

I spent exactly $1.99. Which 2 things did I buy?

Answer: _____

⑪ Nicky

I have 3 loonies and 1 dime. Is it enough for 3 fries?

Answer: _____

Help the cashier give the change to each child with the fewest coins. Show your work.

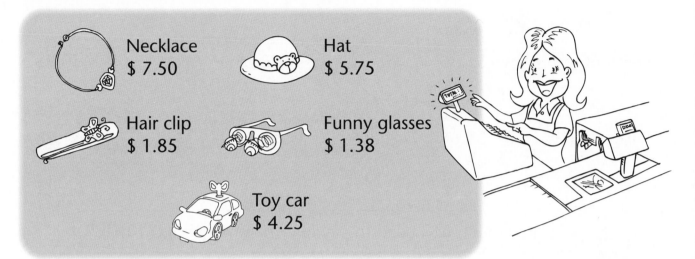

Necklace $ 7.50

Hat $ 5.75

Hair clip $ 1.85

Funny glasses $ 1.38

Toy car $ 4.25

⑫ Joan bought a necklace. What was her change from a $10 bill? What are the coins?

Answer: Joan's change was $ _____ . The coins are _____ twoonie(s) and _____ quarter(s).

⑬ David bought a hat. What was his change from $7.00? What are the coins?

Answer: _____

⑭ Raymond bought 2 toy cars. What was his change from a $10 bill? What are the coins?

Answer: _____

⑮ Lily bought 2 hair clips. What was her change from a $5 bill? What are the coins?

Answer: _____

⑯ Daisy bought 1 pair of funny glasses, 1 hair clip and 1 hat. What was her change from a $10 bill? What are the coins?

Answer: _____

ISBN: 978-1-897164-13-6

Estimate the value of each item. Round each value to the nearest dollar. Then use your calculator to find the exact total for each bill.

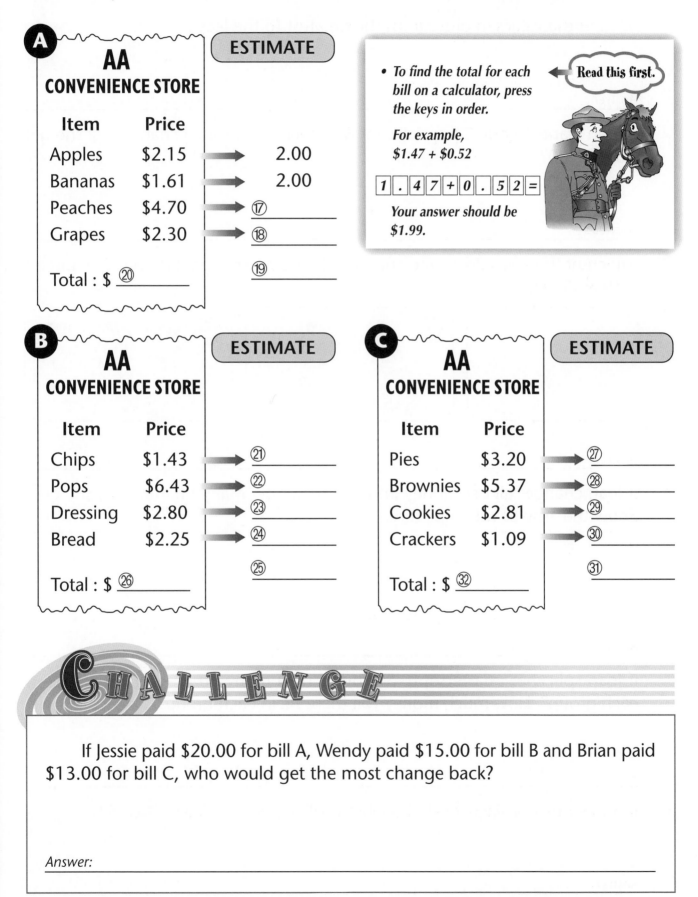

A

AA
CONVENIENCE STORE

Item	Price		ESTIMATE
Apples	$2.15	→	2.00
Bananas	$1.61	→	2.00
Peaches	$4.70	→	⑰ ___
Grapes	$2.30	→	⑱ ___
			⑲ ___
Total : $ ⑳ ___			

- To find the total for each bill on a calculator, press the keys in order.

Read this first.

For example,
$1.47 + $0.52

| 1 | . | 4 | 7 | + | 0 | . | 5 | 2 | = |

Your answer should be $1.99.

B

AA
CONVENIENCE STORE

Item	Price		ESTIMATE
Chips	$1.43	→	㉑ ___
Pops	$6.43	→	㉒ ___
Dressing	$2.80	→	㉓ ___
Bread	$2.25	→	㉔ ___
			㉕ ___
Total : $ ㉖ ___			

C

AA
CONVENIENCE STORE

Item	Price		ESTIMATE
Pies	$3.20	→	㉗ ___
Brownies	$5.37	→	㉘ ___
Cookies	$2.81	→	㉙ ___
Crackers	$1.09	→	㉚ ___
			㉛ ___
Total : $ ㉜ ___			

CHALLENGE

If Jessie paid $20.00 for bill A, Wendy paid $15.00 for bill B and Brian paid $13.00 for bill C, who would get the most change back?

Answer: ___

ISBN: 978-1-897164-13-6

Here is the amount of money that Joan and her friends have. Joan has $2.50, Ann $1.75, Sue $3.30, John $1.50 and Jane $2.70.

① Write these values in order from the greatest to the least.

Answer : _____

② If Joan wants to buy 2 popsicles for 80¢ each, how much change will she get from $2.00?

Answer : _____

③ Which of these would be the change if Joan's mother paid for her 2 popiscles with a $5 bill?

Answer : _____

④ If Joan changes all her money into quarters, how many quarters can she get? Show the answer with a picture.

Answer : _____

⑤ If Joan splits her quarters into 5 groups, how many quarters will there be in each group? How much money will there be in each group?

Answer : _____

⑥ If Ann earns 75¢ each week, how long will it take her to earn $2.25?

Answer : _____

Look at Ann's collection of marbles.

⑦ How many marbles does Ann have?

Answer : _____

⑧ If Ann is given 29 marbles, how many will she have altogether?

Answer : _____

⑨ What fraction of the marbles are black?

Answer : _____

⑩ What fraction of the marbles have a cat's eye?

Answer : _____

⑪ If Ann lost 8 marbles, how many would she have?

Answer : _____

⑫ How many black marbles would Ann have to buy so she would have $\frac{1}{2}$ of her marbles in black?

Answer : _____

⑬ If Ann wants to share her marbles with 2 of her friends, how many marbles will each child get? How many marbles will be left over?

Answer : _____

ISBN: 978-1-897164-13-6

Solve the problems. Show your work.

⑭ Joan has 6 pet mice. If each mouse cost $3.00, how much did they cost in all?

Answer : _____

⑮ Joan spent $24.00 on food for her mice, how much did she spend on each mouse?

Answer : _____

⑯ 2 of Joan's mice each had 4 babies, and she gave 2 of them to a friend. How many baby mice were left?

Answer : _____

⑰ Each of Joan's mice can sell for $5.00. If she sells 5 of them, how much money will she get?

Answer : _____

⑱ How many would Joan need to sell to have $40.00?

Answer : _____

⑲ Joan has $7.00 to buy toys for the mice. Which three of the toys should she choose to spend exactly $7.00?

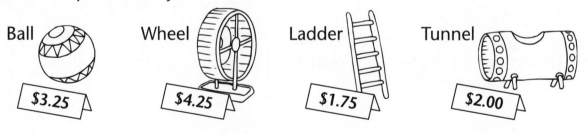

Ball $3.25 Wheel $4.25 Ladder $1.75 Tunnel $2.00

Answer : _____

⑳ Joan bought a ball and a wheel, how much change would she get from $9.00?

Answer : _____

ISBN: 978-1-897164-13-6

Circle the correct answer in each problem.

㉑ Ann earns $2.00 a week. How long will it take her to save $10.00 if she spends $1.00 each week?

A. 5 weeks   B. 10 weeks   C. 15 weeks   D. 8 weeks

㉒ Joan and Ann share 24 marbles equally. How many will each get?

A. 9   B. 10   C. 11   D. 12

㉓ If John joined Joan and Ann, how many should the girls each give up so that they would all have the same number of marbles?

A. 3   B. 4   C. 6   D. 8

㉔ If John has 10 marbles and Joan has 18 marbles, how many should Joan give to John so that they would have the same number of marbles?

A. 4   B. 5   C. 6   D. 7

㉕ Joan has 15 dollars. She wants to spend $\frac{1}{3}$ of her money on candies. How much will she have left?

A. $5.00   B. $10.00   C. $12.00   D. $14.00

㉖ John has $20.00. He spent $5.00 on candies and $3.00 on toys. How much has he spent?

A. $$\frac{8}{20}$$ B. $$\frac{12}{20}$$ C. $$\frac{3}{5}$$ D. $$\frac{5}{23}$$

㉗ Joan has $4.00 and Ann has $12.00. If they each spend $\frac{1}{4}$ of their money, how much will they spend altogether?

A. $2.00   B. $3.00   C. $4.00   D. $5.00

㉘ How much more money does Ann spend than Joan?

A. $1.00   B. $2.00   C. $3.00   D. $4.00

ISBN: 978-1-897164-13-6

UNIT 7

EXAMPLE

Units of measuring
capacity : Litre (L), Millilitre (mL)

| 1 L = 1000 mL |

Units of measuring
mass : Kilogram (kg), Gram (g)

| 1 kg = 1000 g |

 The capacity of this carton is 1L.

A litre of milk has a mass of about 1kg.

Solve the problems. Show your work.

This jug ⌂ holds 1 L and 4 jugs fill this bucket ⌂ .

① What is the capacity of the bucket?

Answer: The capacity is _____ L.

② How much water can 5 jugs hold?

Answer: _____

③ How much water can fill 3 buckets?

Answer: _____

④ How much water can fill 1 jug and 1 bucket?

Answer: _____

⑤ How many millilitres of water can 2 jugs hold?

Answer: _____

⑥ Which hold more, 2 buckets or 5 jugs?

Answer: _____

⑦ Jane fills 3 buckets with water. How many jugs can she fill with the same amount of water?

Answer: _____

Use the pictures to find how much water each container can hold and answer the questions. Show your work.

Containers	Capacity
⑧ vase	L
⑨ bottle	L
⑩ pot	L

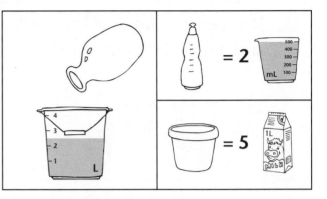

⑪ How much water can 2 vases hold?

Answer: _____

⑫ How much water can 4 bottles hold?

Answer: _____

⑬ How much water can 2 pots hold?

Answer: _____

⑭ How many vases are needed to hold 10 L of water?

Answer: _____

⑮ How many pots are needed to hold 20 L of water?

Answer: _____

⑯ Which container has the greatest capacity?

Answer: _____

⑰ How much greater is the capacity of a pot than that of a vase?

Answer: _____

⑱ How much greater is the capacity of 3 bottles than that of a vase?

Answer: _____

⑲ How many times more water can a pot hold than a vase?

Answer: _____

⑳ How many millilitres of water can a vase hold?

Answer: _____

Decide whether these sentences are about capacity or mass. Write C for capacity and M for mass in the boxes.

㉑ Joan pours 2 glasses of lemonade and has $\frac{1}{2}$ jug of lemonade left.

㉓ When Joan adds 1 cup of juice to her cup, it overflows.

㉒ Joan carries 2 bags in each hand so she can balance.

㉔ Joan can balance on a teeter totter with her 2 baby brothers.

Joan is weighing her books. Answer Joan's questions. Show your work.

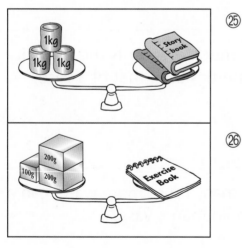

㉕ What is the mass of a story book?

Answer: _____

㉖ What is the mass of an exercise book?

Answer: _____

㉗ How much heavier is a story book than an exercise book?

Answer: _____

㉘ How many exercise books will have about the same mass as a story book?

Answer: _____

ISBN: 978-1-897164-13-6

Look at the pictures and answer the questions.

㉙ Which fruit is lighter than a banana?

Answer: _____ is lighter than a banana.

㉚ Which fruit is heavier than a pineapple?

Answer: _____

㉛ Which fruit is heavier than a banana but lighter than an orange?

Answer: _____

㉜ Put the fruits in order from the heaviest to the lightest.

Answer: _____

CHALLENGE

Joan makes about 250 mL of orange juice with 3 oranges. The mass of 3 oranges is about 1 kg.

① If Joan wants to make 1 L of orange juice, how many oranges does she need?

Answer: _____

② To make 1 L of orange juice, how many kilograms of oranges does she need?

Answer: _____

EXAMPLE

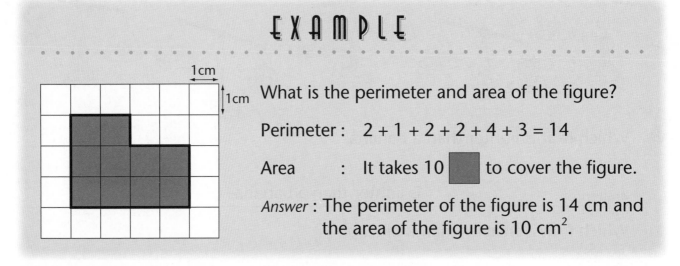

What is the perimeter and area of the figure?

Perimeter : 2 + 1 + 2 + 2 + 4 + 3 = 14

Area : It takes 10 ☐ to cover the figure.

Answer : The perimeter of the figure is 14 cm and the area of the figure is 10 cm².

Use the table below to answer the questions.

Pencil	A	B	C	D	E
Length (cm)	5	3	8	12	15

① Which pencil is the longest?

Answer: Pencil _____ is the longest.

② Which pencil is the shortest?

Answer: _____

③ How much longer is pencil C than pencil A?

Answer: _____

④ How much shorter is pencil B than pencil E?

Answer: _____

⑤ If Jill's pencils get shorter by 1cm each week, how long will it take for pencil A to be the same length as pencil B?

Answer: _____

⑥ How long will it take for pencil E to be the same length as pencil C?

Answer: _____

⑦ If Jill uses pencil D for 7 weeks, how long will it be?

Answer: _____

ISBN: 978-1-897164-13-6

Find the perimeter of each shape by ruler and answer the questions.

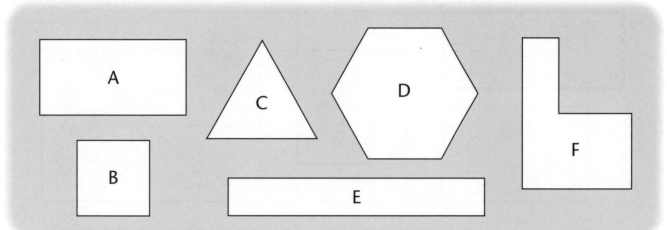

⑧

Shape	A	B	C	D	E	F
Perimeter (cm)						

⑨ Which shape has the greatest perimeter?

Answer: _____

⑩ Which shape has the smallest perimeter?

Answer: _____

⑪ Which two of the shapes have the same perimeter?

Answer: _____

⑫ How much greater is the perimeter of F than that of C?

Answer: _____

⑬ How many times is the perimeter of E greater than that of B?

Answer: _____

⑭ Which shape has a greater perimeter than A, but smaller than E?

Answer: _____

Find the area of each sticker and answer the questions.

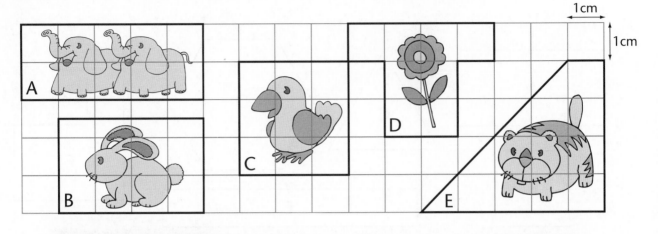

⑮

Sticker	A	B	C	D	E
Area (cm²)					

⑯ Which sticker has the greatest area?

Answer: _____

⑰ Which sticker has the smallest area?

Answer: _____

- 2 ◸ equal to 1 ■   ← Read this first.
  ◸ + ◹ = ■
- 2 ▬ equal to 1 ■
  ▬ + ▬ = ■

⑱ How much smaller is the area of C than that of E?

Answer: _____

⑲ How much greater is the area of B than that of D?

Answer: _____

⑳ Which sticker has a greater area than D, but smaller than A?

Answer: _____

㉑ How many A stickers are needed to cover a piece of paper 4 cm wide and 5 cm long?

Answer: _____

ISBN: 978-1-897164-13-6

Joan has drawn these shapes on her grid paper. Answer the questions.

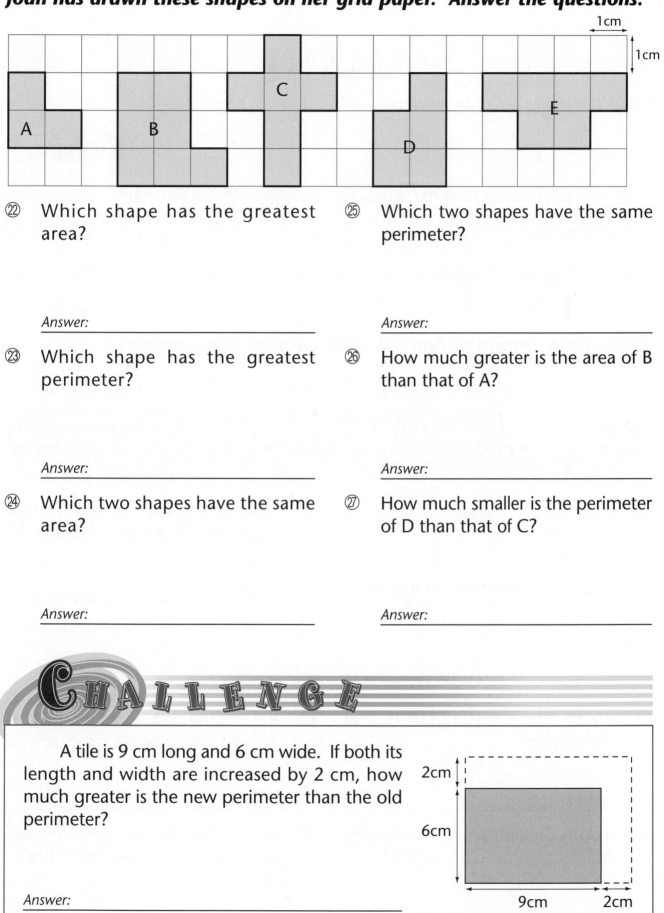

22) Which shape has the greatest area?

Answer: _____

23) Which shape has the greatest perimeter?

Answer: _____

24) Which two shapes have the same area?

Answer: _____

25) Which two shapes have the same perimeter?

Answer: _____

26) How much greater is the area of B than that of A?

Answer: _____

27) How much smaller is the perimeter of D than that of C?

Answer: _____

CHALLENGE

A tile is 9 cm long and 6 cm wide. If both its length and width are increased by 2 cm, how much greater is the new perimeter than the old perimeter?

Answer: _____

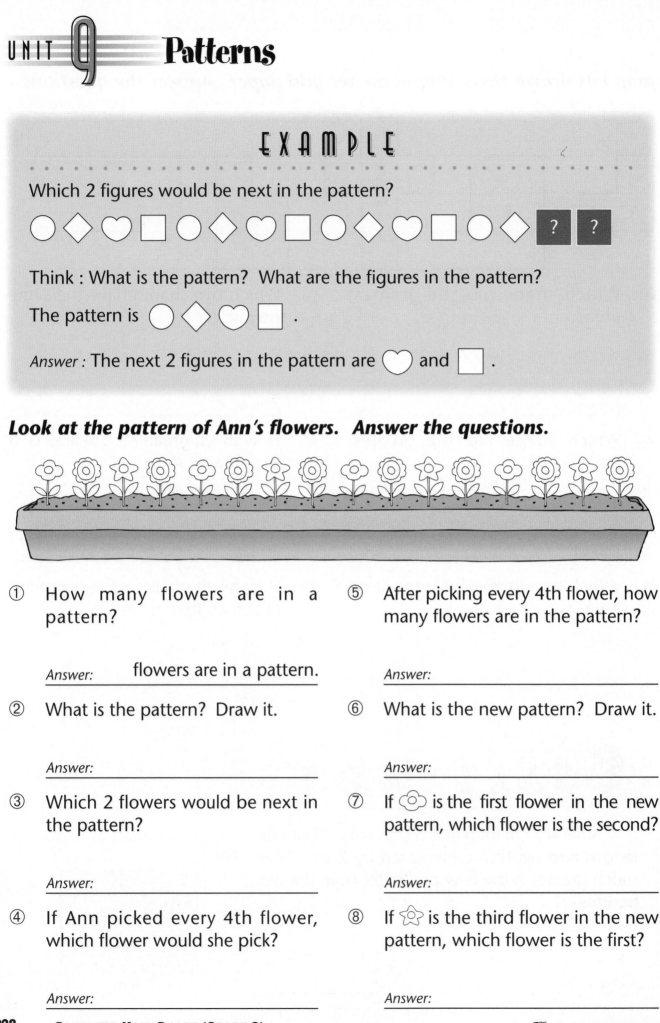

EXAMPLE

Which 2 figures would be next in the pattern?

Think : What is the pattern? What are the figures in the pattern?

The pattern is ⬤ ◇ ♡ ☐ .

Answer : The next 2 figures in the pattern are ♡ and ☐ .

Look at the pattern of Ann's flowers. Answer the questions.

① How many flowers are in a pattern?

Answer: _____ flowers are in a pattern.

② What is the pattern? Draw it.

Answer: _____

③ Which 2 flowers would be next in the pattern?

Answer: _____

④ If Ann picked every 4th flower, which flower would she pick?

Answer: _____

⑤ After picking every 4th flower, how many flowers are in the pattern?

Answer: _____

⑥ What is the new pattern? Draw it.

Answer: _____

⑦ If 🌼 is the first flower in the new pattern, which flower is the second?

Answer: _____

⑧ If ✿ is the third flower in the new pattern, which flower is the first?

Answer: _____

ISBN: 978-1-897164-13-6

Look at the table showing how tall Ann's flowers have grown. Answer the questions.

Flower	Week 1	Week 2	Week 3	Week 4
✿	5 cm	10 cm	15 cm	20 cm
❁	2 cm	4 cm	6 cm	8 cm
✪	4 cm	8 cm	12 cm	16 cm

⑨ Describe the growing pattern of ✿.

Answer: It grows _____ every week.

⑩ Find the height of ✿ in week 6.

Answer: _____

⑪ Describe the growing pattern of ❁.

Answer: _____

⑫ Find the height of ❁ in week 6.

Answer: _____

⑬ Describe the growing pattern of ✪.

Answer: _____

⑭ Find the height of ✪ in week 6.

Answer: _____

⑮ How long will ✿ take to reach a height of 35 cm?

Answer: _____

⑯ How long will ❁ take to reach a height of 12 cm?

Answer: _____

⑰ How long will ✪ take to reach a height of 28 cm?

Answer: _____

Ann and Joan are building towers with blocks. Follow each pattern to add the next set of blocks.

Tower	Step 1	Step 2	Step 3	Step 4
⑱ A				
⑲ B				
⑳ C				

㉑ Complete the chart to show the number of blocks used to build each step of tower A.

4	6	8					

㉒ How many blocks are used in the 10th step to build tower A?

Answer: _____

㉓ Complete the chart to show the number of blocks used to build each step of tower B.

1	4	9					

㉔ How many blocks are used in the 10th step to build tower B?

Answer: _____

㉕ Complete the chart to show the number of blocks used to build each step of tower C.

1	3	6					

㉖ How many blocks are used in the 10th step to build tower C?

Answer: _____

ISBN: 978-1-897164-13-6

Solve the problems. Show your work.

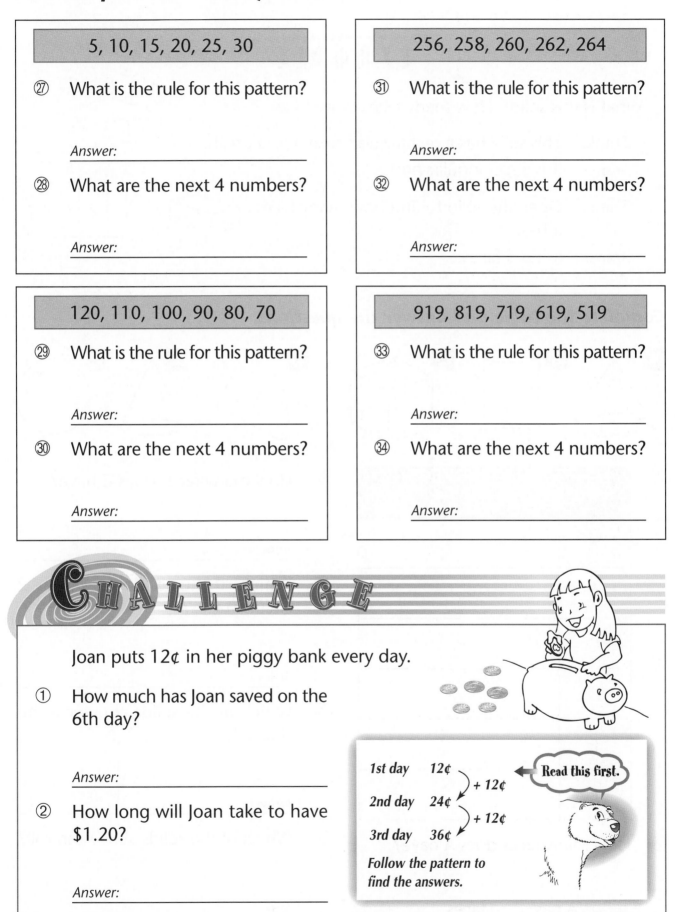

5, 10, 15, 20, 25, 30

㉗ What is the rule for this pattern?

Answer: _____

㉘ What are the next 4 numbers?

Answer: _____

256, 258, 260, 262, 264

㉛ What is the rule for this pattern?

Answer: _____

㉜ What are the next 4 numbers?

Answer: _____

120, 110, 100, 90, 80, 70

㉙ What is the rule for this pattern?

Answer: _____

㉚ What are the next 4 numbers?

Answer: _____

919, 819, 719, 619, 519

㉝ What is the rule for this pattern?

Answer: _____

㉞ What are the next 4 numbers?

Answer: _____

CHALLENGE

Joan puts 12¢ in her piggy bank every day.

① How much has Joan saved on the 6th day?

Answer: _____

② How long will Joan take to have $1.20?

Answer: _____

Read this first.

1st day   12¢
2nd day   24¢   + 12¢
3rd day   36¢   + 12¢

Follow the pattern to find the answers.

ISBN: 978-1-897164-13-6

EXAMPLE

What is this solid? How many faces does it have?

Think: This solid has a rectangular base. It is a prism.

Answer : It is a rectangular prism.

Think: Open the solid to find how many faces it has.

Answer : It has 6 faces.

open →

	5		
1	2	3	4
	6		

Complete the table and answer the questions.

A 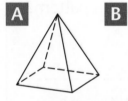 B C 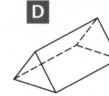 D 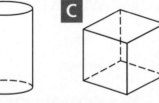 E 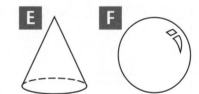 F

①

Solid	Name
A	
B	
C	
D	
E	
F	

② How many faces does A have?

Answer: A has _____ faces.

③ How many faces does C have?

Answer : _____

④ Which of the solids above has 2 circular faces?

Answer : _____

⑤ Which of the solids above can be stacked?

Answer : _____

⑥ Which of the solids above can roll?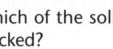

Answer : _____

ISBN: 978-1-897164-13-6

Complete the table and answer the questions.

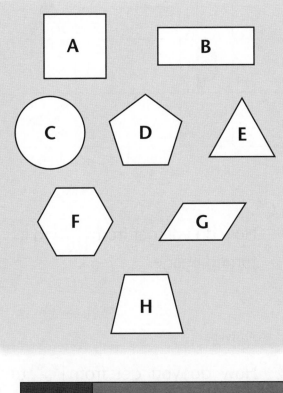

⑦

Shape	Name
A	
B	
C	
D	
E	
F	
G	
H	

⑧ Which of the shapes above has 3 sides?

Answer : _____ has 3 sides.

⑨ Which of the shapes have 4 sides?

Answer : _____

⑩ Which of the shapes have 4 equal sides?

Answer : _____

⑪ How many vertices does F have?

Answer : _____

⑫ How many lines of symmetry are there in a square?

Answer : _____

⑬ How many lines of symmetry are there in a rectangle?

Answer : _____

⑭ Which of the shapes is the top view of a cylinder?

Answer : _____

⑮ If the side view of a triangular prism is B, which one of the shapes is its top view?

Answer : _____

ISBN: 978-1-897164-13-6

Use the grid to answer the questions.

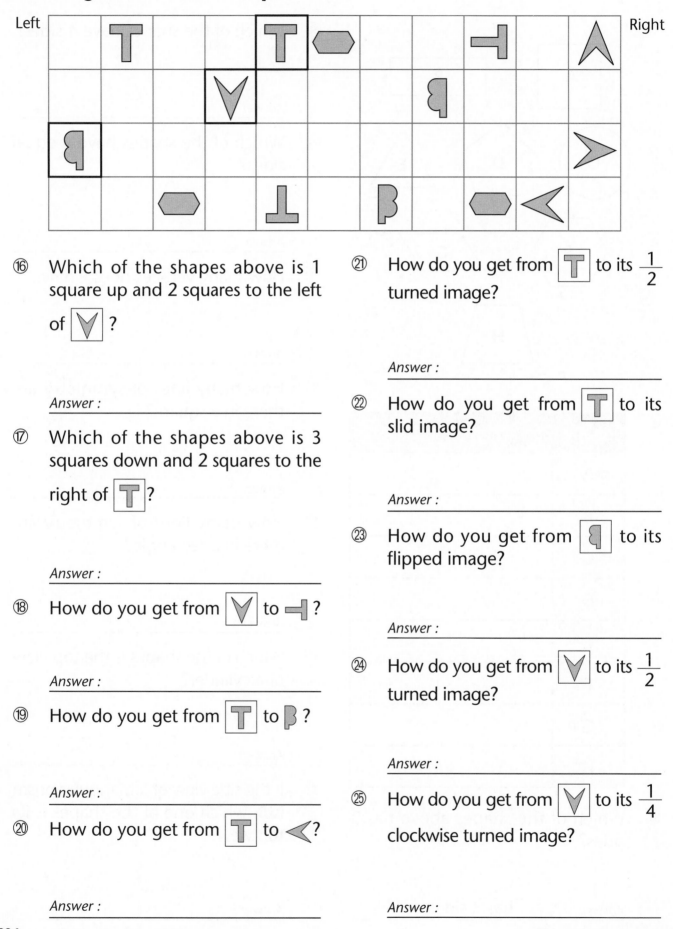

Left   Right

⑯ Which of the shapes above is 1 square up and 2 squares to the left of ⋁ ?

Answer : _____

⑰ Which of the shapes above is 3 squares down and 2 squares to the right of ⊤ ?

Answer : _____

⑱ How do you get from ⋁ to ⊣ ?

Answer : _____

⑲ How do you get from ⊤ to ß ?

Answer : _____

⑳ How do you get from ⊤ to ＜?

Answer : _____

㉑ How do you get from ⊤ to its $\frac{1}{2}$ turned image?

Answer : _____

㉒ How do you get from ⊤ to its slid image?

Answer : _____

㉓ How do you get from ¶ to its flipped image?

Answer : _____

㉔ How do you get from ⋁ to its $\frac{1}{2}$ turned image?

Answer : _____

㉕ How do you get from ⋁ to its $\frac{1}{4}$ clockwise turned image?

Answer : _____

ISBN: 978-1-897164-13-6

㉖ Which of these shapes are symmetrical : ⬡ , ⊤ , ▯ and ∨ ?

Answer : _____

㉗ How many lines of symmetry does ⬡ have?

Answer : _____

㉘ How many lines of symmetry does ⊤ have?

Answer : _____

㉙ How many lines of symmetry does ∨ have?

Answer : _____

㉚ Is ⬡ similar or congruent to ⬡ ?

Answer: _____

㉛ Is ⊤ similar or congruent to ⊥ ?

Answer : _____

㉜ Is ▯ similar or congruent to ▯ ?

Answer : _____

> **Read this first.**
>
> A B C
>
> - **Congruent figures have the same size and shape, e.g. A is congruent to C.**
> - **Similar figures have the same shape, but not the same size, e.g. B is similar to C.**

CHALLENGE

① Jill has the same number of triangles as squares. There are 21 sides altogether. How many does Jill have of each?

Answer : _____

② How many lines of symmetry does a circle have?

Answer : _____

ISBN: 978-1-897164-13-6

EXAMPLE

This graph shows how many marbles Joan has.

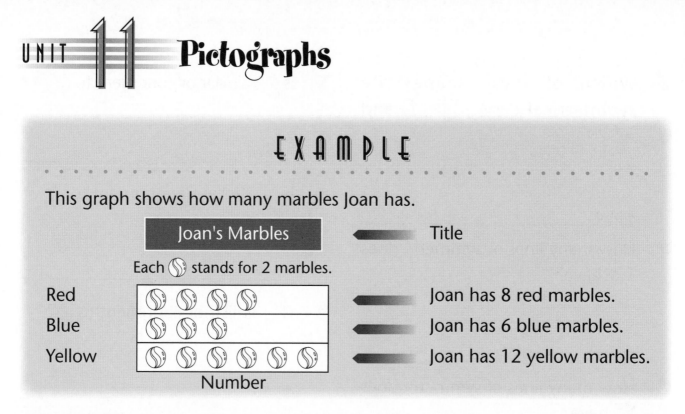

The graph shows the number of vehicles parked at the Pizza King parking lot yesterday. Use the pictograph to answer the questions.

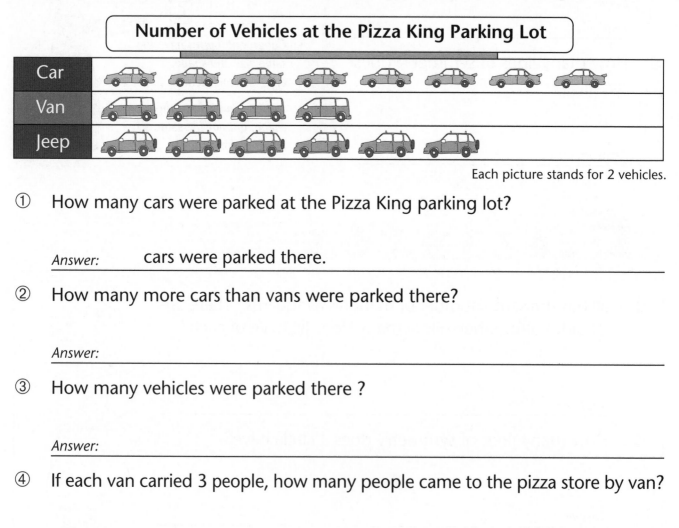

Each picture stands for 2 vehicles.

① How many cars were parked at the Pizza King parking lot?

Answer: _____ cars were parked there.

② How many more cars than vans were parked there?

Answer: _____

③ How many vehicles were parked there ?

Answer: _____

④ If each van carried 3 people, how many people came to the pizza store by van?

Answer: _____

The graph shows the number of pizzas ordered yesterday. Use the pictograph to answer the questions.

Number of Pizzas Ordered	
Small	🍕 🍕 🍕 🍕 🍕 🍕
Medium	🍕 🍕 🍕 🍕 🍕 🍕 🍕 🍕 🍕
Large	🍕 🍕 🍕 🍕 🍕

Each pizza stands for 2 orders.

⑤ What is the title of this pictograph?

Answer: _____

⑥ How many sizes are there?

Answer: _____

⑦ How many order(s) does 🍕 stand for?

Answer: _____

⑧ How many small pizzas were ordered?

Answer: _____

⑨ How many more medium pizzas were ordered than large pizzas?

Answer: _____

⑩ How many pizzas were ordered in all?

Answer: _____

CHALLENGE

Colour the pictograph to show the number of pizzas ordered.

Kind	No. of Pizzas
Pepperoni	~~||||~~ ||
Vegetarian	~~||||~~ ||||
Hawaiian	||||

No. of Pizzas Ordered	🍕 = 2 orders
Pepperoni	🍕 🍕 🍕 🍕 🍕
Vegetarian	🍕 🍕 🍕 🍕 🍕
Hawaiian	🍕 🍕 🍕 🍕 🍕

ISBN: 978-1-897164-13-6

EXAMPLE

The graph shows the number of stickers collected by the children.

Here are the points to remember :
- Write the title.
- Label the two axes.
- Write the scale.
- Draw the bars with the same width.

The owner of Pizza King used a bar graph to show customers' choice of one-topping pizzas last week. Use his bar graph to answer the questions.

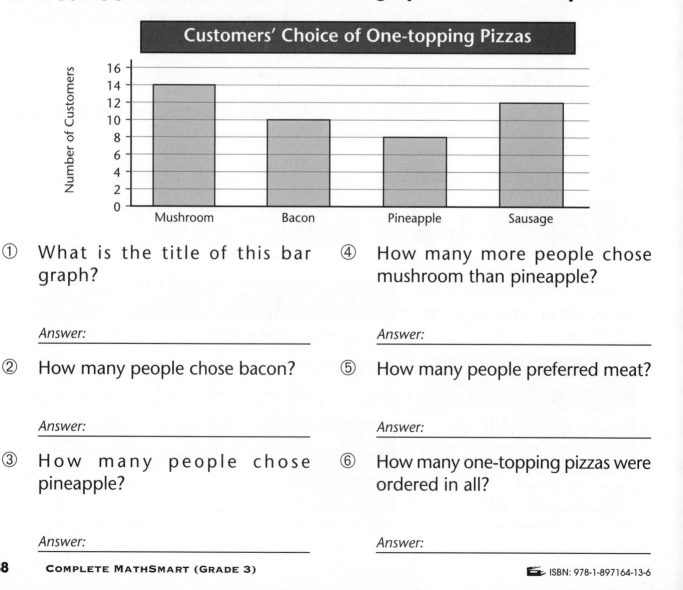

① What is the title of this bar graph?

Answer: _____

② How many people chose bacon?

Answer: _____

③ How many people chose pineapple?

Answer: _____

④ How many more people chose mushroom than pineapple?

Answer: _____

⑤ How many people preferred meat?

Answer: _____

⑥ How many one-topping pizzas were ordered in all?

Answer: _____

ISBN: 978-1-897164-13-6

Joan asked her friends how many crackers they had for snack yesterday. Use the information below to complete the bar graph and answer the questions.

	Paul	Gary	Lesley	Irene
⑦ Number of crackers	⊞⊞	⊞ I	⊞ ⊞ II	⊞ III

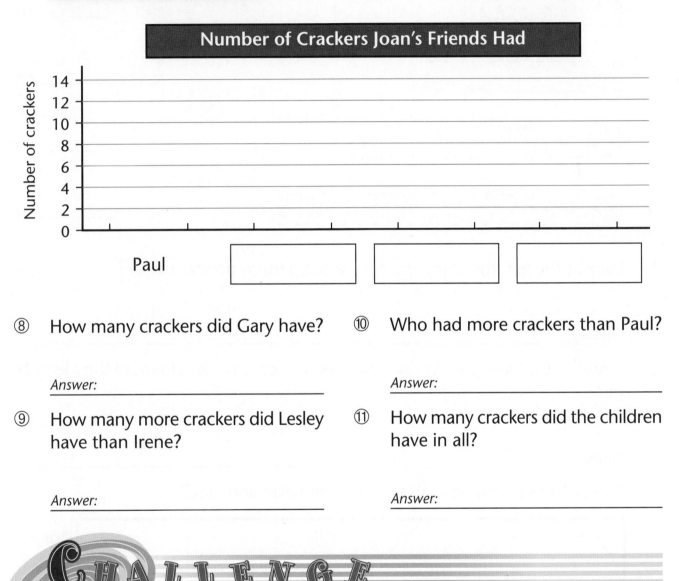

Number of Crackers Joan's Friends Had

Number of crackers

Paul

⑧ How many crackers did Gary have?

Answer: _____

⑨ How many more crackers did Lesley have than Irene?

Answer: _____

⑩ Who had more crackers than Paul?

Answer: _____

⑪ How many crackers did the children have in all?

Answer: _____

CHALLENGE

Joan had more crackers than Gary but fewer than Irene. How many crackers did she have? Explain.

Answer: _____

ISBN: 978-1-897164-13-6

Ann has 5 pencils. Help her measure the length of each pencil to the nearest centimetre.

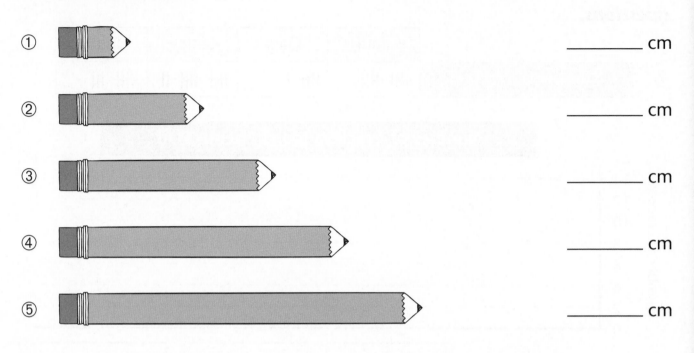

① _____ cm

② _____ cm

③ _____ cm

④ _____ cm

⑤ _____ cm

⑥ Look at the lengths of the pencils. What pattern do you notice?

Answer : _____

⑦ If Ann got 2 more pencils that followed the pattern, what would their lengths be?

Answer : _____

⑧ This is Ann's pencil box. What is its perimeter and area?

1cm

1cm

Answer : _____

ISBN: 978-1-897164-13-6

Look at Ann's birthday gifts. Then check ✓ the side of each scale that would tip down.

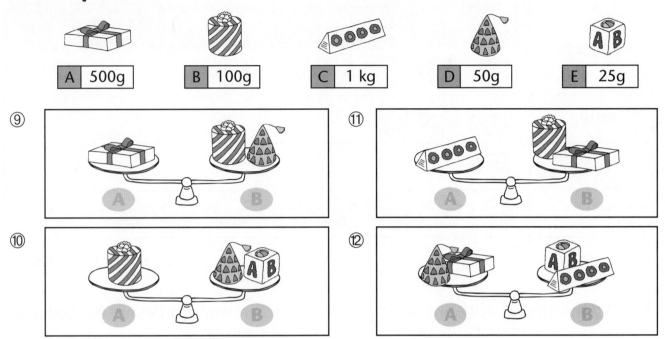

Look at Ann's birthday gifts again and answer the questions.

⑬ What is the shape of gift B? How many faces does it have?

Answer : _____

⑭ What is the shape of gift C? How many faces does it have?

Answer : _____

⑮ What is the shape of gift E? How many faces does it have?

Answer : _____

⑯ John says, 'The gift I bought for Ann can roll and its two ends are flat.' Which gift did John buy for Ann?

Answer : _____

⑰ Katie says, 'The gift I bought for Ann cannot roll and it has 5 faces.' Which gift did Katie buy for Ann?

Answer : _____

Use the pictograph to answer the questions.

	Capacity of Containers
Jug	🍵 🍵 🍵 🍵 🍵 🍵
Bottle	🍵 🍵 🍵
Glass	🍵
Vase	🍵 🍵 🍵 🍵 🍵 🍵 🍵 🍵

Each 🍵 holds 500 mL

⑱ What is the capacity of a jug?

Answer : _____

⑲ What is the capacity of a vase?

Answer : _____

⑳ How many millilitres are there in a litre?

Answer : _____

㉑ Which container has a capacity of less than 1 L?

Answer : _____

㉒ How many times is the capacity of a jug more than that of a bottle?

Answer : _____

㉓ How many bottles are needed to fill 3 L of juice?

Answer : _____

㉔ Which hold more, 2 bottles or 5 glasses?

Answer : _____

㉕ 2 jugs can fill a bucket. What is the capacity of a bucket?

Answer : _____

㉖ 4 bowls can fill a vase. What is the capacity of a bowl?

Answer : _____

ISBN: 978-1-897164-13-6

Use the information below to complete the bar graph and answer the questions.

	Joan	Jane	Katie	George	David
Number of glasses of water	50	45	60	55	40

㉗

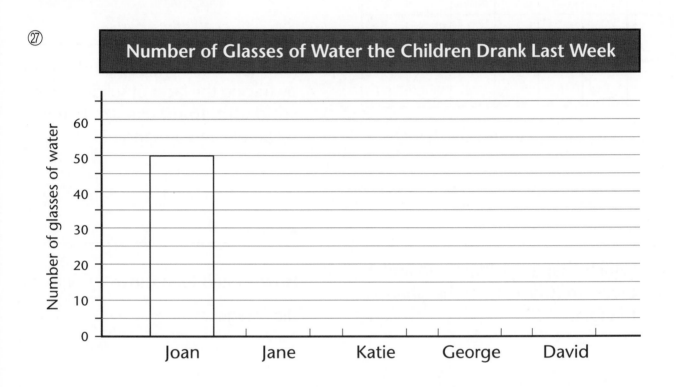

㉘ How many more glasses of water did George drink than David?

Answer : _____

㉙ If 6 glasses of water can fill a bottle, how many bottles of water did Katie drink?

Answer : _____

㉚ How many glasses of water did the children drink in all?

Answer : _____

㉛ What fraction of the total number of glasses of water did Joan drink?

Answer : _____

ISBN: 978-1-897164-13-6

Look at the grid and answer the questions.

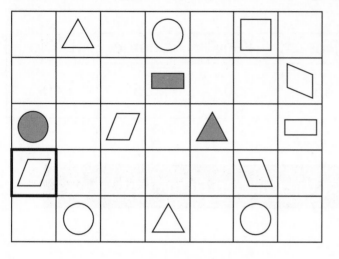

㉜ How many triangles are there?

Answer : _____

㉝ Which shape is 2 blocks up and 1 block to the left of the shaded triangle?

Answer : _____

㉞ Which shape is 1 block up and 2 blocks to the right of the shaded rectangle?

Answer : _____

㉟ How do you move from the shaded triangle to another triangle which is the farthest?

Answer : _____

㊱ How do you move from the shaded circle to another circle which is the closest?

Answer : _____

㊲ Joan drew the shapes on the grid by tracing the faces of solids. Which solid did Joan use to trace a rectangle and a triangle?

Answer : _____

㊳ How should Joan move ⬜ to its slid image?

Answer : _____

㊴ How should she move ⬜ to its flipped image?

Answer : _____

㊵ How should she move ⬜ to its $\frac{1}{4}$ anti-clockwise turned image?

Answer : _____

ISBN: 978-1-897164-13-6

1. Addition and Subtraction

↪ Children learn to add or subtract 3-digit whole numbers.

↪ To do addition,

1st   align the numbers on the right-hand side.

2nd add numbers from right to left (starting with the ones place).

3rd   carry groups of 10 from one column to the next column.

Example

Align the numbers.	Add the ones; then carry 1 ten to the tens column.	Add the tens; then carry 1 hundred to the hundreds column.	Add the hundreds.
3 4 7 + 5 9	1 3 4 7 + 5 9 6 ↑ 7 + 9 = 16	1 1 3 4 7 + 5 9 0 6 ↑ 1 + 4 + 5 = 10	1 3 4 7 + 5 9 4 0 6 ↑ 1 + 3 = 4

347 + 59 = 406

↪ To do subtraction,

1st   align the numbers on the right-hand side.

2nd subtract the number from right to left (starting with the ones place).

3rd   if the number is too small to subtract, borrow 1 from the column on the left.

Example

Align the numbers.	Borrow 1 ten from the tens column; subtract the ones.	Borrow 1 hundred from the hundreds column; subtract the tens.	Subtract the hundreds.
4 1 2 – 6 8	0 12 4 1 2 – 6 8 4 ↑ 12 – 8 = 4	3 10 4 1 2 – 6 8 4 4 ↑ 10 – 6 = 4	3 4 1 2 – 6 8 3 4 4

412 – 68 = 344

2. Multiplication

↪ Children should understand that multiplication is repeated addition and be familiar with multiplying 1-digit whole numbers.

They should know that:

a. the product of two even numbers is even.

    Example $2 \times 8 = 16$

b. the product of an even number and an odd number is even.

    Example $4 \times 7 = 28$

c. the product of two odd numbers is odd.

    Example $3 \times 9 = 27$

d. the product of any number multiplied by 5 has 0 or 5 at the ones place.

    Example $4 \times 5 = 20$

ISBN: 978-1-897164-13-6

- Even if the order of multiplication changes, the product remains the same.

  Example $6 \times 7 = 7 \times 6 = 42$

- When multiplying a 2-digit number by a 1-digit number, first multiply the ones, and then multiply the tens. Remember to carry if necessary.

  Example

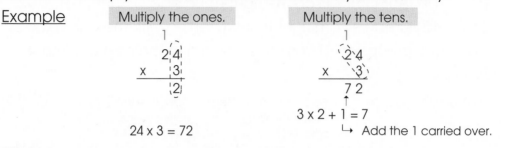

| Multiply the ones. | Multiply the tens. |

$$24 \times 3 = 72 \qquad 3 \times 2 + 1 = 7$$

Add the 1 carried over.

3. Division

- Children should understand that division is the opposite of multiplication. They can recall the multiplication facts to do division. To do division, they should multiply the divisor by a number to get a product closest to the dividend. They can take the following steps to do division.

  | 1st Divide | 2nd Multiply | 3rd Subtract | 4th Bring down |

- When the dividend is smaller than the divisor, put 0 in the quotient.

  Example

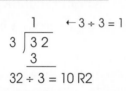

  Divide the tens.

  $$\begin{array}{r} 1 \\ 3\ \overline{\smash{)}32} \\ 3 \\ \hline \end{array}$$ ← $3 \div 3 = 1$

  $32 \div 3 = 10\ \text{R}2$

  Divide the ones.

  $$\begin{array}{r} 10 \\ 3\ \overline{\smash{)}32} \\ 3 \\ \hline 2 \end{array}$$ ← Dividend 2 is smaller than the divisor 3. Put 0 in the quotient.

4. Mixed Operations

- When an expression involves several operations, it must be done in the following order:

  1st   do multiplication and division from left to right.

  2nd do addition and subtraction from left to right.

  Example $30 - 5 \times 2 = 30 - 10$ ← First, do the multiplication (5×2).

  $\qquad\qquad\qquad = 20$ ← Then do the subtraction ($30 - 10$).

5. Measurement

- Children learn to use centimetres, metres or kilometres in measuring lengths and distances. They need to know how to calculate the perimeters and areas of 2-dimensional figures and write them out using appropriate units.

- When the dimensions of a figure are not in the same unit, children should change them to the same unit before doing any calculation.

  Example

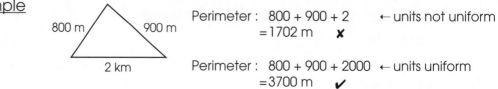

  Perimeter : $800 + 900 + 2$ ← units not uniform
  $\qquad\qquad\ = 1702\ \text{m}$ ✗

  Perimeter : $800 + 900 + 2000$ ← units uniform
  $\qquad\qquad\ = 3700\ \text{m}$ ✔

   ISBN: 978-1-897164-13-6

6. Time

↦ Children learn to estimate and measure the passage of time in five-minute intervals, and in days, weeks, months and years. They also learn how to tell and write time to the nearest minute using analog and digital clocks. Parents should give children daily practice to consolidate their knowledge of time.

Example

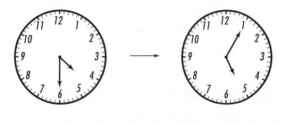

Duration : 35 minutes

7. Capacity

↦ In using standard units such as millilitre or litre to measure and record capacity of containers, children should know that the capacity of a 10-cm cube is 1 litre. Encourage children to make observations of different kinds of containers and let them recognize how much 1-litre is.

8. Shapes

↦ Children investigate the similarities and differences among a variety of prisms or pyramids using concrete materials and drawings. They also learn to name and describe prisms and pyramids by the shapes of their bases or ends. Parents should remind their children that prisms and pyramids are named by the shapes of the ends or bases.

Example

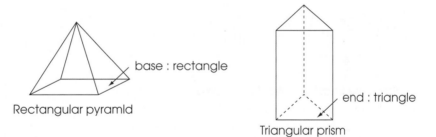

base : rectangle

Rectangular pyramid

end : triangle

Triangular prism

9. Transformations

↦ Children learn to draw the lines of symmetry in 2-dimensional shapes and identify transformations, such as flips, slides and turns, using concrete materials and drawings. Rotations are limited to quarter turn, half turn and three-quarter turn only.

Example

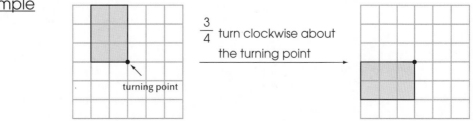

$\frac{3}{4}$ turn clockwise about the turning point

turning point

ISBN: 978-1-897164-13-6

10. Coordinate Geometry

↝ Children learn to describe how to get from one point to another on a grid and the location of a point on a grid as an ordered pair of numbers. Through games and activities, children can learn this topic effectively.

<u>Example</u>

The ☆ is in the square (3 , 2).

↑ ↑
horizontal number vertical number

11. Bar Graphs and Circle Graphs

↝ At this stage, children should know the quantity represented by each picture on a graph with many-to-one correspondence. They should also know how to use scales with multiples of 2,5 or 10, and interpret data and draw conclusions from the graphs. At this stage, children do not need to construct circle graphs, but they should be able to interpret them.

<u>Examples</u>

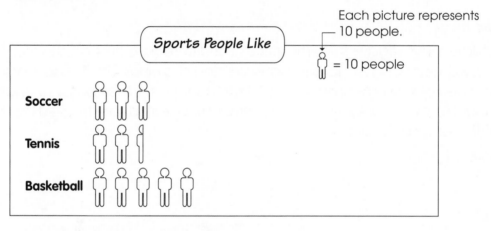

Each picture represents 10 people.

Sports People Like

Soccer

Tennis

Basketball

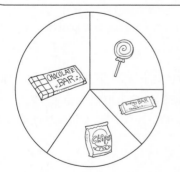

Favourite Snacks in Mrs Vann's Class

The most popular snack is chocolate.
A quarter of the students like lollipops.

ISBN: 978-1-897164-13-6

1 Addition and Subtraction

1. Cedarbrae School
2. Brownsville School
3. 1050 − 426 = 624 ; 624
4. 1025 − 50 = 975 ; 975
5. 1330 + 50 = 1380 ; 1380
6. 1040 − 250 = 790 ; 790
7. 1245 − 319 = 926 ; 926
8. 582 + 1429 = 2011 ; 2011
9. 394 + 1066 = 1460 ; 1460
10. 1325 + 849 = 2174 ; 2174
11. 582 + 394 + 1325 = 2301 ; 2301
12. 1429 + 1066 + 849 = 3344 ; 3344
13. 3344 − 2301 = 1043 ; 1043
14. 3579
15. 3600
16. 4110
17. 4820
18. 3718
19. 3800
20. 1020
21. 3792
22. 4244
23. 3769
24. 892
25. 1855
26. 2778
27. 4002
28. 2439
29. 3021
30. 1978
31. 1144
32. Math is such fun!
33. 3590 + 2945 = 6535 ; 6535
34. 1782 + 2595 = 4377 ; 4377
35. 2595 − 1782 = 813 ; 813
36. 2945 − 1827 = 1118 ; 1118
37. 3590 + 260 = 3850 ; 3850
38. 1782 − 290 = 1492 ; 1492

2 4-digit Numbers

1. 3268
2. 1986
3. 2371
4. 5734
5. 5734 ; 3268 ; 2371 ; 1986
6. 6541
7. 3068
8. 9523
9. 1274
10. Two thousand three hundred forty-one
11. Four thousand one hundred two
12. Seven thousand nine
13. 1200
14. 2050
15. 3400
16. 2025

17. 3
18. 9
19. 3
20. 9 big jars, 3 medium jars and 8 small jars.

3 Multiplication

1a. 3 ; 6 ; 9 ; 12 ; 15 ; 18
 b. 6
 c. 6 ; 18
2a. 4 ; 8 ; 12 ; 16 ; 20 ; 24 ; 28
 b. 7
 c. 7; 28
3a. 8 ; 16 ; 24 ; 32 ; 40 ; 48
 b. 6
 c. 6 ; 48
4a. 7 ; 14 ; 21 ; 28 ; 35
 b. 5
 c. 5 ; 35
5a. 2 ; 4 ; 6 ; 8 ; 10 ; 12 ; 14 ; 16
 b. 8
 c. 8 ; 16
6. B ; D ; 18
7. B ; C ; 20
8. A ; D ; 28
9. B ; D ; 27
10. A ; B ; 12
11. B ; C ; 24
12a. 8 ; 64
 b. 2 ; 16
13a. 2 ; 18
 b. 5 ; 45
14a. 3 ; 18
 b. 6 ; 36
15a. 4 ; 12
 b. 3 ; 9
16a. 4 ; 28
 b. 2 ; 14
17. 3 x 6 = 18 ; 18
18. 4 x 8 = 32 ; 32
19. 5 x 5 = 25 ; 25
20. 7 x 8 = 56 ; 56
21. 5 x 9 = 45 ; 45

4 Division

1a. 3 b. 3 2a. 2 b. 2
3a. 4 b. 4 4a. 7 b. 7
5a. 3 b. 3 6a. 3 b. 3
7. 9
8.

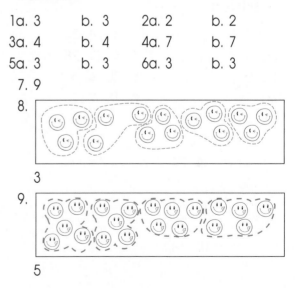

3

9.

5

10.

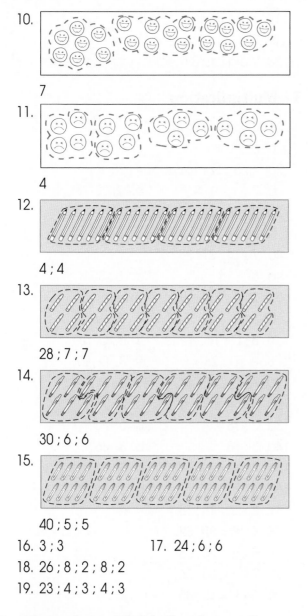

7

11.

4

12.

4 ; 4

13.

28 ; 7 ; 7

14.

30 ; 6 ; 6

15.

40 ; 5 ; 5

16. 3 ; 3   17. 24 ; 6 ; 6
18. 26 ; 8 ; 2 ; 8 ; 2
19. 23 ; 4 ; 3 ; 4 ; 3

5 More about Multiplication and Division

1a. 3 ; 8   b. 3 ; 24 ; 24
2a. 4 ; 7   b. 4 ; 28 ; 28
3a. 20   b. 20 ; 4 ; 4
4a. 18   b. 18 ; 2 ; 2
 5. 48 ÷ 8 = 6 ; 6
 6. 3 x 9 = 27 ; 27
 7. 8 x 3 = 24 ; 24
 8. 36 ÷ 4 = 9 ; 9
 9. 6 x 7 = 42 ; 42
10. 25 ÷ 5 = 5 ; 5
11. 3 x 6 = 18 ; 18

Midway Review

 1. 1171 ; 1172 ; 1174
 2. 2788 ; 2888 ; 3088
 3. 8214 ; 6214 ; 4214
 4. 4014 ; 4010 ; 4006
 5. 3   6. 3947
 7. 5068   8. 8373
 9. 2   10. 9263
11. 7483
12. Eight thousand three hundred seventy-three
13. Eight hundred ninety
14.

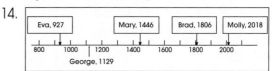

15. 927 + 2018 = 2945 ; 2945
16. 2018 − 927 = 1091 ; 1091
17. 1806 + 1446 = 3252 ; 3252
18. 1806 − 1446 = 360 ; 360
19. 1806 + 1129 = 2935 ; 2935
20. 927 + 2018 + 1446 = 4391 ; 4391
21a. 6 ; 18 ; 18   b. 24 ; 8 ; 8
22a. 5 ; 35 ; 35   b. 28 ; 4 ; 4
23a. 3 ; 27 ; 27   b. 18 ; 2 ; 2
24a. 12   b. 12
  c. 4   d. 6
25a. 18   b. 18
  c. 9   d. 3
26a. 24   b. 24
  c. 3   d. 4
27. 8 ; 4 ; 4   28. 9 ; 54 ; 54
29. 63 ; 9 ; 9   30. 4 ; 36 ; 36

6 Money

1a.

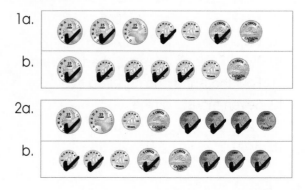

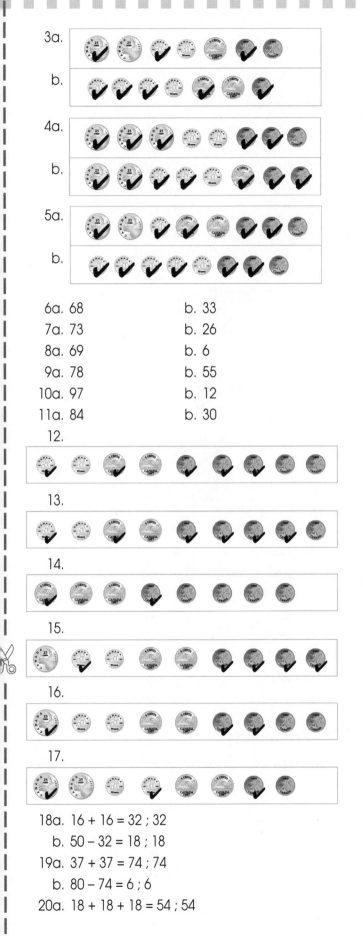

3a.

b.

4a.

b.

5a.

b.

6a. 68   b. 33
7a. 73   b. 26
8a. 69   b. 6
9a. 78   b. 55
10a. 97   b. 12
11a. 84   b. 30

12.

13.

14.

15.

16.

17.

18a. 16 + 16 = 32 ; 32
  b. 50 − 32 = 18 ; 18
19a. 37 + 37 = 74 ; 74
  b. 80 − 74 = 6 ; 6
20a. 18 + 18 + 18 = 54 ; 54

b. 100 − 54 = 46 ; 46
21a. 29 + 29 + 29 = 87 ; 87
  b. 100 − 87 = 13 ; 13

7 Measurement

1.   2.

3. metre   4. hour
5. minute   6. 60
7. 24   8. 15
9. 44   10. 24
11. the flour   12. the cocoa
13. the sugar

14a.

b.

15. 1 hour 30 minutes
16a. 26   b. 22
17. the kitchen

8 Fractions and Decimals

1 – 10. (Suggested answers)

1.   2.

3.   4.

5.   6.

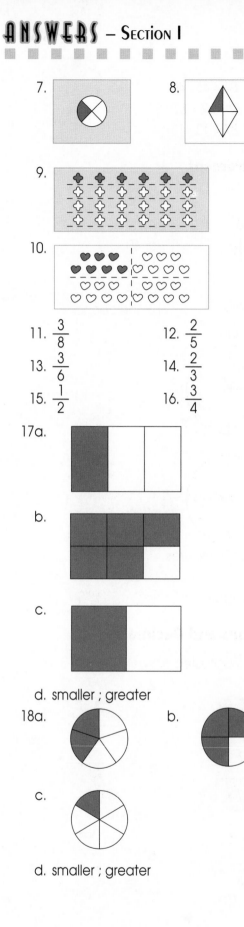

7.

8.

9.

10.

11. $\frac{3}{8}$

12. $\frac{2}{5}$

13. $\frac{3}{6}$

14. $\frac{2}{3}$

15. $\frac{1}{2}$

16. $\frac{3}{4}$

17a.

b.

c.

d. smaller ; greater

18a.

b.

c.

d. smaller ; greater

19. 7

20. $\frac{5}{7}$

21. $\frac{3}{7}$

22. $\frac{4}{7}$

23. $\frac{4}{7}$

24. $\frac{2}{7}$

25. $\frac{1}{7}$

26. 0.3

27. 0.5

28. 0.8

29. 0.8

30. 0.7

31. 0.4

32. 0.5

33. 0.4

34 – 36. (Suggested answers)

34.

35.

36.

37. four

38. seven

39. eight

40. 2.35

41. 2.61

42. less

43. smaller

44. 3.09

45. 3.25

46. less

47. smaller

48. 0.75

49. 2.50

50. 1.75

51. less

52. more

53. smaller

54. greater

9 Probability

1. No

2. 4

3. 5

4. 1

5. 3

6. No

7. 4

8. 5

9. 1

10. B

11. A

12. C

ISBN: 978-1-897164-13-6

13. C   14. B
15. D   16. A

10 Graphs

1. Number of Heads Each Child Got
2. 4   3. 6
4. 3   5. 5
6. Gerrie   7. Iris
8. 2   9. 3
10. Sales of Doughnuts in Doug's Doughnut Shop Yesterday
11. Bar graph   12. 30
13. 50   14. Jellied
15. Sour dough   16. Honey
17. 240
18. 9 ; 6 ; 7 ; 5   19. Swimming
20. Hiking   21. 27
22.

Favourite Summer Activities in Mrs Feler's Class

Favourite Activity									
Swimming	▩	▩	▩	▩	▩	▩	▩	▩	▩
Soccer	▩	▩	▩	▩	▩	▩	▩		
Cycling	▩	▩	▩	▩	▩	▩	▩	▩	
Hiking	▩	▩	▩	▩	▩				
	1	2	3	4	5	6	7	8	9

Number of Children

23.

Students Having Been to Florida

Bar graph — Number of Students: Grade 1 = 8, Grade 2 = 12, Grade 3 = 16, Grade 4 = 14

24. Students Having Been to Florida
25. 3   26. 1
27. 14   28. 5
29. 50

Final Review

1. 67   2. 29
3. 49   4. 32
5a. $100 - 67 = 33$; 33
  b.
6a. $100 - 49 - 32 = 19$; 19
  b.
7a. $100 - 29 - 29 = 42$; 42
  b.
8a.
  b. 34
9a.
  b. 38
10a. 13   b. 9
11. B   12. A
13. 18   14. 5
15. 10   16. 2
17. Time for Homework Yesterday
18. Pictograph
19. 5   20. 13
21. 2
22.

Time for Homework Yesterday

less than half an hour	half an hour	one hour	one and a half hours	two hours

Time Spent

23. $\frac{2}{10}$; 0.2   24. $\frac{6}{10}$; 0.6
25. $\frac{5}{10}$; 0.5   26. $\frac{9}{10}$; 0.9
27. No   28. Red
29. White   30. Yes

31. No

32. Red

33. 11

34. $\frac{4}{11}$

35. $\frac{3}{11}$

36a.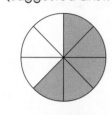

b.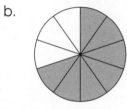

37 (Suggested answers)

a.

b.

38. 4 ; 11 ; 7 ; 14

39. 7

40. 36

41. 92

ISBN: 978-1-897164-13-6

1 Introducing Multiplication

1. 8 ; 8 ; 8
2. 12 , 15 ; 15 ; 15
3. 15 , 20 , 25 , 30 , 35 ; 35 ; 35
4. 12 , 16 , 20 , 24 ; 24 ; 24
5. 2 , 2 , 2 , 2 ; 5 ; 10
6. 4 , 4 , 3 ; 12
7. 5 , 5 , 3 ; 15
8. 6 ; 2 ; 12
9. 5 , 20 ; 5 , 20
10. 3 , 18 ; 3 , 18
11. 2 , 14 ; 2 , 14
12. 8 , 24 ; 8 , 24
13. 2 , 2 , 2 , 2 , 2 ; 6 ; 12
14. 3 , 3 , 3 , 3 ; 5 ; 15
15. 4 , 4 , 4 , 4 ; 5 ; 20
16. 5 , 5 , 3 ; 15
17. 5 ; 5 ; 5 , 45
18. 7 ; 7 ; 7 , 56
19. 4 ; 4 ; 4 , 20
20. 6 ; 6 ; 6 , 18
21. B
22. F
23. D
24. I
25. A
26. G
27. E
28. H
29. C
30. 5 ; 3 ; 5 , 3 ; 5 , 3 ; 15 ; 15

Just for Fun

1. | + || + ||| = |||| or (dashed grouping)
2. ||||| — || — | = ||

2 Multiplying by 2 or 5

1. 1 ; 1 ; 2
2. 2 ; 2 ; 4
3. 3 ; 3 ; 6
4. 4 ; 8
5. 5 ; 10
6. 6 ; 12
7. 7 ; 14
8. 8 ; 16
9. 9 ; 18
10. 2 , 4 , 6 , 8 , 10 , 12 , 14 , 16 , 18
11. 1 ; 1 ; 5
12. 2 ; 2 ; 10
13. 3 ; 3 ; 15
14. 4 ; 4 ; 20
15. 5 ; 5 ; 25
16. 6 ; 6 ; 30
17. 7 ; 7 ; 35
18. 8 ; 8 ; 40
19. 9 ; 9 ; 45
20. 5 , 10 , 15 , 20 , 25 , 30 , 35 , 40 , 45
21. 16
22. 20
23. 35
24. 10
25. 15
26. 12
27. 25
28. 4
29. 8
30. 40
31. 6
32. 10
33. 2
34. 45
35. 30
36. 18
37. 5
38. 14
39. 10
40. 10
41. 6
42. 18
43. 16
44. 25
45. 15
46. 40
47. 8
48. 12
49. 4
50. 14
51. 35
52. 20
53. 5
54. 18
55. 30
56. 2
57. 4 , 5 ; 20 ; 20
$$\begin{array}{r} 5 \\ \times\ 4 \\ \hline 2\,0 \end{array}$$
58. 6 , 2 ; 12 ; 12
$$\begin{array}{r} 2 \\ \times\ 6 \\ \hline 1\,2 \end{array}$$
59. 4 , 2 ; 8 ; 8
$$\begin{array}{r} 2 \\ \times\ 4 \\ \hline 8 \end{array}$$
60. 3 , 5 ; 15 ; 15
$$\begin{array}{r} 5 \\ \times\ 3 \\ \hline 1\,5 \end{array}$$

Just for Fun

9 ; 2 ; 5 ; 4 ; 6 ; 1 ; 7 ; 3 ; 8

3 Multiplying by 3 or 4

2. 2 ; 2 ; 6
3. 3 ; 3 ; 9

4. 4 ; 4 ; 12
5. 5 ; 5 ; 15
6. 6 ; 6 ; 18
7. 7 ; 7 ; 21

8. 8 ; 8 ; 24

9. 3 ; 6 ; 9 ; 12 ; 15 ; 18 ; 21 ; 24 ; 27
10. 4
11. 8 ; 8
12. 12 ; 3 ; 12
13. 16 ; 4 ; 16
14. 20 ; 5 ; 20
15. 24 ; 6 ; 24
16. 28 ; 7 ; 28
17. 32 ; 8 ; 32
18. 36 ; 9 ; 36
19.
8 ; 12 ; 16 ; 20 ; 24 ; 28 ; 32 ; 36 ; 40
20. 15
21. 28
22. 16
23. 9
24. 6
25. 12.
26. 24
27. 32
28. 21
29. 4
30. 12
31. 18
32. 24
33. 36
34. 20
35. 27
36. 3
37. 8
38. 20
39. 24
40. 27
41. 21
42. 9
43. 32
44. 24
45. 36
46. 18
47. 28
48. 16
49. 15
50. 12
51. 3
52. 6
53. 4
54. 12
55. 8
56. 5 , 4 ; 20 ; 20
$$\begin{array}{r} 4 \\ \times\ 5 \\ \hline 2\,0 \end{array}$$
57. 4 , 3 ; 12 ; 12
$$\begin{array}{r} 3 \\ \times\ 4 \\ \hline 1\,2 \end{array}$$
58. 7 , 4 ; 28 ; 28
$$\begin{array}{r} 4 \\ \times\ 7 \\ \hline 2\,8 \end{array}$$
59. 8 , 3 ; 24 ; 24
$$\begin{array}{r} 3 \\ \times\ 8 \\ \hline 2\,4 \end{array}$$

Just for Fun

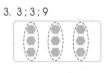

4 Multiplying by 6 or 7

1. 1 ; 1 ; 6
2. 2 ; 2 ; 12
3. 3 ; 3 ; 18
4. 4 ; 24
5. 5 ; 30
6. 6 ; 36
7. 7 ; 42
8. 8 ; 48
9. 9 ; 54
10. 6 ; 12 ; 18 ; 24 ; 30 ; 36 ; 42 ; 48 ; 54
11. 7
12. 14 ; 14
13. 21 ; 3 ; 21
14. 28 ; 4 ; 28
15. 35 ; 5 ; 35
16. 42 ; 6 ; 42
17. 49 ; 7 ; 49
18. 56 ; 8 ; 56
19. 63 ; 9 ; 63
20.

→	7	14	20	26	40	58
	12	21	28	34	56	63	→
	19	27	35	42	49	54	

21. 24
22. 35
23. 21

24. 18   25. 36   26. 56   27. 14
28. 48   29. 54   30. 28   31. 7
32. 30   33. 12   34. 42   35. 49
36. 42   37. 63   38. 6   39. 21
40. 30   41. 18   42. 54   43. 14
44. 35   45. 15   46. 20   47. 6
48. 7   49. 24   50. 63   51. 36
52. 48   53. 49   54. 6   55. 56
56. 42   57. 12   58. 28   59. 42
60. 8 x 6 ; 48 ; 48   61. 5 x 7 ; 35 ; 35
62. 4 x 6 ; 24 ; 24   63. 6 x 7 ; 42 ; 42

Just for Fun

1. – , –   2. – , +   3. + , –   4. + , +

5 Multiplication Facts to 49

1a. 4 ; 8   b. 2 ; 8

c. 4 ; 2 ; 8
2a. 5 ; 15

b. 3 ; 15

c. 5 ; 3 ; 15
3a. 3 ; 12   b. 4 ; 12

c. 3 ; 4 ; 12
4. 10 ; 10 ; 5   5. 18 ; 18 ; 6   6. 28 ; 28 ; 4
7. 14 ; 14 ; 7   8. 30 ; 30 ; 6, 5   9. 20 ; 20 ; 4 ; 5
10. 7 ; 21   11. 4 ; 24   12. 6 ; 12
13. 5 ; 35   14. 6 ; 24   15. 9 ; 18
16. F   17. T   18. T   19. T
20. T   21. F   22. T   23. T
24a. 9 ; 9 ; 18   b. 6 ; 6 ; 18

c. 3 ; 3 ; 18   d. 9 ; 6 ; 3 ; 18

25a. 8 ; 8 ; 24   b. 6 ; 6 ; 24

c. 4 ; 4 ; 24   d. 8 ; 6 ; 4 ; 24

26. 7   27. 6   28. 5   29. 3
30. 9

Just for Fun

4x6 — 8x3
3x7 — 7x3
4x5 — 5x4
6x3 — 9x2

6 Multiplying by 8, 9, 0 or 1

1. 8 ; 8 ; 8 ; 8   2. 8 ; 8 ; 0 ; 0
3. 8 ; 8 ; 64 ; 64   4. 9 ; 9 ; 72 ; 72
5. 1 ; 8   6. 2 ; 16   7. 3 ; 24   8. 4 ; 32
9. 5 ; 40   10. 6 ; 48   11. 7 ; 56
12. 8 ; 16 ; 24 ; 32 ; 40 ; 48 ; 56 ; 64 ; 72
13. 1 ; 9   14. 2 ; 18   15. 3 ; 27   16. 4 ; 36
17. 5 ; 45   18. 6 ; 54   19. 7 ; 63   20. 8 ; 72
21. 81
22. 4   23. 0   24. 0   25. 3
26. 24   27. 36   28. 64   29. 18
30. 81   31. 16   32. 54   33. 72
34. 0   35. 8   36. 0   37. 7
38. 5   39. 27   40. 32   41. 0
42. 45   43. 0   44. 6   45. 56
46. 6 X 9 ; 54 ; 54   47. 9 X 0 ; 0 ; 0

```
      9                        0
    x 6                      x 9
    ───                      ───
     54                        0
```

48. 7 x 1 ; 7 ; 7   49. 3 x 8 ; 24 ; 24

```
      1                        8
    x 7                      x 3
    ───                      ───
      7                       24
```

Just for fun

7 More Multiplying

1. 30   2. 50   3. 40   4. 70
5. 3   6. 0   7. 60   8. 10
9. 90   10. 80   11. 56   12. 27
13. 42   14. 10
15.

	1	2	3	4	5	6	7	8	9	10
1	1	2	3	4	5	6	7	8	9	10
2	2	4	6	8	10	12	14	16	18	20
3	3	6	9	12	15	18	21	24	27	30
4	4	8	12	16	20	24	28	32	36	40
5	5	10	15	20	25	30	35	40	45	50
6	6	12	18	24	30	36	42	48	54	60
7	7	14	21	28	35	42	49	56	63	70
8	8	16	24	32	40	48	56	64	72	80
9	9	18	27	36	45	54	63	72	81	90
10	10	20	30	40	50	60	70	80	90	100

16. B ; E   17. A ; C   18. D ; F
19. 4 , 9 ; 36 ; 9 , 4 , 36
20. 4 , 8 ; 32 ; 8 , 4 ; 32
21. 42   22. 27   23. 40
24. 0   25. 9   26. 70
27. 45   28. 18   29. 72
30. 14   31. 0   32. 18
33. 90   34. 28   35. 3 ; 21
36. 1 ; 8 37. 3 ; 6 38. 0 ; 0
39. 10 ; 8 40. 10 ; 20
41. 10 x 0 ; 0 ; 0   42. 5 x 6 ; 30 ; 30
43. 8 x 4 ; 32 ; 32   44. 7 x 6 ; 42 ; 42
45. 4 x 9 ; 36 ; 36   46. 7 x 3 ; 21 ; 21

ISBN: 978-1-897164-13-6

Just for Fun

1. 2 , 2 ; 2 , 2   2. 1 , 2 , 3 ; 1 , 2 , 3

8   Introducing Division

2. 3

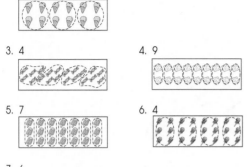

3. 4   4. 9

5. 7   6. 4

7. 6

8. 5

9. 6

10. 4

11. 8

12. 5 ; 2

13. 8   14. 6   15. 4 ; 4
16. 3 ; 3 ; 3   17. 3 ; 3 ; 3   18. 6 ; 6 ; 6
19. 3 ; 3   20. 12 ; 12 , 4 ; 3 ; 3
21. 18 ; 18 , 3 ; 6 ; 6   22. 15 ; 15 , 5 ; 3 ; 3
23. 15 ; 15 , 3 ; 5 ; 5   24. 10 ; 10 , 5 ; 2 ; 2

Just for Fun

1. 6 ; 24 ; 0   2. 9 ; 45 ; 45

Midway Review

1. 2 , 4 , 12 , 14   2. 15 , 18 , 21 , 27
3. 25 , 30 , 40 , 45   4. 18 , 24 , 42 , 48
5. 21 , 28 , 49 , 56   6. 4 , 16 , 20 , 28
7. 18 , 54 , 63 , 72   8. 24 , 32 , 64 , 72
9. 5   10. 1
11. 0   12. 2 ; 4 ; 6 ; 8
13. 56   14. 0   15. 50   16. 30
17. 9   18. 14   19. 24   20. 12
21. 30   22. 8   23. 35   24. 18
25. 24   26. 45   27. 18   28. 28
29. 10   30. 21   31. 27   32. 0

33. 20   34. 12   35. 63   36. 7
37. 32   38. 18   39. 6   40. 40
41. 48   42. 36   43. 54
44. 1   45. 0   46. 0   47. 35
48. 40   49. 54   50. 4 ; 32   51. 4 ; 36
52. 0 ; 0   53. 10 ; 6   54. 3 ; 6   55. 6 ; 42
56. B   57. D   58. D   59. A
60. 8 ; 8 , 4 ; 2 ; 2   61. 12 ; 12 , 3 ; 4 ; 4
62. 6 ÷ 3 ; 2 ; 2   63. 6 x 4 ; 24 ; 24
64. 5 x 8 ; 40 ; 40   65. 3 x 7 ; 21 ; 21
66. 4

9   Multiplication and Division Fact Families

1. 3 ; 3   2. 5 ; 5   3. 3 ; 3   4. 4 ; 4
5. 5 ; 5   6. 2 ; 2   7. 4 ; 4
8. 15 ; 5 , 3 ; 15 ; 15 , 3 ; 5 ; 15 , 5 ; 3
9. 16 ; 8 , 2 ; 16 ; 16 , 2 ; 8 ; 16 , 8 ; 2
10. 3 , 7 ; 21 ; 7 , 3 ; 21 ; 21 , 3 ; 7 ; 21 , 7 ; 3
11. 3 , 6 ; 18 ; 6 , 3 , 18 ; 18 , 3 ; 6 ; 18 , 6 ; 3
12. 4 , 6 ; 24 ; 6 , 4 ; 24 ; 24 , 6 ; 4 ; 24 , 4 ; 6
13. 4 , 5 ; 20 ; 5 , 4 ; 20 ; 20 , 5 ; 4 ; 20 , 4 ; 5
14. 6 ; 3   15. 4 ; 9   16. 8 ; 6
17. 7 ; 4   18. 3 ; 8   19. 7 ; 5
20. 54 ; 9   21. 40 ; 5   22. 32 ; 4
23. 27 ; 9   24. 42 ; 6   25. 45 ; 9
26. 4 ; 4   27. 6 ; 6   28. 7 ; 7
29. 9 ; 9   30. 3 ; 3   31. 6 ; 6
32. 9 ; 9 ; 81   33. 8 ; 8   34. 6 ; 6 ; 36
35. 7 , 8 ; 56 ; 8 , 7 , 56 ; 56 , 8 ; 7 ; 56 , 7 ; 8
36. 8 , 9 ; 72 ; 9 , 8 ; 72 ; 72 , 9 ; 8 ; 72 , 8 ; 9
37.- 40. (Suggested answers)
37. 6 , 2 ; 12 ; 12 , 2 ; 6   38. 8 , 5 ; 40 ; 40 , 5 ; 8
39. 5 , 6 ; 30 ; 30 , 6 ; 5   40. 9 , 5 ; 45 ; 45 , 5 ; 9

Just for Fun

10   Dividing by 1, 2 or 3

2. 8 ; 4

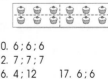

3. 4 ; 4   4. 6 ; 3

5. 12 ; 4   6. 8 ; 4

7. 5 ; 5   8. 12 ; 4

9. 5 ; 5 ; 5   10. 6 ; 6 ; 6
11. 9 ; 9 ; 9   12. 7 ; 7 ; 7
14. 7   15. 8   16. 4 ; 12   17. 6 ; 6
18. 9 ; 18   19. 7 ; 7   20. 3 ; 6   21. 9 ; 27
22. 8   23. 8   24. 2   25. 10
26. 4   27. 3   28. 6   29. 4

ISBN: 978-1-897164-13-6

30. 2   31. 9   32. 6   33. 2
34. 1   35. 3   36. 5   37. 1
38. 5   39. 5

40.
```
    4
3 ) 1 2
    1 2
```
41.
```
    4
2 ) 8
    8
```
42.
```
    4
1 ) 4
    4
```
43.
```
    7
2 ) 1 4
    1 4
```

44.
```
    3
3 ) 9
    9
```
45.
```
    7
3 ) 2 1
    2 1
```
46.
```
    9
3 ) 2 7
    2 7
```
47.
```
    8
1 ) 8
    8
```

48.
```
    8
2 ) 1 6
    1 6
```
49.
```
    3
1 ) 3
    3
```
50.
```
    3
2 ) 6
    6
```
51.
```
    2
3 ) 6
    6
```

52. 24 , 3 ; 8 ; 8
```
    8
3 ) 2 4
    2 4
```
53. 16 , 2 ; 8 ; 8
```
    8
2 ) 1 6
    1 6
```

54. 6 , 1 ; 6 ; 6
```
    6
1 ) 6
    6
```
55. 12 , 2 ; 6 ; 6
```
    6
2 ) 1 2
    1 2
```

Just for Fun
16

11 Dividing by 4 or 5

2. 20 ; 4

3. 30 ; 6

4. 16 ; 4

5. 24 ; 6

6. 15 ; 3

7. 12 ; 3

8.

	1	2	3	4	5	6	7	8	9
4	4	8	12	16	20	24	28	32	36
5	5	10	15	20	25	30	35	40	45

9. 2   10. 4   11. 3
12. 8   13. 6   14. 4
15. 8   16. 7   17. 9
18. 5   19. 9   20. 7
21. 6   22. 1   23. 3
24. 1   25. 5   26. 2
27.
```
    4
4 ) 1 6
    1 6
```
28.
```
    6
5 ) 3 0
    3 0
```
29.
```
    5
4 ) 2 0
    2 0
```
30.
```
    9
5 ) 4 5
    4 5
```
31.
```
    8
4 ) 3 2
    3 2
```
32.
```
    5
5 ) 2 5
    2 5
```
33.
```
    9
4 ) 3 6
    3 6
```
34.
```
    8
5 ) 4 0
    4 0
```
35.
```
    6
4 ) 2 4
    2 4
```

36.
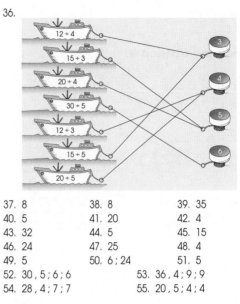

37. 8   38. 8   39. 35
40. 5   41. 20   42. 4
43. 32   44. 5   45. 15
46. 24   47. 25   48. 4
49. 5   50. 6 ; 24   51. 5
52. 30 , 5 ; 6 ; 6   53. 36 , 4 ; 9 ; 9
54. 28 , 4 ; 7 ; 7   55. 20 , 5 ; 4 ; 4

Just for Fun
1. – , + , –   2. – , + , –   3. – , + , + or + , – , –
4. + , – , +   5. + , + , –   6. + , + , +

12 Dividing by 6 or 7

2.   21 ; 3 ; 3 ; 21

3.   18 ; 3 ; 3 ; 18

4.   28 ; 4 ; 4 ; 28

5. 9 ; 9   6. 6 ; 6
7. 7 ; 7   8. 9 ; 6 x 9 = 54
9. 6 ; 7 x 6 = 42   10. 4 ; 6 x 4 = 24
11. 4 ; 7 x 4 = 28   12. 5 ; 6 x 5 = 30
13. 3 ; 7 x 3 = 21   14. 3 ; 6 x 3 = 18
15. 2 ; 7 x 2 = 14   16. 8 ; 6 x 8 = 48
17. 2   18. 5   19. 7
20. 1   21. 1   22. 8
23.
```
    6
6 ) 3 6
    3 6
```
24.
```
    3
7 ) 2 1
    2 1
```
25.
```
    7
7 ) 4 9
    4 9
```
26.
```
    4
7 ) 2 8
    2 8
```
27.
```
    9
6 ) 5 4
    5 4
```
28.
```
    3
6 ) 1 8
    1 8
```
29. ✓   30. ✗ ; 8
31. ✓   32. ✗ ; 6
33. ✓   34. ✗ ; 8
35. 30   36. 7   37. 48
38. 21   39. 6   40. 7
41. 6   42. 56   43. 7
44. 7   45. 30   46. 54
47. 7   48. 7   49. 7
50. 8   51. 3 ; 21   52. 6
53. 54 , 6 ; 9 ; 9; check: 6 x 9 = 54

ISBN: 978-1-897164-13-6

54. 56 , 7 ; 8 ; 8; check: 7 x 8 = 56
55. 24 , 6 ; 4 ; 4; check: 6 x 4 = 24
56. 35 , 7 ; 5 ; 5; check: 7 x 5 = 35

Just for Fun

A ; E

13 Dividing by 8 or 9

1. 9 ; 3
2. 4 , 8 ; 8 , 4
3. 45 , 5 ; 9 ; 45 , 9 ; 5
4. 40 , 5 ; 8 ; 40 , 8 ; 5
5. 8 ; 8
6. 8 ; 8
7. 4 ; 4
8. 5 ; 5
9. 4 ; 4
10. 7 ; 7
11. 3 ; 3
12. 2 ; 2
13. 3 ; 3
14. 5 ; 5
15. 2 ; 2
16. 6 ; 6
17. 1 ; 1
18. 6 ; 6
19. 9 ; 9
20. 7 ; 7
21. 9 ; 9
22. 1 ; 1

23.
$$8 \overline{)16} \quad 2$$
$$\underline{16}$$

24.
$$8 \overline{)72} \quad 9$$
$$\underline{72}$$

25.
$$9 \overline{)36} \quad 4$$
$$\underline{36}$$

26.
$$9 \overline{)54} \quad 6$$
$$\underline{54}$$

27.
$$9 \overline{)45} \quad 5$$
$$\underline{45}$$

28.
$$8 \overline{)64} \quad 8$$
$$\underline{64}$$

29.
$$8 \overline{)56} \quad 7$$
$$\underline{56}$$

30.
$$9 \overline{)81} \quad 9$$
$$\underline{81}$$

31.
$$8 \overline{)32} \quad 4$$
$$\underline{32}$$

32. E ; F ; G ; I
33. A ; D ; H ; L
34. B ; C ; J ; K
35. 54 , 9 ; 6 ; 6
36. 56 , 8 ; 7 ; 7
37. 45 , 9 ; 5 ; 5

Just for Fun

1. 96
2. 103
3. 1036
4. 601

14 Division with Remainders

2.
14 ; 4R2

3.
27 ; 3R3

4.
26 ; 5R1

5.
20 ; 3R2

6. 6 ; 1
7. 5 ; 5
8. 8R8
9. 3R2
10. 8R3
11. 5R2
12. 6R2
13. 5R1
14. 8R1
15. 5R6
16. 7R4
17. 7R1

18.
$$9 \overline{)25} \quad 2R7$$
$$\underline{18}$$
$$7$$

19.
$$3 \overline{)19} \quad 6R1$$
$$\underline{18}$$
$$1$$

20.
$$5 \overline{)46} \quad 9R1$$
$$\underline{45}$$
$$1$$

21.
$$6 \overline{)55} \quad 9R1$$
$$\underline{54}$$
$$1$$

22.
$$7 \overline{)52} \quad 7R3$$
$$\underline{49}$$
$$3$$

23.
$$4 \overline{)38} \quad 9R2$$
$$\underline{36}$$
$$2$$

24.
$$8 \overline{)79} \quad 9R7$$
$$\underline{72}$$
$$7$$

25.
$$6 \overline{)39} \quad 6R3$$
$$\underline{36}$$
$$3$$

26.
$$3 \overline{)19} \quad 6R1$$
$$\underline{18}$$
$$1$$

27.
$$3 \overline{)17} \quad 5R2$$
$$\underline{15}$$
$$2$$

28.
$$7 \overline{)22} \quad 3R1$$
$$\underline{21}$$
$$1$$

29.
$$4 \overline{)38} \quad 9R2$$
$$\underline{36}$$
$$2$$

30.
$$9 \overline{)55} \quad 6R1$$
$$\underline{54}$$
$$1$$

31.
$$6 \overline{)44} \quad 7R2$$
$$\underline{42}$$
$$2$$

32.
$$8 \overline{)65} \quad 8R1$$
$$\underline{64}$$
$$1$$

33.
$$5 \overline{)26} \quad 5R1$$
$$\underline{25}$$
$$1$$

34.
$$2 \overline{)19} \quad 9R1$$
$$\underline{18}$$
$$1$$

35.
$$3 \overline{)29} \quad 9R2$$
$$\underline{27}$$
$$2$$

36.
$$6 \overline{)53} \quad 8R5$$
$$\underline{48}$$
$$5$$

37.
$$4 \overline{)13} \quad 3R1$$
$$\underline{12}$$
$$1$$

38.
$$7 \overline{)53} \quad 7R4$$
$$\underline{49}$$
$$4$$

39.
$$8 \overline{)38} \quad 4R6$$
$$\underline{32}$$
$$6$$

40.
$$9 \overline{)46} \quad 5R1$$
$$\underline{45}$$
$$1$$

41.
$$5 \overline{)41} \quad 8R1$$
$$\underline{40}$$
$$1$$

42. cupboard
43. 20 ÷ 6 ; 3R2 ; 3 ; 2
44. 12 ÷ 5 ; 2R2 ; 2 ; 2
45. 89 ÷ 9 ; 9R8 ; 9 ; 8

Just for Fun

1. 50 , 53 , 58 , 80 , 83 , 85
2. 308 , 350 , 358 , 380 , 508 , 530 , 538 , 580
3. 803 , 805 , 830 , 835 , 850 , 853

15 More Dividing

1. 24 ; 24
2. 6R1 ; 6 x 3 = 18 ; 18 + 1 = 19
3. 6R3 ; 6 x 7 = 42 ; 42 + 3 = 45
4. 7R4 ; 7 x 5 = 35 ; 35 + 4 = 39
5. 8R3 ; 8 x 5 = 40 ; 40 + 3 = 43
6. 7R7 ; 7 x 9 = 63 ; 63 + 7 = 70
7. 6R1 ; 6 x 4 = 24 ; 24 + 1 = 25
8. 7R1 ; 7 x 2 = 14 ; 14 + 1 = 15

9.
$$9 \overline{)73} \quad 8R1$$
$$\underline{72}$$
$$1$$

10.
$$4 \overline{)28} \quad 7$$
$$\underline{28}$$

11.
$$5 \overline{)15} \quad 3$$
$$\underline{15}$$

12.
$$3 \overline{)26} \quad 8R2$$
$$\underline{24}$$
$$2$$

13.
$$6 \overline{)39} \quad 6R3$$
$$\underline{36}$$
$$3$$

14.
$$8 \overline{)48} \quad 6$$
$$\underline{48}$$

15.
$$2 \overline{)18} \quad 9$$
$$\underline{18}$$

16.
$$7 \overline{)29} \quad 4R1$$
$$\underline{28}$$
$$1$$

17.
$$4 \overline{)34} \quad 8R2$$
$$\underline{32}$$
$$2$$

18.
```
    5 R4
5 ) 29
    25
    ─
     4
```

19.
```
     6
3 ) 18
    18
```

20.
```
    4 R4
9 ) 40
    36
    ─
     4
```

21.
```
     8
6 ) 48
    48
```

22.
```
    4 R2
8 ) 34
    32
    ─
     2
```

23.
```
    5 R1
2 ) 11
    10
    ─
     1
```

24.
```
     5
7 ) 35
    35
```

25.
```
    5 R2
4 ) 22
    20
    ─
     2
```

26.
```
    9 R2
5 ) 47
    45
    ─
     2
```

27. $18 \div 4 = 4R2 \longrightarrow 36 \div 6 = 6 \longrightarrow 27 \div 7 = 3R6 \longrightarrow 54 \div 9 = 6$
$\longrightarrow 42 \div 6 = 7 \longrightarrow 13 \div 2 = 6R1 \longrightarrow 21 \div 3 = 7 \longrightarrow 35 \div 8 =$
$4R3 \longrightarrow 27 \div 3 = 9 \longrightarrow 45 \div 9 = 5$

28. $24 \div 8 = 3$
29. $46 \div 5 = 9R1$ ✓
30. $30 \div 6 = 5$
31. $56 \div 8 = 7$
32. $27 \div 9 = 3$
33. $26 \div 4 = 6R2$ ✓
34. $38 \div 7 = 5R3$ ✓

Just for Fun

$1 + 4 = 5 ; 2 \times 3 = 6$

16 More Multiplying and Dividing

1.
```
   0
 x 8
 ───
   0
```

2.
```
   7
 x 6
 ───
  42
```

3.
```
     8
7 ) 56
    56
```

4.
```
     9
4 ) 36
    36
```

5.
```
     6
3 ) 18
    18
```

6.
```
     8
6 ) 48
    48
```

7.
```
     7
5 ) 35
    35
```

8.
```
     7
9 ) 63
    63
```

9.
```
     6
2 ) 12
    12
```

10.
```
     9
8 ) 72
    72
```

11.
```
   5
 x 2
 ───
  10
```

12.
```
   3
 x 0
 ───
   0
```

13.
```
  10
 x 5
 ───
  50
```

14.
```
   1
 x 9
 ───
   9
```

15a. 20   b. 4, 5 ; 20   c. 20 ; 4   d. 20 ; 5
16a. 9, 3 ; 27
  c. 27, 3 ; 9   b. 3, 9 ; 27
                        d. 27, 9 ; 3
17a. 3, 4 ; 12
  c. 12, 3 ; 4   b. 4, 3 ; 12
                        d. 12, 4 ; 3
18a. 3, 5 ; 15
  c. 15, 5 ; 3   b. 5, 3 ; 15
                        d. 15, 3 ; 5
19. C   20. D   21. A   22. E
23. B   24. H   25. F   26. I
27. G
28. $3 \times 8 ; 24 ; 24$ 29. $12 \div 6 ; 2 ; 2$
30. $4 \times 8 ; 32 ; 32$ 31. $28 \div 5 ; 5R3 ; 3$

Just for fun

$1 + 7 = 8 ; 9 - 4 = 5 ; 2 \times 3 = 6$

Final Review

1. 20, 30, 35, 40   2. 27, 54, 63, 72
3. 14, 10, 8, 6   4. 28, 24, 16, 12

5. 72, 48, 32, 24
6. 4   7. 9   8. 8   9. 28
10. 18   11. 35   12. 9   13. 8
14. 9   15. 24   16. 20   17. 20
18. 9   19. 8   20. 7   21. 24
22. 48   23. 15   24. 0   25. 7R2
26. 6R4   27. 8R1   28. 7R3

29.
```
     8
6 ) 48
    48
```

30.
```
     7
5 ) 35
    35
```

31.
```
     4
7 ) 28
    28
```

32.
```
     9
2 ) 18
    18
```

33.
```
     8
4 ) 32
    32
```

34.
```
     6
3 ) 18
    18
```

35.
```
     7
8 ) 56
    56
```

36.
```
     4
9 ) 36
    36
```

37.
```
   6
 x 7
 ───
  42
```

38.
```
   8
 x 2
 ───
  16
```

39.
```
   1
 x 5
 ───
   5
```

40.
```
   9
 x 9
 ───
  81
```

41.
```
   3
 x 9
 ───
  27
```

42.
```
   4
 x 9
 ───
  36
```

43.
```
   0
 x 7
 ───
   0
```

44.
```
   5
 x 6
 ───
  30
```

45.
```
     7
9 ) 63
    63
```

46.
```
     7
2 ) 14
    14
```

47.
```
     9
5 ) 45
    45
```

48.
```
     8
3 ) 24
    24
```

49.
```
    8 R1
6 ) 49
    48
    ─
     1
```

50.
```
    8 R1
4 ) 33
    32
    ─
     1
```

51.
```
    5 R5
8 ) 45
    40
    ─
     5
```

52.
```
     8
7 ) 56
    56
```

53. 9, 5 ; 45 ; 5, 9 ; 45 ; 45, 9 ; 5 ; 45, 5 ; 9
54. 8, 4 ; 32 ; 4, 8 ; 32 ; 32, 8 ; 4 ; 32, 4 ; 8
55. 7 ; 7   56. 8 ; 8   57. 9 ; 9   58. 6 ; 6
59. 7 ; 7   60. 9 ; 9   61. 7 ; 7   62. 9 ; 9
63. 5 ; 5   64. 36   65. 2   66. 3
67. 4   68. 5   69. 7   70. 6
71. x   72. 2   73. 32   74. ÷
75. 0   76. 1   77. 10   78. 6
79. 4 ; 32   80. 2 ; 12   81. 0 ; 0   82. 6 ; 3
83. 4 ; 4   84. 0 ; 0   85. 20 ; 3   86. 8 ; 9
87. – 88. (Suggested answers)
87. 6, 8 ; 48 ; 48, 6 ; 8   88. 5, 7 ; 35 ; 35, 7 ; 5
89. $2 \times 8 ; 16 ; 16$ 90. $9 \times 4 ; 36 ; 36$
91. $36 \div 6 ; 6 ; 6$ 92. $34 \div 4 ; 8R2 ; 8 ; 2$

ISBN: 978-1-897164-13-6

Review

1. 6	2. 1	3. 14
4. 6	5. 7	6. 5
7. 8:00	8. 8:30	9. 8:15

10. 9 ; 11 ; 13 ; 15 ; up ; 2
11. 30 ; 40 ; 50 ; 60 ; up ; 10
12. 12 ; 10 ; 8 ; 6 ; down ; 2

13. 20 ; Cone	14. 5 ; Cylinder
15. 15 ; Cube	16. Sometimes
17. Often	18. Never
19. smaller	20. 45
21. 30	22. 2
23. 3	24. 38 + 25 = 63 ; 63

25. 38 – 25 = 13 ; 13   26. 36 + 43 = 79 ; 79
27. 43 – 36 = 7 ; 7
28. 29 + 46 = 75 ; 75   29. 46 – 29 = 17 ; 17

30.

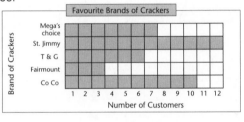

31. Favourite Brands of Crackers

32. 5	33. 6	34. 4
35. 4	36. St. Jimmy	37. 38

1 Numbers to 100

1. Twenty-two	2. Thirty-six
3. Forty-five	4. Sixty
5. Seventy-two	6. Eighty-four
7. Eighty-eight	8. Ninety-nine

9. 74 ; 76 ; 80 ; 82 ; 85   10. 40 ; 42 ; 45 ; 48 ; 50
11. 85 ; 87 ; 89 ; 92 ; 96   12. 47 ; 50 ; 53 ; 56 ; 60

13. 50 ; 54 ; 56	14. 70 ; 85 ; 90
15. 50 ; 60 ; 80	16. 88 ; 90 ; 94
17. 60	18. 100
19. 20	20. 84

21. 85 ; 80 ; 75 ; 70 ; 65   22. 34 ; 32 ; 30 ; 28 ; 26
23. 60 ; 50 ; 40 ; 30 ; 20   24. 65 ; 60 ; 55 ; 50 ; 45
25. 62 ; 60 ; 58 ; 56 ; 54   26. 48 ; 46 ; 44 ; 42 ; 40

27. 30 ; 25 ; 20 ; 15 ; 10	28. 19 ; 24 ; 53 ; 64
29. 30 ; 55 ; 70 ; 81	30. 51 ; 62 ; 70 ; 73
31. 13 ; 25 ; 36 ; 48	32. 22 ; 32 ; 74 ; 92
33. 6 ; 27 ; 8 ; 28	34. 9 ; 10 ; 10
35. 3 ; 10	36. 52, 80, 50, 67, 63
37. 16, 52, 36, 80, 50	38. 80

39. 67, 63		40. 52
41. 16, 36		

42a. thirty-fifth   b. thirty-sixth   c. thirty-seventh
  d. thirty-eighth   e. thirty-ninth   f. fortieth

43. 33rd	44. 41st
45. 3	46. 1
47. 4	48. 38th

Mind Boggler

1. 34	2. Alex

2 Addition and Subtraction

1. 41	2. 55
3. 35	4. 61
5. 16	6. 19
7. 55	8. 55
9. 81	10. 55
11. 59	12. 64
13. 50	14. 55
15. 92	16. 55

17. batter
18. 79 ; 79 – 23 = 56 or 79 – 56 = 23
19. 73 ; 73 – 34 = 39 or 73 – 39 = 34
20. 63 ; 63 + 27 = 90
21. 37 ; 37 + 46 = 83
22. 80 ; 80 – 56 = 24 or 80 – 24 = 56
23. 7 ; 7 + 35 = 42

24. 25	25. 19
26. 18	27. 18
28. 38	29. 34
30. 43 ; 80 – 40 = 40	31. 72 ; 30 + 50 = 80
32. 9 ; 80 – 70 = 10	33. 15 ; 40 – 30 = 10
34. 46 + 38 ; 84 ; 84	35. 46 – 38 ; 8 ; 8
36. 25 + 36 ; 61 ; 61	37. 36 – 25 ; 11 ; 11
38. 85 – 36 ; 49 ; 49	39. 36 – 17 ; 19 ; 19
40. 85 – 16 ; 69 ; 69	41. 39 + 16 ; 55 ; 55
42. 4.16	43. 1.45
44. 10.30	45. 6.28
46. 8.09	47. 7.06
48. 3.50	49. 4.18
50. 1.47	51. 7.68
52. 5.65	53. 2.94

Mind Boggler

9.15

3 Multiplication

1. 4 ; 4 ; 4 ; 4 ; 12   2. 2 ; 2 ; 2 ; 2 ; 2 ; 8
3. 3 ; 3 ; 3 ; 3 ; 3 ; 3 ; 15   4. 7 ; 7 ; 7 ; 7 ; 7 ; 28
5. 5 ; 5 ; 5 ; 5 ; 5 ; 5 ; 5 ; 35

6. 6 ; 5 ; 6 ; 5 ; 30
7. 7 ; 6 ; 7 ; 6 ; 42
8. 5 ; 8 ; 5 ; 8 ; 40
9. 6 ; 9 ; 6 ; 9 ; 54
10. 7 ; 4 ; 7 ; 4 ; 28
11. 4 ; 2 ; 4 ; 2 ; 8
12. 5 ; 3 ; 5 ; 3 ; 15
13. 2 ; 7 ; 2 ; 14
14. 5 ; 4 ; 5 ; 20
15. 6 ; 3 ; 6 ; 18
16. 4 ; 6 ; 4 ; 24
17. 3 ; 5 ; 3 ; 15
18. 1 ; 5 ; 5
19. 2 ; 5 ; 10
20. 3 ; 5 ; 15
21. 4 ; 5 ; 20
22. 5 ; 5 ; 25
23. 6 ; 5 ; 30
24. 1 ; 7 ; 7
25. 2 ; 7 ; 14
26. 3 ; 7 ; 21
27. 4 ; 7 ; 28
28. 5 ; 7 ; 35
29. 6 ; 7 ; 42
30. 8
31. 10
32. 24
33. 16
34. 21
35. 35
36. 48
37. 9
38. 12
39. 25
40. 14
41. 18
42. 28
43. 27
44. 36
45. 12
46. 35
47. 6
48. 24 ;
$$\begin{array}{r} 3 \\ \times\ 8 \\ \hline 2\ 4 \end{array}$$
49. 27 ;
$$\begin{array}{r} 9 \\ \times\ 3 \\ \hline 2\ 7 \end{array}$$
50. 12 ;
$$\begin{array}{r} 2 \\ \times\ 6 \\ \hline 1\ 2 \end{array}$$
51. 18 ;
$$\begin{array}{r} 3 \\ \times\ 6 \\ \hline 1\ 8 \end{array}$$
52. 20 ;
$$\begin{array}{r} 5 \\ \times\ 4 \\ \hline 2\ 0 \end{array}$$

Mind Boggler

1. 60
2. 245
3. 144

4 Measurement I

1. km
2. cm
3. cm
4. cm
5. mm
6. km
7. m
8.-10. (Estimate: Individual answers)
8. 83
9. 75
10. 63
11. 20
12. A
13. 14 ; 12
14. 18 ; 20
15. 20 ; 15
16. 16 ; 9
17. C ; B ; D ; A
18. B ; C ; A ; D
19a. 250 mL ; 375 mL ; 341 mL
b. B ; C ; A
20a. 1 L ; 4 L ; 2 L ; 3 L
b. B ; D ; C ; A
21. mL ; L
22. L ; L
23. mL ; L
24. L
25a. 750 g ; 250 g ; 450 g
b. A ; C ; B
26a. 2 kg ; 3 kg ; 4 kg ; 1 kg
b. C ; B ; A ; D

Mind Boggler

1. 200
2. 100

5 Geometry I

1. Square
2. Parallelogram
3. Triangle
4. Rectangle
5. Rhombus
6. Circle
7. Trapezoid
8. Pentagon
9.-14. (Suggested drawings)

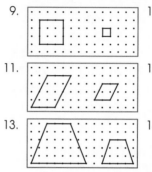
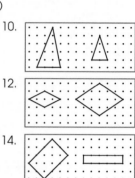

15. 3 ; 3 ; 4 ; 4 ; 4 ; 4 ; 4
16. 3 ; 3 ; 4 ; 4 ; 4 ; 4 ; 4
17. No ; Yes ; Yes ; Yes ; No ; Yes ; No
18. ✔
19. ✘
20. ✘
21. ✔
22. ✔

23.
24.
25.
26.

27. 2 ; 3 ; 3
28. 3 ; 1 ; 2
29. 1 ; 1 ; 2
30. B
31. C
32. B
33. A
34. 1 ; right ; 3 ; up
35. 2 ; left ; 3 ; up
36. 4 ; right ; 4 ; down or 4 ; left ; 4 ; up

Mind Boggler

B ; D

6 Division

1. 6 ; 2
2. 12 ; 4
3. 15 ; 3
4.

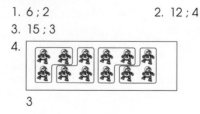

3

ISBN: 978-1-897164-13-6

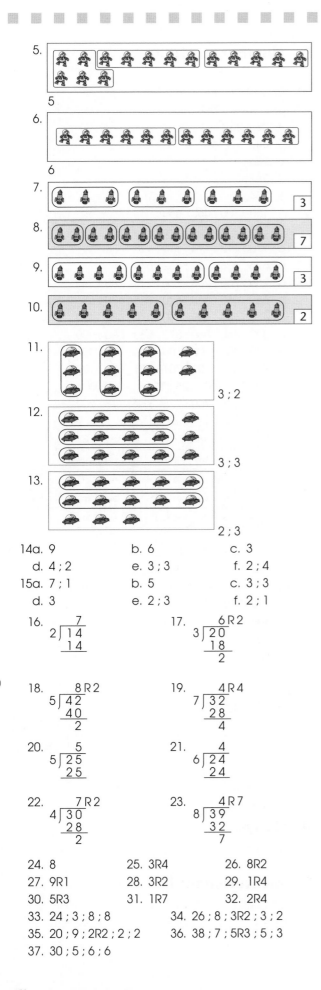

14a. 9   b. 6   c. 3
d. 4 ; 2   e. 3 ; 3   f. 2 ; 4
15a. 7 ; 1   b. 5   c. 3 ; 3
d. 3   e. 2 ; 3   f. 2 ; 1

16. $\frac{7}{2\overline{)14}}$ $\frac{14}{}$ 17. $\frac{6R2}{3\overline{)20}}$ $\frac{18}{2}$

18. $\frac{8R2}{5\overline{)42}}$ $\frac{40}{2}$ 19. $\frac{4R4}{7\overline{)32}}$ $\frac{28}{4}$

20. $\frac{5}{5\overline{)25}}$ $\frac{25}{}$ 21. $\frac{4}{6\overline{)24}}$ $\frac{24}{}$

22. $\frac{7R2}{4\overline{)30}}$ $\frac{28}{2}$ 23. $\frac{4R7}{8\overline{)39}}$ $\frac{32}{7}$

24. 8   25. 3R4   26. 8R2
27. 9R1   28. 3R2   29. 1R4
30. 5R3   31. 1R7   32. 2R4
33. 24 ; 3 ; 8 ; 8   34. 26 ; 8 ; 3R2 ; 3 ; 2
35. 20 ; 9 ; 2R2 ; 2 ; 2   36. 38 ; 7 ; 5R3 ; 5 ; 3
37. 30 ; 5 ; 6 ; 6

Mind Boggler

6 ; 5

7 Data Management

1. Number of Customers Last Week
2. 5   3. 40   4. 45
5. 20   6. 13   7. Sunday
8. Thursday   9. 100
10. 55 ; 30 ; 35 ; 40 ; 25 ; 50 ; 45

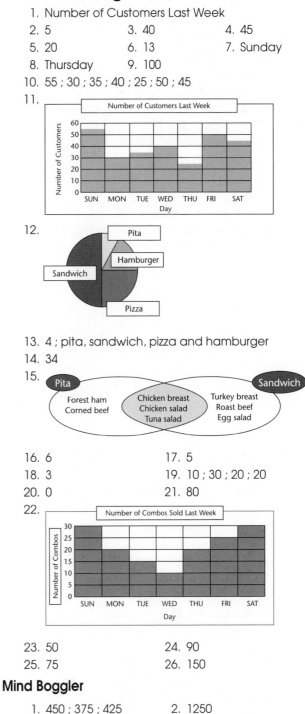

13. 4 ; pita, sandwich, pizza and hamburger
14. 34
16. 6   17. 5
18. 3   19. 10 ; 30 ; 20 ; 20
20. 0   21. 80

23. 50   24. 90
25. 75   26. 150

Mind Boggler

1. 450 ; 375 ; 425   2. 1250

Progress Test

1. 90 ; 75 ; 70 ; 55
2. 70 ; 60 ; 40
3. 52 ; 56 ; 58 ; 60
4. 90 ; 88 ; 84 ; 78
5. 91 ; Ninety-one

6. 28 ; Twenty-eight

7. 19 ; Nineteen

8. 77 ; Seventy-seven

9. 45 ; Forty-five

10. 6 ; Six

11. 92 ; Ninety-two

12. 57 ; Fifty-seven

13. 54 ; Fifty-four

14. 64 ; Sixty-four

15. 38 ; Parallelogram ; 4 ; 4

16. 50 ; Triangle ; 3 ; 3

17. 37 ; Trapezoid ; 4 ; 4

18. 225 mL ; 950 mL ; 3 L

19. 400 g ; 250 g ; 2 kg

20. C

21. B

22a. 3 + 3 + 3 + 3 ; 8 ; 8 ; 3 ; 24 b. 8 c. 3

23a. 5 + 5 + 5 + 5 ; 7 ; 5 ; 7 ; 5 ; 35 b. 7 c. 5

24a. 7 ; 4 ; 7 ; 4 ; 7 ; 28 b. 4 c. 7

25.
$$\begin{array}{r} 7 \\ \times\ 4 \\ \hline 2\,8 \end{array}$$

26.
$$\begin{array}{r} 6 \\ \times\ 5 \\ \hline 3\,0 \end{array}$$

27.
$$5\overline{)\begin{array}{l} 8 \\ 4\,0 \\ 4\,0 \end{array}}$$

28.
$$6\overline{)\begin{array}{l} 7 \\ 4\,2 \\ 4\,2 \end{array}}$$

29.
$$7\overline{)\begin{array}{l} 5 \\ 3\,5 \\ 3\,5 \end{array}}$$

30.
$$9\overline{)\begin{array}{l} 2\,R7 \\ 2\,5 \\ 1\,8 \\ \hline 7 \end{array}}$$

31.
$$\begin{array}{r} 3 \\ \times\ 9 \\ \hline 2\,7 \end{array}$$

32.
$$\begin{array}{r} 4 \\ \times\ 8 \\ \hline 3\,2 \end{array}$$

33. 24 34. 2R2 35. 3R2

36. 45 37. 21 38. 18

39. 8 40. 2R6 41. 4R7

42. 20

43. Mrs. Green's Earnings

44. 40 ; 50 ; 20 ; 45 ; 0 ; 65 ; 25

45. Thursday 46. 245

47. 5 48. $4\frac{1}{2}$

49. 3.31 ; 2.31 ; 5.62 50. 1.27 ; 2.54

51. 4.47 ; 0.35 ; 4.82 52. 28

53. 85 54. 7

55. 35 56. 3 ; 2

57. 32 58. 12

59. 6 ; 2

8 Numbers to 1000

1. 2 ; 3 ; 6 ; 236

2. 3 ; 4 ; 7 ; 347

3. 2 ; 5 ; 4 ; 254

4. 236, 254

5. 347

6. 236

7. 347

8. 254

9. 150 ; 300 ; 450 ; 650

10. 206 ; 218 ; 234 ; 256

11a. 110 ; 112 ; 114 ; 116 ; 118

b. 626 ; 628 ; 630 ; 632 ; 634

12a. 255 ; 260 ; 265 ; 270 ; 275 ; 280 ; 285

b. 655 ; 660 ; 665 ; 670 ; 675 ; 680 ; 685

13a. 430 ; 440 ; 450 ; 460 ; 470 ; 480 ; 490

b. 840 ; 850 ; 860 ; 870 ; 880 ; 890 ; 900

14a. 300 ; 400 ; 500 ; 600 ; 700 ; 800 ; 900

b. 401 ; 501 ; 601 ; 701 ; 801 ; 901 ; 1001

15a. 50 ; 75 ; 100 ; 125 ; 150 ; 175 ; 200

b. 650 ; 675 ; 700 ; 725 ; 750 ; 775 ; 800

16.-17.

Jason's route					Helen's route		
950	800	750	600	300	350	300	200
1000	900	800	700	600	400	250	200
900	650	600	550	500	450	400	300
700	700	550	400	400	300	200	100
800	750	700	450	350	200	300	100

18a. 293, 239, 329, 392, 923, 932

b. 932, 923, 392, 329, 293, 239

19a. 446, 464, 644 b. 644, 464, 446

20a. 507, 570, 705, 750 b. 750, 705, 570, 507

21. Yes

22. Yes

23. No

24. 268

25. 219

26. 532 ; 428 ; 280 ; 705

27.

			Tim		Helen	Jason		Mabel
0	100	200	300	400	500	600	700	

28. Mabel 29. Tim

30. 628 ; No 31. 5

Mind Boggler

1. 505 2. 120

9 Measurement II

1a. 12:35 b. 1:05 c. 30

2a. 4:15 b. 4:25 c. 10

ISBN: 978-1-897164-13-6

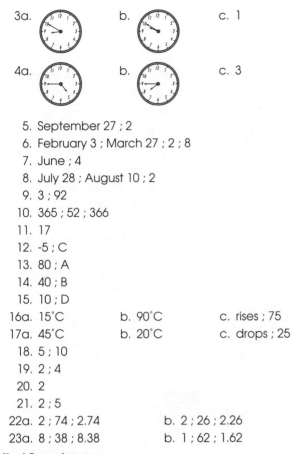

3a. (clock) b. (clock) c. 1

4a. (clock) b. (clock) c. 3

5. September 27 ; 2
6. February 3 ; March 27 ; 2 ; 8
7. June ; 4
8. July 28 ; August 10 ; 2
9. 3 ; 92
10. 365 ; 52 ; 366
11. 17
12. -5 ; C
13. 80 ; A
14. 40 ; B
15. 10 ; D
16a. 15°C   b. 90°C   c. rises ; 75
17a. 45°C   b. 20°C   c. drops ; 25
18. 5 ; 10
19. 2 ; 4
20. 2
21. 2 ; 5
22a. 2 ; 74 ; 2.74   b. 2 ; 26 ; 2.26
23a. 8 ; 38 ; 8.38   b. 1 ; 62 ; 1.62

Mind Boggler

5.20

10 More about Addition and Subtraction

1.
```
  1 1 4
+ 2 4 8
-------
  3 6 2
```
2.
```
    8 7
+ 1 6 2
-------
  2 4 9
```
3.
```
  5 4 0
+ 3 6 3
-------
  9 0 3
```
4.
```
  2 5 5
+   9 6
-------
  3 5 1
```

5. 379
6. 438
7. 747
8. 631
9. 441
10. 360
11. 485
12. 481
13. 620
14. 300
15. 373
16. 607
17. 790
18. 541
19. 151
20. 131
21. 158
22. 32
23. 157
24. 109
25. 88
26. A, B, C, E
27. D
28. 215 ; 215 + 376 = 591
29. 135 ; 135 + 119 = 254
30. 584 ; 584 + 88 = 672
31. 135 ; 135 + 268 = 403
32. 283 ; 283 + 146 = 429

33. 76 ; 76 + 158 = 234
34.
```
  3 9 9   ;   4 0 0   ; 526
+ 1 2 7     + 1 3 0
-------     -------
  5 2 6       5 3 0
```
35.
```
    8 9   ;     9 0   ; 488
+ 3 9 9     + 4 0 0
-------     -------
  4 8 8       4 9 0
```
36.
```
  2 0 0   ;   2 0 0   ; 12
- 1 8 8     - 1 9 0
-------     -------
    1 2         1 0
```
37.
```
  3 0 0   ;   3 0 0   ; 92
- 2 0 8     - 2 1 0
-------     -------
    9 2         9 0
```
38.
```
  2 0 8   ;   2 1 0   ; 59
- 1 4 9     - 1 5 0
-------     -------
    5 9         6 0
```
39.
```
    8 9   ;     9 0   ; 277
+ 1 8 8     + 1 9 0
-------     -------
  2 7 7       2 8 0
```

40. 982 − 656 ; 326 ; 326
41. 863 − 288 ; 575 ; 575
42. 126 + 38 ; 164 ; 164
43. 225 + 225 ; 450 ; 450
44. 923 − 475 ; 448 ; 448
45. 295 + 295 ; 590 ; 590
46. 109 + 216 ; 325 ; 325

Mind Boggler

1.
```
  2 5 6
+ 1 6 9
-------
  4 2 5
```
2.
```
  6 3 3
- 1 5 8
-------
  4 7 5
```
3.
```
  5 0 1
- 2 6 4
-------
  2 3 7
```

11 Geometry II

1.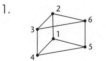
Triangular prism

2.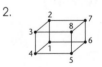
Rectangular prism

3. 6 ; 9 ; 5 ; 3 ; 2
4. 8 ; 12 ; 6 ; 6 ; 0
5. Yes
6. Yes
7. triangular ; 4 ; 6 ; 4
8. rectangular ; 5 ; 8 ; 5
9. square ; 5 ; 8 ; 5
10. (Suggested answer)

	red		
blue	yellow	blue	yellow
		red	

11. 3   12. ✗   13. ✗   14. ✔

15. ✔   16. ✔   17. ✗

18.-19. (Suggested answers)

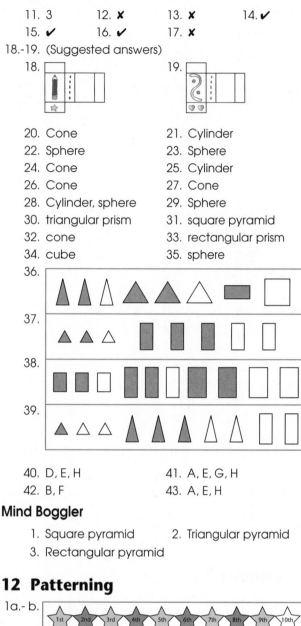

18.   19.

20. Cone   21. Cylinder
22. Sphere   23. Sphere
24. Cone   25. Cylinder
26. Cone   27. Cone
28. Cylinder, sphere   29. Sphere
30. triangular prism   31. square pyramid
32. cone   33. rectangular prism
34. cube   35. sphere

36.
37.
38.
39.

40. D, E, H   41. A, E, G, H
42. B, F   43. A, E, H

Mind Boggler

1. Square pyramid   2. Triangular pyramid
3. Rectangular pyramid

12 Patterning

1a.- b.

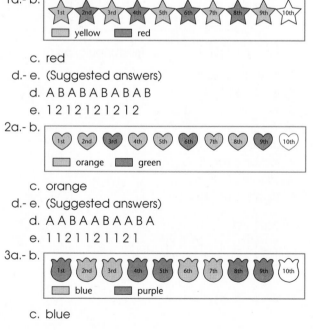

    yellow   red

c. red

d.- e. (Suggested answers)

d. A B A B A B A B A B

e. 1 2 1 2 1 2 1 2 1 2

2a.- b.

    orange   green

c. orange

d.- e. (Suggested answers)

d. A A B A A B A A B A

e. 1 1 2 1 1 2 1 1 2 1

3a.- b.

    blue   purple

c. blue

d.- e. (Suggested answers)

d. A B B A A B B A A B

e. 1 2 2 1 1 2 2 1 1 2

4. inside the circle, outside the circle ; dots, stripes

5. big, small ; on the rectangle, under the rectangle

6. small, big, big ; up, up, down

7. big, small, small ; left, right, right

8. in front of the circle, behind the circle, behind the circle ; left, left, right

9a. 4, 8, 12, 16, 20, 24, 28, 32, 36, 40, 44, 48, 52, 56, 60, 64, 68, 72, 76, 80, 84, 88, 92, 96, 100

b. increases ; 4

10a. 6, 12, 18, 24, 30, 36, 42, 48, 54, 60, 66, 72, 78, 84, 90, 96

b. increases ; 6

11a. 12, 24, 36, 48, 60, 72, 84, 96

b. increases ; 12

12a. 25 ; 30 ; 35 ; 40   b. increase ; 5

13a. 9 ; 8 ; 7 ; 6   b. decreases ; 1

14a. 2 ; 4 ; 6 ; 8 ; 10 ; 12 ; 14 ; 16 ; 18 ; 20

b. 0 ; 2 ; 4 ; 6 ; 8

15.

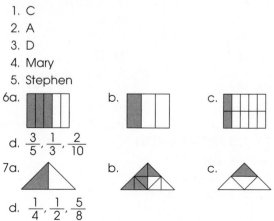

16. increases ; 1

17. decreases ; 1

18. 2 ; 3 ; 4 ; 5 ; 6

19. 5 ; 4 ; 3 ; 2 ; 1

20. 3 ; 6 ; 10 ; 15 ; 21

Mind Boggler

1 ; 4 ; 9 ; 16 ; 25 ; 36

13 Fractions

1. C
2. A
3. D
4. Mary
5. Stephen

6a.   b.   c.

d. $\frac{3}{5}$, $\frac{1}{3}$, $\frac{2}{10}$

7a.   b.   c.

d. $\frac{1}{4}$, $\frac{1}{2}$, $\frac{5}{8}$

          ISBN: 978-1-897164-13-6

8a. 5   b. 2 ; 2

9a. 2   b. 7 ; $\frac{7}{10}$

10a. 4 ; 4   b. 3 ; 4 ; $\frac{3}{4}$

11a. $\frac{1}{4}$ b. $\frac{3}{4}$

12a. $\frac{2}{5}$ b. $\frac{3}{5}$

13a. $\frac{3}{4}$ b. $\frac{1}{4}$

14a.

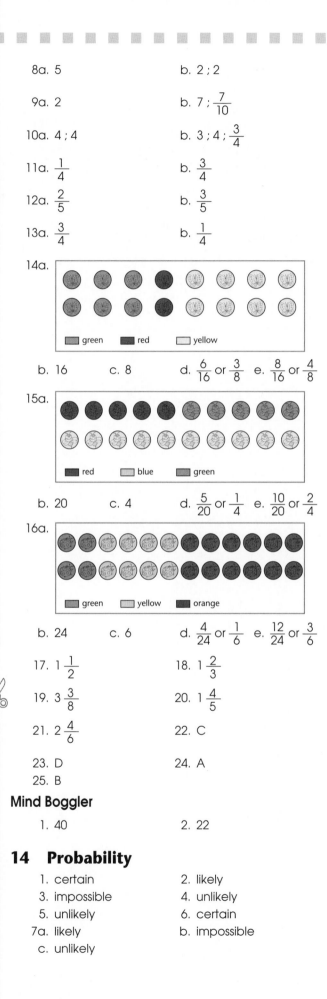

□ green   ■ red   □ yellow

b. 16   c. 8   d. $\frac{6}{16}$ or $\frac{3}{8}$ e. $\frac{8}{16}$ or $\frac{4}{8}$

15a.

■ red   □ blue   ■ green

b. 20   c. 4   d. $\frac{5}{20}$ or $\frac{1}{4}$ e. $\frac{10}{20}$ or $\frac{2}{4}$

16a.

■ green   □ yellow   ■ orange

b. 24   c. 6   d. $\frac{4}{24}$ or $\frac{1}{6}$ e. $\frac{12}{24}$ or $\frac{3}{6}$

17. $1\frac{1}{2}$ 18. $1\frac{2}{3}$

19. $3\frac{3}{8}$ 20. $1\frac{4}{5}$

21. $2\frac{4}{6}$ 22. C

23. D   24. A

25. B

Mind Boggler

1. 40   2. 22

14   Probability

1. certain   2. likely

3. impossible   4. unlikely

5. unlikely   6. certain

7a. likely   b. impossible

c. unlikely

8a. 4 ; 4 ; 4 ; 0   b. 3
c. Yes   d. No

9a. 0 ; 9 ; 0 ; 2   b. 2
c. Yes   d. No

10. A   11. B

12. B   13. B

14. B   15. A

16. C   17. D

18. A   19. D

20. No   21. Yes

22. Yes   23. No

24. Yes   25. 30

26.

Card	Tally	Total
1	卌	5
2	卌 卌	10
3	卌 卌 卌	15

27. Yes   28. No   29. 1

Mind Boggler

1. A

2. Janet has the greatest chance to pick 3 and the least chance to pick 1 . Therefore she has more 3 than 2 or 1 .

Final Test

1. B   2. D

3. C   4. A

5. C   6. D

7. D   8. A

9. D   10. A

11. B   12. C

13. A   14. D

15. B   16. C

17. 348   18. 544

19. 109   20. 466

21. 35

22.
$$\begin{array}{r} 6\,R\,4 \\ 6\,\overline{)40} \\ \underline{36} \\ 4 \end{array}$$
23.
$$\begin{array}{r} 8 \\ 3\,\overline{)24} \\ \underline{24} \end{array}$$

24. 54   25. 384

26. 181   27. 51

28. 651   29. 16

30. 20   31. 5R1

32. 4R1   33. 90 ; 84 ; 82 ; 78

34. 70 ; 75 ; 85 ; 95   35. 404 ; 407 ; 408 ; 410

36. 20°C

37. 15°C

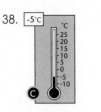

38.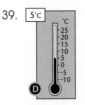

39. (5°C thermometer)

66.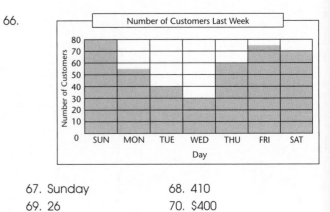

Number of Customers Last Week

40. A ; B ; D ; C
41. 209 + 347 ; 556 ; 556
42. 347 − 209 ; 138 ; 138
43. 3 x 6 ; 18 ; 18
44. 20 ÷ 4 ; 5 ; 5

45a. (image)   b. (image)

46a. 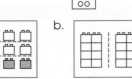   b. (image)

47a. 24   b. 24
48. Rectangular pyramid
49. Triangular prism
50. Cylinder
51. Rectangular prism
52. C
53a. small, small, big
 b. stripes, stripes, dots
54a. under the prism, on the prism
 b. big, small

67. Sunday   68. 410
69. 26   70. $400

55.

Gift	Tally	Total
(pyramid)	II	2
(prism)	IIII	4
(die)	IIII	4
(brick)	HHH HHH II	12

56. Yes
57. No
58. No

59a. Yes   b. smaller

60. $\frac{2}{22}$

61. $\frac{4}{22}$

62. $\frac{16}{22}$

63. $\frac{6}{22}$

64a. 11   b. 6   c. $\frac{6}{11}$

65a. 10:25   b. 4:55

ISBN: 978-1-897164-13-6

Unit 1

1. Lesley, Gary Paul, Joe, Joan, Ann
2. 110, 100, 90, 80
3. Height : 145 – 130 = 15   Paul would have to grow 15 cm.
4. Difference : 145 – 120 = 25   The difference in height between the tallest student and the shortest student is 25 cm.
5. Paul, Joe, Lesley, Ann, Gary
6. No. of marbles : 513 – 100 = 413
   Lesley has 100 fewer marbles than Joe.
7. No. of marbles : 270 + 40 = 310
   Ann has 40 more marbles than Gary.
8. I will get to Ann's number first.
9. Joe can match Paul's score by winning 10 marbles.

Challenge

If Ann gives 10 to Gary, Ann will have 300 and Gary will have 280. ✗
If Ann gives 20 to Gary, Ann will have 290 and Gary will have 290. ✓
If Ann gives 20 marbles to Gary, they will have the same number of marbles.

Unit 2

1. There are 27 animals in all.
2. There are 15 4-legged animals.
3. No. of ducks : 15 + 9 = 24   There are 24 ducks altogether.
4. No. of animals : 3 + 9 = 12   There are 12 animals with wings.
5. No. of cows : 20 – 8 = 12   12 cows are still in the barn.
6. No. of animals : 15 – 12 = 3
   There are 3 more 4-legged animals than 2-legged ones.
7. He should buy : 64 – 39 = 25   He should buy 25 more goats.
8. No. of animals : 68 + 23 = 91   He has 91 animals now.
9. No. of birds : 24 + 34 + 59 = 117   He has 117 birds.
10. Peter sold : 47 + 59 = 106   Peter sold 106 cows and goats altogether.
11. No. of gulls : 196 – 98 + 105 = 203   There are 203 gulls altogether.
12. No. of gulls : 312 + 64 = 376   There were 376 gulls at the start.
13. No. of gulls : 305 – 84 = 221   221 gulls are left.
14. No. of gulls : 576 – 153 – 283 = 140   140 gulls remain.
15. No. of gulls : 413 + 311 + 136 = 860   There are 860 gulls altogether.
16. ducks
17. cows
18. chickens
19. goats
20. sheep
21. pigs
22. He should use field B because 48 is closer to 50.
23. No. of trees : 150 – 68 = 82
    He can plant 82 more trees there afterwards.
24. No. of trees : (25 + 50) – 68 = 7
    He can plant 7 more trees there afterwards.
25. No. of trees : 53 + 75 = 128
    He should choose field C because it can hold more than 100 trees.
26. No. of trees : 150 – 128 = 22   He can plant 22 more trees there.
27. No. of peach trees : 91 – 36 = 55
    No. of trees : 100 – 55 = 45   He can plant 45 more trees.

Challenge

No. of ducks	No. of sheep	No. of legs	
1	8	2 + 32 = 34	✗
2	7	4 + 28 = 32	✓

There are 2 ducks and 7 sheep.

Unit 3

1.		5 x 4	20
2.		5 x 6	30
3.		3 x 4	12
4.		4 x 7	28
5.		3 x 5	15
6.		6 x 2	12

7. 5 plates with 3 apples each. 5 x 3 = 15
   There are 15 apples in all.
8. 6 plates with 4 oranges each. 6 x 4 = 24
   There are 24 oranges in all.
9. 7 baskets with 2 pears each. 7 x 2 = 14
   There are 14 pears in all.
10. 6 bags with 1 watermelon each. 6 x 1 = 6
    There are 6 watermelons in all.
11. 3 plates with 8 cherries each. 3 x 8 = 24
    There are 24 cherries in all.
12. 6 x 8 = 48   There are 48 apples.
13. 9 x 7 = 63   There are 63 oranges.
14. 5 x 3 = 15   3 children will get 15 candies in all.
15. 7 x 4 = 28   4 children will get 28 crackers in all.
16. 5 x 5 = 25   5 children will get 25 chicken nuggets in all.
17. 6 x 5 = 30   5 children will get 30 cookies in all.
18. 2 x 7 = 14   7 children will get 14 cheese sticks in all.
19. 3 x 2 = 6   2 children will get 6 brownies in all.
20. 8 x 6 = 48   6 children will get 48 marshmallows in all.
21. 4 x 4 = 16   4 children will get 16 pretzels in all.
22. 6 x 6 = 36   There are 36 chips.
23. 2 x 7 = 14   There are 14 pieces of cheese.
24. 5 x 8 = 40   There are 40 grams of marshmallows.
25. 6 x 5 = 30   A plate of candies costs 30¢.

Challenge

He saved : 10 + 20 + 30 = 60   Terry saved 60¢ altogether.

Unit 4

1.
10 ÷ 5 = 2
Each child will get
2 cupcakes.

2.
12 ÷ 3 = 4
Each boy will get
4 cookies.

3.
20 ÷ 5 = 4
There are 4 candies
in each group.

4.
18 ÷ 6 = 3
Each child will get
3 crackers.

5. 24 ÷ 3 = 8 She needs 8 baskets.
6. 24 ÷ 4 = 6 She needs 6 baskets.
7. 24 ÷ 6 = 4 She needs 4 baskets.
8. 24 ÷ 8 = 3 She needs 3 baskets.
9. No. of chocolate doughnuts : 8 ÷ 2 = 4
   There are 4 chocolate doughnuts in each group.
10. No. of honey doughnuts : 16 ÷ 2 = 8
    There are 8 honey doughnuts in each group.
11. No. of chocolate doughnuts : 8 ÷ 4 = 2
    No. of honey doughnuts : 16 ÷ 4 = 4
    There are 2 chocolate doughnuts and 4 honey doughnuts in each group.
12. 24 ÷ 5 = 4...4
    There are 4 groups, and 4 students are left over.
13. 30 ÷ 4 = 7...2
    Each student can get 7 crayons, and 2 crayons are left over.
14. 48 ÷ 9 = 5...3
    Each student can get 5 markers, and 3 markers are left over.
15. 61 ÷ 7 = 8...5
    Each student can get 8 markers, and 5 markers are left over.
16. There are 6 pencils. If each student gets 2 pencils, Mrs Winter can give them to 3 students.
17. There are 7 glue sticks. If each student gets 1 glue stick, Mrs Winter can give them to 7 students.

18. No. of erasers : $19 - 7 \times 2 = 19 - 14 = 5$
    5 erasers are left over; no glue sticks are left over.
19. $36 \div 4 = 9$ He would need 9 small boxes.
20. $36 \div 6 = 6$ He would need 6 big boxes.
21. $48 \div 4 = 12$ He would need 12 small boxes.
22. $18 \div 4 = 4...2$ He would need 5 small boxes.
23. $26 \div 4 = 6...2$ He would need 7 small boxes.
24. $26 \div 6 = 4...2$ He would need 5 big boxes.

Challenge

1. No. of boxes : $12 \div 4 = 3$ I paid : $3 \times 3 = 9$
   I would buy 3 small boxes and pay $9.
2. No. of boxes : $12 \div 6 = 2$ I paid : $2 \times 4 = 8$
   I would buy 2 big boxes and pay $8.
3. The big box is a better deal. It costs less to buy 12 cupcakes in big boxes.

Unit 5

1. 3; 3; $\frac{2}{3}$ 2. 8; 8; $\frac{5}{8}$ 3. 6; 6; $\frac{3}{6}$

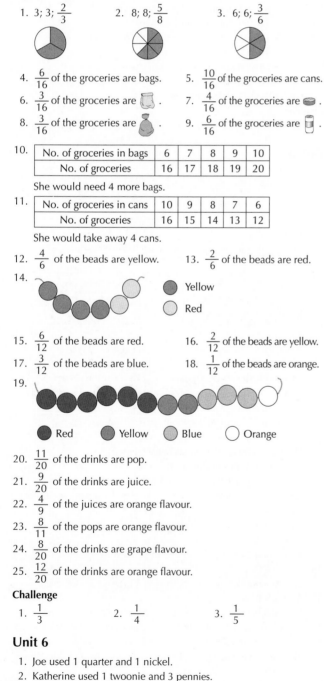

4. $\frac{6}{16}$ of the groceries are bags.
5. $\frac{10}{16}$ of the groceries are cans.
6. $\frac{3}{16}$ of the groceries are 🛍.
7. $\frac{4}{16}$ of the groceries are 🥫.
8. $\frac{3}{16}$ of the groceries are 🍾.
9. $\frac{6}{16}$ of the groceries are 🥫.

10.

No. of groceries in bags	6	7	8	9	10
No. of groceries	16	17	18	19	20

She would need 4 more bags.

11.

No. of groceries in cans	10	9	8	7	6
No. of groceries	16	15	14	13	12

She would take away 4 cans.

12. $\frac{4}{6}$ of the beads are yellow.
13. $\frac{2}{6}$ of the beads are red.

14.
    ○ Yellow
    ○ Red

15. $\frac{6}{12}$ of the beads are red.
16. $\frac{2}{12}$ of the beads are yellow.
17. $\frac{3}{12}$ of the beads are blue.
18. $\frac{1}{12}$ of the beads are orange.

19.
    ● Red   ● Yellow   ● Blue   ○ Orange

20. $\frac{11}{20}$ of the drinks are pop.
21. $\frac{9}{20}$ of the drinks are juice.
22. $\frac{4}{9}$ of the juices are orange flavour.
23. $\frac{8}{11}$ of the pops are orange flavour.
24. $\frac{8}{20}$ of the drinks are grape flavour.
25. $\frac{12}{20}$ of the drinks are orange flavour.

Challenge

1. $\frac{1}{3}$ 2. $\frac{1}{4}$ 3. $\frac{1}{5}$

Unit 6

1. Joe used 1 quarter and 1 nickel.
2. Katherine used 1 twoonie and 3 pennies.

---

3. William used 1 twoonie, 1 loonie, 1 dime and 1 nickel.
4. Ann used 1 loonie, 3 quarters, 1 nickel and 1 penny.
5. Cost : $2.20 + 2.20 = 4.40$
   Natasha used 2 twoonies, 1 quarter, 1 dime and 1 nickel.
6. Cost : $1.86 + 1.28 = 3.14$ Jane needs to pay $3.14.
7. Cost : $1.68 + 0.95 = 2.63$ They cost $2.63.
8. Cost : $2.75 + 2.75 + 1.86 = 7.36$ Susan needs to pay $7.36.
9. Change : $10.00 - 1.68 - 1.28 = 7.04$ Tom got $7.04 change.
10. If Daisy bought fries, she would have $0.95 ($1.99 - 1.04 = 0.95$) left. Pop costs $0.95. Daisy bought fries and pop.
11. Cost for 3 fries : $1.04 + 1.04 + 1.04 = 3.12 > 3.1$ (Money Nicky has)
    No. It is not enough for 3 fries.
12. Change : $10 - 7.5 = 2.5$ Joan's change was $2.50.
    The coins are 1 twoonie and 2 quarters.
13. Change : $7 - 5.75 = 1.25$ David's change was $1.25.
    The coins are 1 loonie and 1 quarter.
14. Change : $10 - 4.25 - 4.25 = 1.5$ Raymond's change was $1.50.
    The coins are 1 loonie and 2 quarters.
15. Change : $5 - 1.85 - 1.85 = 1.3$ Lily's change was $1.30.
    The coins are 1 loonie, 1 quarter and 1 nickel.
16. Change : $10 - 1.38 - 1.85 - 5.75 = 1.02$
    Daisy's change was $1.02.   The coins are 1 loonie and 2 pennies.
17. 5.00   18. 2.00   19. 11.00   20. 10.76
21. 1.00   22. 6.00   23. 3.00   24. 2.00
25. 12.00   26. 12.91   27. 3.00   28. 5.00
29. 3.00   30. 1.00   31. 12.00   32. 12.47

Challenge

Jessie's change   Wendy's change   Brian's change
$20 - 10.76 = 9.24$ $15 - 12.91 = 2.09$ $13 - 12.47 = 0.53$
Jessie would get the most change back.

Midway Review

1. $3.30, $2.70, $2.50, $1.75, $1.50
2. Change : $2 - 0.8 - 0.8 = 0.4$ She will get $0.40 (40¢) change.
3. Change : $5 - 0.8 - 0.8 = 3.4$ B would be the change.
4. 🪙🪙🪙🪙🪙🪙🪙🪙🪙🪙   She can get 10 quarters.
5. No. of quarters : $10 \div 5 = 2$; Value : $0.25 + 0.25 = 0.5$
   Each group has 2 quarters and its value is $0.50 (50¢).
6. (1 week; $0.75) ⟶ (2 weeks; $1.50) ⟶ (3 weeks; $2.25)
   She will take 3 weeks to earn $2.25.
7. Ann has 13 marbles.
8. No. of marbles : $13 + 29 = 42$ She will have 42 marbles altogether.
9. $\frac{5}{13}$ of marbles are black.
10. $\frac{4}{13}$ of marbles have a cat's eye.
11. No. of marbles : $13 - 8 = 5$ She would have 5 marbles.
12.

No. of marbles in black	5	6	7	8
No. of marbles in all	13	14	15	16

Ann would have to buy 3 black marbles.

13. No. of marbles : $13 \div 3 = 4...1$
    Each child will get 4 marbles and 1 marble will be left over.
14. Cost : $3 \times 6 = 18$ They cost $18.00 in all.
15. She spent : $24 \div 6 = 4$ She spent $4.00 on each mouse.
16. No. of baby mice : $4 \times 2 - 2 = 6$ 6 baby mice were left.
17. Amount : $5 \times 5 = 25$ She will get $25.00.
18. No. of mice : $40 \div 5 = 8$ She would need to sell 8 mice.
19. Ball, ladder, tunnel : $3.25 + 1.75 + 2 = 7$
    She should choose a ball, a ladder and a tunnel.
20. Change : $9 - 3.25 - 4.25 = 1.5$ She would get $1.50 change.
21. B   22. D   23. B   24. A
25. B   26. A   27. C   28. B

Unit 7

1. Capacity : 1 x 4 = 4   The capacity is 4 L.
2. Capacity : 1 x 5 = 5   5 jugs can hold 5 L of water.
3. Capacity : 4 x 3 = 12   12 L of water can fill 3 buckets.
4. Capacity : 1 + 4 = 5   5 L of water can fill 1jug and 1 bucket.
5. 2 jugs hold : 1000 x 2 = 2000   2 jugs hold 2000 millilitres of water.
6. 2 buckets : 8 L   5 jugs : 5 L   2 buckets hold more.
7. No. of jugs : 4 x 3 = 12   She can fill 12 jugs.
8. 2.5 L   9. 1 L   10. 5 L
11. Capacity : 2.5 + 2.5 = 5   2 vases can hold 5 L of water.
12. Capacity : 1 + 1 + 1 + 1 = 4   4 bottles can hold 4 L of water.
13. Capacity : 5 + 5 = 10   2 pots can hold 10 L of water.
14.

No. of vases	1	2	3	4
Capacity	2.5	5	7.5	10

4 vases are needed.
15. No. of pots : 20 ÷ 5 = 4   4 pots are needed.
16. The pot has the greatest capacity.
17. Difference : 5 – 2.5 = 2.5
    A pot can hold 2.5 L more water than a vase.
18. Difference : 3 – 2.5 = 0.5
    3 bottles can hold 0.5 L more water than a vase.
19. A pot can hold 5 L; a vase can hold 2.5 L.
    A pot can hold 2 times more water than a vase.
20. Water a vase can hold : 1000 + 1000 + 500 = 2500
    A vase can hold 2500 millilitres of water.
21. C   22. M   23. C   24. M
25. Mass : (1000 + 1000 + 1000) ÷ 2 = 1500
    The mass of a story book is 1500 g (1.5 kg).
26. Mass : 100 + 200 + 200 = 500
    The mass of an exercise book is 500 g.
27. Difference : 1500 – 500 = 1000
    A story book is 1000 g heavier than an exercise book.
28. (1 exercise book; 500 g) ⟶ (2 exercise books; 1000 g) ⟶
    (3 exercise books; 1500 g)
    3 exercise books will have about the same mass as a story book.
29. A strawberry is lighter than a banana.
30. A watermelon is heavier than a pineapple.
31. An apple is heavier than a banana but lighter than an orange.
32. Watermelon, pineapple, orange, apple, banana, strawberry.

Challenge

1.

No. of oranges	3	6	9	12
Orange juice	250mL	500mL	750mL	1000mL

She needs 12 oranges.
2. (3 oranges; 1 kg) ⟶ (12 oranges; 4 kg)   She needs 4 kg of oranges.

Unit 8

1. Pencil E is the longest.
2. Pencil B is the shortest.
3. Difference : 8 – 5 = 3   Pencil C is 3 cm longer than Pencil A.
4. Difference : 15 – 3 = 12   Pencil B is 12 cm shorter than Pencil E.
5. 5 cm $\xrightarrow{\text{after 1 week}}$ 4 cm $\xrightarrow{\text{after 1 week}}$ 3 cm
    It will take 2 weeks.
6. No. of weeks : 15 – 8 = 7   It will take 7 weeks.
7. Length : 12 – 7 = 5   It will be 5 cm long.
8. 12; 8; 9; 12; 16; 13
9. Shape E has the greatest perimeter.
10. Shape B has the smallest perimeter.
11. Shape A and shape D have the same perimeter.
12. Difference : 13 – 9 = 4
    The perimeter of F is 4 cm greater than that of C.
13. Times : 16 ÷ 8 = 2   The perimeter of E is 2 times greater than that of B.

14. F has a greater perimeter than A, but smaller than E.
15. 10; 10; 9; 8; 12
16. Sticker E has the greatest area.
17. Sticker D has the smallest area.
18. Difference : 12 – 9 = 3
    The area of sticker C is 3 cm² smaller than that of sticker E.
19. Difference : 10 – 8 = 2
    The area of sticker B is 2cm² greater than that of sticker D.
20. C has a greater area than that of D, but smaller than that of A.
21. 2 A stickers are needed.   22. Shape B has the greatest area.
23. Shape C has the greatest perimeter.
24. Shape C and shape E have the same area.
25. Shape B and shape E have the same perimeter.
26. Difference : 7 – 3 = 4   The area of B is 4 cm² greater than that of A.
27. Difference : 14 – 10 = 4
    The perimeter of D is 4 cm smaller than that of C.

Challenge

Perimeter : (2 + 6) x 2 + (9 + 2) x 2 – (6 + 9) x 2 = 8
The new perimeter is 8 cm greater than the old perimeter.

Unit 9

1. 4 flowers are in a pattern.   2. 🌸🌸🌸🌸
3. 🌼🌸 🌸🌼   4. 🌼
5. 3 flowers are in the pattern.   6. 🌸🌸🌼🌸
7. 🌼 is the second.   8. 🌼 is the first.
9. It grows 5 cm every week.
10. Height : 20 + 5 + 5 = 30   The height will be 30 cm.
11. It grows 2 cm every week.
12. Height : 8 + 2 + 2 = 12   The height will be 12 cm.
13. It grows 4 cm every week.
14. Height : 16 + 4 + 4 = 24   The height will be 24 cm.
15.

Week	4	5	6	7
Height (cm)	20	25	30	35

It will take 7 weeks.
16.

Week	4	5	6
Height (cm)	8	10	12

It will take 6 weeks.
17.

Week	4	5	6	7
Height (cm)	16	20	24	28

It will take 7 weeks.
18.   19.   20.

21. 10; 12; 14; 16; 18
22. (8th) 18 ⟶ (9th) 20 ⟶ (10th) 22   22 blocks are used.
23. 16; 25; 36; 49; 64
24. (8th) 64 ⟶ (9th) 81 ⟶ (10th) 100   100 blocks are used.
25. 10; 15; 21; 28; 36
26. (8th) 36 ⟶ (9th) 45 ⟶ (10th) 55   55 blocks are used.
27. The numbers get bigger by 5.
28. The next 4 numbers are 35, 40, 45 and 50.
29. The numbers get smaller by 10.
30. The next 4 numbers are 60, 50, 40 and 30.
31. The numbers get bigger by 2.
32. The next 4 numbers are 266, 268, 270 and 272.
33. The numbers get smaller by 100.
34. The next 4 numbers are 419, 319, 219 and 119.

Challenge

1.

Day	1	2	3	4	5	6
Saved ¢	12	24	36	48	60	72

Joan has saved 72¢ ($0.72) on the 6th day.

2.

Day	6	7	8	9	10
Saved ¢	72	84	96	108	120

Joan will take 10 days to have 120¢ ($1.20).

Unit 10

1. A : Rectangular pyramid   B : Cylinder
   C : Cube   D : Triangular prism
   E : Cone   F : Sphere
2. A has 5 faces.   3. C has 6 faces.
4. B has 2 circular faces.   5. B, C and D can be stacked.
6. B, E and F can roll.
7. A : Square   B : Rectangle
   C : Circle   D : Pentagon
   E : Triangle   F : Hexagon
   G : Parallelogram   H : Trapezoid
8. E has 3 sides.   9. A, B, G and H have 4 sides.
10. A has 4 equal sides.   11. F has 6 vertices.
12. There are 4 lines of symmetry.   13. There are 2 lines of symmetry.
14. C is the top view of a cylinder.   15. E is its top view.
16. 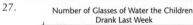   17.
18. 1 square up and 5 squares to the right.
19. 3 squares down and 2 squares to the right.
20. 3 squares down and 5 squares to the right.
21. 3 squares down.   22. 3 squares to the left.
23. 1 square down and 6 squares to the right.
24. 1 square up and 7 squares to the right.
25. 2 squares down and 6 squares to the right.
26. ⬡ , T and V are symmetrical.
27. It has 2 lines of symmetry.   28. It has 1 line of symmetry.
29. It has 1 line of symmetry.   30. It is similar to ⬡ .
31. It is congruent to ⊥ .   32. It is congruent to B.

Challenge

1. No. of sides of a triangle and a square : 3 + 4 = 7
   No. of each shape : 21 ÷ 7 = 3   Jill has 3 triangles and 3 squares.
2. A circle has many lines of symmetry.

Unit 11

1. No. of cars : 8 x 2 = 16   16 cars were parked there.
2. Difference : 16 – 8 = 8   There were 8 more cars than vans.
3. No. of vehicles : 18 x 2 = 36   There were 36 vehicles.
4. No. of people : 8 x 3 = 24
   24 people came to the pizza store by van.
5. Number of pizzas ordered.   6. There are 3 sizes.
7. It stands for 1 order.
8. No. of pizzas : 6 x 2 = 12   12 small pizzas were ordered.
9. Difference : 18 – 9 = 9
   9 more medium pizzas were ordered than large pizzas.
10. No. of pizzas : 12 + 18 + 9 = 39   39 pizzas were ordered in all.

Challenge

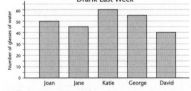

Unit 12

1. Customers' choice of one-topping pizzas.

2. 10 people chose bacon.   3. 8 people chose pineapple.
4. Difference : 14 – 8 = 6
   6 more people chose mushroom than pineapple.
5. No. of people : 10 + 12 = 22   22 people preferred meat.
6. No. of pizzas : 14 + 10 + 8 + 12 = 44
   44 pizzas were ordered in all.
7.

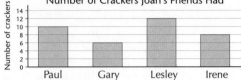

8. Gary had 6 crackers.
9. Difference : 12 – 8 = 4   Lesley had 4 more crackers than Irene.
10. Lesley had more crackers than Paul.
11. No. of crackers : 10 + 6 + 12 + 8 = 36
    The children had 36 crackers in all.

Challenge

Gary had 6 crackers and Irene had 8 crackers, so Joan had 7 crackers.

Final Review

1. 2   2. 4   3. 6   4. 8   5. 10
6. The lengths of the pencils increase by 2 cm.
7. Their lengths would be 12 cm and 14 cm.
8. Perimeter : 15 + 5 + 15 + 5 = 40   Area : 75
   Its perimeter is 40 cm and its area is 75 cm².
9. A   10. A   11. A   12. B
13. It is a cylinder. It has 3 faces.
14. It is a triangular prism. It has 5 faces.
15. It is a cube. It has 6 faces.
16. John bought gift B for Ann.   17. Katie bought gift C for Ann.
18. Capacity : 500 x 6 = 3000   The capacity of a jug is 3000 mL (3 L).
19. Capacity : 500 x 8 = 4000   The capacity of a vase is 4000 mL (4 L).
20. There are 1000 millilitres in a litre.
21. A glass has a capacity of less than 1 L.
22. A jug can fill 6 cups; a bottle can fill 3 cups. The capacity of a jug
    is 2 times more than that of a bottle.
23. A bottle can hold 1500 mL. Two bottles can hold 3000 mL.
    2 bottles are needed to hold 3 L of juice.
24. 2 bottles can hold 3 L; 5 glasses can hold 2.5 L. 2 bottles hold more.
25. Capacity : 3 + 3 = 6   The capacity of a bucket is 6 L.
26. 2 cups can fill a bowl. The capacity of a bowl is 1 L.
27.

28. Difference : 55 – 40 = 15
    George drank 15 more glasses of water than David.
29. No. of bottles : 60 ÷ 6 = 10   Katie drank 10 bottles of water.
30. No. of glasses : 50 + 45 + 60 +55 + 40 = 250
    The children drank 250 glasses of water in all.
31. Joan drank $\frac{50}{250}$ of the total number of glasses of water.
32. There are 3 triangles.   33. ◯   34. ☐
35. 2 blocks up and 3 blocks to the left.
36. 2 blocks down and 1 block to the right.
37. Joan used a triangular prism.
38. 1 block up and 2 blocks to the right.
39. 5 blocks to the right.
40. 2 blocks up and 6 blocks to the right.